G000255958

'With his customary wit and nerve to tell it as it is, David Wilbourne well catches John Habgood, who, despite his alleged coldness, was one of the most genuine and gentle of men.'
Gordon Bates, Bishop of Whitby (1983–1999)

'Few are better placed than David Wilbourne to open up the life of one of the twentieth-century's great Anglican figures. Scientist of precocious prodigy, shooter of silent looks, sincerely loved pastor and friend; all the sides of the astonishing man that was John Habgood are brought to life here with wit, poignancy and affection.'
Fergus Butler-Gallie, author of *A Field Guide to the English Clergy*

'In this excellent biography, the true John Habgood emerges . . . I count it a huge privilege to have worked closely with John, a wise human being and clearly one of the outstanding archbishops of the twentieth century.'
Lord Carey, Archbishop of Canterbury (1991–2002)

'John Habgood was a man of great intellectual and moral substance, who played a key role at a difficult time for the Church of England. David Wilbourne, his former chaplain, catches the essence of the man with admiration, affection and humour in this highly readable and important biography.'
Lord Richard Harries, Bishop of Oxford (1987–2006)

'With his perceptive insights and sometimes wry sense of humour, David Wilbourne brings *Just John* to life as a towering intellect, a pastor, priest and bishop bearing the huge burdens and responsibilities of both the Church and state, yet never succumbing to the pettiness of factions, disputes and differences – and always seeking to bring and hold people together.'
Lord David Hope, Archbishop of York (1995–2005)

'John Habgood was a giant of the twentieth century and no one is better placed to write his biography than David Wilbourne . . . David has poetry in his soul and writes beautifully as well as perceptively.'
John Inge, Bishop of Worcester

'Someone described a biography as a novel with an index! As John Habgood's last episcopal appointment, I can vouch that this is no novel. Bishop David Wilbourne, once his chaplain, captures faithfully the public face and the private thoughts of one of the greatest bishops of the twentieth century. David ministered with him and to him. He shows how John Habgood shaped the Church of England and defined its role and relationship to the state. In these pages you'll hear the Archbishop's wisdom, feel his pastoral touch and see his vision for a Church immersed and baptized into God's world.'
James Jones, Bishop of Liverpool (1998–2013)

'This biography is perceptive, sensitive, wide-ranging, intelligent and honest, qualities that John Habgood himself possessed in abundance. It captures him magnificently and shows how very fortunate the Church of England – and the wider Church – was to have this prayerful, thoughtful, highly articulate apologist as one of its leaders, even if it did not always appreciate the great gifts he put at its disposal.'
Barry Morgan, Archbishop of Wales (2003–2017)

'An absolutely beautiful piece of work that well catches Archbishop Habgood, the last Anglican theologian I used to make the walk to the Lords' chamber to hear speak. Lord Habgood would smile with pleasure and amusement to read it.'
Matthew Parris

'Lord Habgood was a towering presence, physically, intellectually and spiritually, and David paints a wonderful picture of this sorely missed servant of God.'
John Sentamu, Archbishop of York (2005–2020)

'A sensitive, insightful and loving portrait of a great Archbishop of York.'
George Stack, RC Archbishop of Cardiff

'As Archbishop's Chaplain, the author was privileged to know and understand him. For those who stood in awe of Archbishop John and thought him aloof, this book portrays a man of prayer and personal simplicity,

devoted to his family and a caring pastor. The author tells the story of John Habgood with admiration, affection and humour that bring both tears of laughter and tears of sadness at the loss of a great and wise archbishop.'
Dame Mary Tanner

'A beautifully crafted and intimate portrait of one of the Church of England's most profound thinkers of recent times.'
Canon Angela Tilby

'David Wilbourne's rooted biography has taught me much about John the human being, who delighted in the sacrament of the present moment, and who seems to go on teaching me how to be a Christian and a bishop.'
Graham Usher, Bishop of Norwich

'Beautiful, humorous, touching and revealing.'
Justin Welby, Archbishop of Canterbury

'With all the wit and originality of his earlier books, David Wilbourne offers a warm, perceptive portrait of one of the great Anglican intellects of the last hundred years. Those who thought John Habgood only a cerebral and rather remote personality will find a very three-dimensional figure here; and we are given some sense of just what a rich – and sometimes even risky – contribution he made to the good of both society and the Church.'
Lord Rowan Williams, Master of Magdalene College, Cambridge, and Archbishop of Canterbury (2002–2012)

David Wilbourne's life has included a veritable grand tour of Yorkshire, including living in Saltburn, Hull, the South Riding, York and its Vale, Scarborough, Middlesbrough, Pontefract and Helmsley. Along the way, he worked as a management trainee at Barclays Bank, studied Natural Sciences and Theology at Cambridge University, taught Ancient Greek in Cambridge and York, and worked as a parish priest in several places in Yorkshire. He acted as chaplain/adviser to three Archbishops of York and was appointed a canon of York Minster. From 2009, he was an assistant bishop in Cardiff and the South Wales valleys before returning to be an assistant bishop in the York Diocese in 2017, based in Scarborough. He is married to Rachel, a history teacher, and they have three adult daughters. A keen cyclist, hill walker and writer, David has had seven books and three courses published since 1995, and is a regular newspaper columnist and book reviewer, TV and radio broadcaster and after-dinner speaker, combining the humorous and poignant.

JUST JOHN

The authorized biography of John Habgood,
Archbishop of York, 1983–1995

David Wilbourne

First published in Great Britain in 2020

Society for Promoting Christian Knowledge
36 Causton Street
London SW1P 4ST
www.spck.org.uk

Scripture quotation is author's own translation.

British Library Cataloguing-in-Publication Data
A catalogue record for this book is available from the British Library

ISBN 978–0–281–05828–0
eBook ISBN 978–0–281–08392–3

1 3 5 7 9 10 8 6 4 2

Typeset by Manila Typesetting Company
First printed in Great Britain by TJ International
Subsequently digitally reprinted in Great Britain

eBook by Manila Typesetting Company

Produced on paper from sustainable forests

Contents

Plates

Plates

Plates

Preface

John Habgood, ninety-fifth Archbishop of York, played a giant to my grasshopper, his mind gigabyte to my kilobyte. Ever since he became Archbishop in 1983, I have been fascinated by him and worked closely with him in the four heady years up to his retirement in 1995. What I witnessed couldn't be contained by those years, and spilled out into my *Archbishop's Diary* (1995) and ten years of diary columns in the *Church Times*. In 2005, John asked me to write his authorized biography and, over three years, we spent several days meeting and discussing, with me scribbling down his every word. He had kept a substantial archive for pretty well the whole of his life, and we selected material together that caught his voice well. I interviewed a host of people who had been connected with him, with others making written submissions following a general invitation for material in the *Church Times*.

The biography then simmered during my eight years as Assistant Bishop of Llandaff, my appreciation of John's episcopacy being informed by my own direct experience of episcopacy. In the last decade, I have reviewed over 200 books for the *Church Times*, by various authors, whose immensity gave emphasis to John's greater immensity. John's death in March 2019 gave me the impetus to set down a remarkable life that had a remarkable effect on Church and State for half a century, complete with a lot of surprises which will drive us to reassess the past and shape a future that so needs people of John's calibre.

The biography is chronological, though occasionally a few doors open and let John's future in. From time to time, to give a change of voice, I have included verbatim reflections from those on whom John had an enormous impact. During his ministry John produced and published a mass of material. I have quoted from it sparingly, because I sensed it was impertinent to try and paraphrase it, and his genius required it to stand alone. His writings are readily available for those who yearn for more.

Occasionally I play the devil's advocate and present a counter-argument to John's – no doubt were he still alive, he would shoot me down in flames!

When I was consecrated a bishop in 2009, John gave me the cope and mitre he had worn as Bishop of Durham and Archbishop of York. As I wear it, I often think, 'What would John say? What would John do?' I am not of the calibre to inherit his mantle; I just touch the hem of his garment, which I try to do in this book.

Acknowledgements

I am deeply grateful for the remarkable encouragement of the Most Reverends Justin Welby and Rowan Williams, the two Archbishops of Canterbury whose tenure coincided with my writing this biography.

Thanks to Alison Barr, publisher at SPCK, for being such a patient and brilliant midwife throughout the 14 years this biography has taken to come to birth. Thanks too to the Society of Authors and the Authors' Foundation for their very generous financial support of this project, and for their helpful and highly professional advice throughout my writing career. Also, thanks to John Pritchard, former Bishop of Oxford and Chair of SPCK, for his warm and practical advice on combining a busy episcopacy with writing a major work. Thanks to John Habgood's family and friends for so generously trusting me with John's soul, and to all those named in the book whose views fashioned my view. I am very grateful to Paul Handley, Editor of the *Church Times*, for his kind permission to quote from the *Church Times'* extensive coverage of John's career. Thanks too to John Peart-Binns for so generously sharing with me all the material he used for his 1987 book on John, *Living with Paradox*. Thirty years ago I found his book a great inspiration, which whetted my appetite for all things Habgoodian. Rather than repeating detail he included, I have tried to complement what he set out.

I am particularly grateful to the Dean of King's College, Cambridge, the Very Reverend Stephen Cherry, and his archivist, Patricia McGuire, for her painstaking research. Also to the Dean of St Albans, the Very Reverend Jeffrey John and his archivist, Rob Piggott, who took tremendous trouble to help when the biography took a very surprising turn in my quest to discern John's path to greatness. St Albans popping up shouldn't have been too surprising, however, given that John Habgood strongly felt the Church of England had made a fatal mistake in not making Jeffrey John a bishop.

Acknowledgements

I am very grateful to our eldest daughter, Ruth, for transcribing John Habgood's 20,000-word diary of his Middle Eastern trip, meticulously deciphering his hurried handwritten text. But my greatest debt is to my wife, Rachel, not just for proofreading and editing the book but also for her enthusiastic energy, cheering the project and me at every stage.

1
John's genes

'The people of Crete unfortunately make more history than they can consume locally,' jests Arlington Stringham, in one of Saki's short stories. The genes of John Habgood, ninety-fifth Archbishop of York, are so saturated with history that history was bound to spill out in a packed life which bridged science and religion.

The first record of a Habgood (probably an eponymous surname for someone who happened on something good) dates from 1252, when one James Habgood sold his house. Eight centuries on there are just under 700 Habgoods in the UK, concentrated in Latton, whose parish church records 101 Habgood burials prior to the twentieth century, three Habgood chest tombs, two Habgood memorial windows and nearly 40 Habgood memorials. In April 1991 the Archbishop preached at Evensong there, gladly helping with a fundraising campaign to restore the Cotswold tiled roof, gleefully chattering at the bunfight with Habgood clones galore, an ecclesiastical version of *The Boys from Brazil*. The Latton Habgood family motto is *Vincit Omnia Veritas* (Truth conquers all). Though distant relatives obviously thronged there, John Habgood's motto crest in Bishopthorpe Palace, *Per Aspera Virtus* (Strength through difficulty), is drawn from another clutch of Habgoods in Wimborne, whose famous minster contains a Habgood family vault. One James Habgood from Wimborne eloped with a schoolgirl in 1760, then remarried following her death and the death of their only child, begetting a son, John, in his old age, who inherited Towse's House, a farm in Chewton Mendip. The youngest of John's 13 children, Henry, was a GP who married his partner's daughter Sarah, with whom he had seven children, including John Habgood's father, Arthur, born in 1882. When Henry died in 1935, he left the considerable sum of £28K.

Arthur was schooled at Dover College and read Medicine at Jesus College, Cambridge, enjoying acting in Cambridge Footlights. He served in the University Rifle Volunteers, joining the troops lining the streets for Queen Victoria's funeral in 1901. He completed his medical training at the London Hospital, qualifying in 1908, also commissioned as a captain, a Special Reserve in the Royal Army Medical Corps. When war broke out in 1914, Arthur was given five days to report for duties, initially serving as a doctor in the British Expeditionary Force, known as the Old Contemptibles because the Kaiser dismissed them as a contemptible little army. During the war he served at Ypres, Arras, the Somme and Cambrai, was hospitalized with septicaemia in 1915, then trained newly enlisted doctors in Colchester for war work before returning to the Front as lieutenant colonel in command of the 142 Field Ambulance. Awarded a DSO in 1917, he kept a diary, now preserved in the Imperial War Museum, charting a chaotic time of constant movement with long marches, deploying horse-drawn ambulances to mop up after the bloodiest engagements, with prolonged periods without sleep or food. In August 1918 he was badly wounded in the thigh, with a fellow doctor managing to stem a tear in his femoral artery and stop him bleeding to death. Awarded a year's wound pension, he returned as a doctor to Colchester Military Hospital. He left the army in 1920 and briefly served as a medical officer in Battersea before working with the Red Cross in war-torn Romania, where he was awarded a signed history of Romania by Queen Marie. Medical standards were primitive, with midwifery undertaken by 'wise women' 'whose only qualification is they are old and have attended many confinements'. He made the pioneering discovery that the mortality rate of young children was significantly lower than that of older ones, concluding that breast-fed infants were more resistant to infection.

In 1921 he was appointed an emergency officer and skin specialist in the London Hospital, and in 1922 secured a partnership with Horace Gooch in Stony Stratford. Frequent visits are recorded to a young widow, Vera Hatton (née Vera Chetwynd-Stapylton), whose late husband had died of tetanus after accidentally shooting himself in the foot. Those post-mortem trysts were clearly for romantic rather than medical reasons, in that they wed at St Marylebone, London, in September 1924, a somewhat chaotic affair caused by the fact that Arthur had forgotten to inform the vicar that a marriage was to take place.

It was Vera's genes that were soaked in history. Edward III made her fourteenth-century ancestor, Brian Stapylton, a Knight of the Garter for slaughtering a Saracen assassin. The good Brian, having served as Warden of Calais during the French wars, purchased the manor at Wighill, west of York, presenting the Dominican Priory at York with a relic of Mary Magdalene's hand, which presumably he had picked up during one of the Crusade's quieter moments. In 1536 his descendant, William, served as a popular captain in the Pilgrimage of Grace, a peaceful movement that objected to Henry VIII's dissolution of the monasteries. He mustered 500 men who besieged Hull before marching on Doncaster with a larger force, where the Duke of Norfolk, representing Henry, deceitfully sued for terms, and William returned to Wighill.

In Elizabethan times another ancestor, Sir Robert Stapylton, had a fierce and long-standing dispute with Edward Sandys, Archbishop of York, over leasing church lands. Sir Robert lured the Archbishop to discuss the matter at his friend's house in Doncaster, where by night the host's wife invaded the Archbishop's bedroom. Sir Robert and the host then burst in and 'discovered' them together, and blackmailed the compromised Archbishop into ceding his acres and paying off the cuckolded husband. The Archbishop, when faced by further blackmail, boldly took the case to Royal Council, claiming the whole thing was a honeytrap, and was exonerated. To emphasize he was happily married, Sandys is the only archbishop to appear with his stony-faced wife on his official portrait in Bishopthorpe, little realizing that four centuries later a portrait of a descendant of his arch-enemy would appear beside him.

Sir Robert's grandson, Sir Philip, was MP for Boroughbridge in the Long Parliament, joined the Roundhead ranks at the Battle of Edgehill, fell out with Cromwell, was impeached by Fairfax, before finally escaping to Calais, niftily fathering ten children along the way.

His great, great, great, granddaughter, Martha, married Granville Chetwynd, the son of an Irish baron, a major general in the York Fencible Regiment who tried to suppress the Irish Rebellion in 1798, but suffered heavy losses. He and Martha took the name Chetwynd-Staplyton, but a lavish lifestyle forced the sale of their Wighill country seat. Their youngest son, William (John Habgood's great grandfather), was a prize-winning rower at Eton and then Merton, Oxford, where he captained the college crew, achieving an unbeaten eleven bumps in nine days, and was promptly made a fellow for his sporting if not his academic prowess. He was then ordained by that scourge of Darwin and Huxley, 'Soapy' Sam Wilberforce, Bishop of Oxford, who appointed him vicar of the Merton College living of Old Malden. He ministered there for 44 years, where, like many pioneering Victorian clerics, he rebuilt the entire church and parish.

William's daughter Ella married Henry Cockburn, of Cockburn's Port, and their son Archibald was John Habgood's godfather, presenting him and Rosalie with a dozen bottles of 1927 port as a wedding present.

His son Edward was a stockbroker. John Habgood only met his grandfather once as a little boy, gamely taking him for a spin in his bath chair around Hove seafront, recalling his strange sticking-up eyebrows. Ironically John Habgood himself went on to develop these, using them as a form of communication and disapproval when words failed him – in my time working at Bishopthorpe Palace a member of staff was sacked simply on the basis of a Habgood raised eyebrow.

John Habgood's mother, Vera, was the fifth of Edward's six children. Richard, the eldest, became a stockbroker, and his daughter Helen married Sir/Lord Michael Adeane, Assistant Private Secretary to George VI and then Private Secretary to Elizabeth II from 1953 to 1972, played by Will Keen in Netflix's *The Crown*. Their son Edward was Private Secretary to the Prince and Princess of Wales. Michael's grandfather, Lord Stamfordham, had been Private Secretary to Victoria and George V, who praised him as 'the man who taught me to be King'.

Vera, nicknamed Poppy because of her red cheeks, was curiously loaned as a child to Edward's cousin, Maddy Abel Smith, to be a bright companion to her lonely daughter, May. The two girls shared a governess, and clearly Poppy was the life and soul of a very privileged party – the Abel Smiths were wealthy bankers, directors of the National Provincial, occupying Coleorton Hall near Ashby de la Zouch. Vera had her coming out party at Welbeck Abbey in the presence of the King of Spain, and then went on to finishing school in Paris. The Abel Smiths were utterly bereaved when Vera, at the tender age of 19, left them to be married.

'Do you know what it is to lose her sweet brightness?' Maddy wrote in a letter to Edgar Hutton, Vera's future husband. 'She is the most absolutely unselfish girl that ever lived, and always happy and contented, besides being perfectly lovely. You are too lucky for words.' Vera and May kept in close touch, with their friendship lasting a lifetime. Vera attended the society wedding of May's younger brother Henry to Lady May Cambridge in 1931, when Princess Elizabeth was a bridesmaid. Also in attendance was Edward, Prince of Wales, and Queen Mary (who disapproved of aristocracy marrying anyone named Smith), and countless other exotic European royals who had cannily managed to avoid being assassinated/executed in the aftermath of the Great War.

Vera's own wedding in the grounds of Coleorton Hall (complete with its own church) was lavish, with 750 guests, a flower festival and a cricket match. Her husband, Edgar, 13 years her senior, proposed to Vera in the most romantic of settings, a grotto in Charleville Castle's garden. Edgar was the nephew of the Earl of Charleville, with the castle and its vast park on the edge of Tullamore, the family seat. Who was set to inherit and why has more twists and turns than a Gospel genealogy – time fails me to tell of dead corpses mislaid on trains, and commoner husbands disinherited for refusing to defer to their titled wives. The traits of a galaxy of colourful characters are most acutely concentrated in Edgar's cousin, Charles. Educated at Eton and Sandhurst, he served in the 6th Rifles in India, went illicitly to Tibet (then closed to foreigners) and sailed for 600 miles up the Omsk to lead a hunting party through the Tian Shan Mountains in order to bag wild sheep. En route he also picked up a small bear, which he took back to Ireland: it grew to be seven feet tall and Charles regularly wrestled with it. In 1924, this adventurer of *Boys' Own* proportions prepared the way for Malory and Irvine's ill-fated attempt to conquer Everest, discovering the Yeti and naming it 'the abominable snowman' *en passant*. His other achievements ranged from serving as an MP for Wolverhampton and Chelmsford to running a citrus farm in Tunisia, where he was a confidante of its first president. Notoriously gay, he once, unsuccessfully, tried to seduce John Habgood's half-brother, Bill, deploying his butler as the advance party, who arrived in Bill's room armed with a large dish of butter (shades of *Last Tango in Paris*) and a hopeful smile. His love for Bill unrequited, he dropped dead in 1963.

Edgar was more staid than his cousin, working as a director of the agricultural equipment firm Mann Egerton in Norwich, persuaded by his new wife to replace his bedtime tot of whisky with cocoa. He and Vera ultimately resided at Oxnead Hall in Norfolk, whose underground tunnels Vera sheltered in from Zeppelin raids during Edgar's undistinguished service as a lieutenant in the Royal Artillery in France. Following the war, they moved to Hainford Lodge until Edgar's unfortunate death in 1923.

Vera and Edgar had two children, Bunny and Bill, whose genes John Habgood had a half-share in. Bunny, educated at Thornton College, a Roman Catholic convent school, worked as a mannequin for a time in London, before marrying a GP, Arthur's junior partner, in 1932, with John Habgood a pageboy in a sailor suit. They had three children: Madeleine, a GP, Diana, a radiologist, and David, a regular soldier. In the 1970s one of Diana's sons was punished at school for lying, in that he had claimed both his uncles lived in castles. He was, of course, actually telling the truth, in that at that stage his Uncle Bill occupied Charleville Castle and his Uncle John Auckland Castle.

Madeleine had a brilliant son, William, who had excelled at Oxford and was teaching in the USA until his tragic death in an air crash in 1994. The death deeply affected John Habgood; I recall him breaking off from his scripted sermon at a confirmation in Bridlington Priory that December and talking about William, that such deaths were 'intolerable, simply intolerable'. This was followed by a very long and quite awkward silence, during which he looked with great intensity at a young mother in the front pew, who was due to be confirmed with her son. I always prepared notes on the candidates for the Archbishop, but was never quite sure he took much notice of my ramblings. I had noted that the young mother candidate had cancer, and had only weeks to live, and the Archbishop's look combined such love and such sorrow it spoke mountains.

John Habgood was clearly deeply fond of 'Brother Bill', who bravely fought against the Nazis in Europe prior to Dunkirk, and was badly wounded in the right thigh. After he had recovered, he then engaged in the horrors of jungle warfare in Burma, where he was again badly wounded in his right leg, permanently losing the use of his knee. The stiff leg didn't stop him driving or striding across Irish bogs. After the war, he visited

Eton to lecture on the Burma campaign, and gave the headmaster and John Habgood (by then a pupil there) a lift to the lecture hall in his rickety car. To John Habgood's embarrassment the glove compartment fell open, depositing a joint of raw meat on the headmaster's lap. In 1963 Bill inherited and occupied Charleville Castle, developing a quasi-religious attitude to preserving the land, with a sensitivity to ecology ahead of his time. Despite being English, president of the British Legion and devotee of the Church in Ireland, he proved highly popular with the locals, not least because he treated Protestant and Catholic tradesmen with identical courtesy. At his funeral in 1982, the local head of the IRA told John Habgood, 'I hated everything he stood for, but God, what a man!' Years later, when he dedicated a cross in Tullamore Church in Bill's memory, the Archbishop of Dublin praised

> his personal goodness and faithfulness, transcending all division and class and creed, which lays claim upon universal appreciation and affection. It is no easy destiny to bear the honour and responsibility of a great name with grace and distinction . . . but this Bill succeeded in doing eminently.

Since we are surrounded by so great a cloud of history-makers, let John Habgood now run with perseverance the race that is set before him.

2

Unfolding John

Arthur and Poppy had two children of their own: Pam, born in 1925, followed two years later by John. The two children bonded well, and attended much-hated dancing lessons, culminating in a concert where John was decked out as an elf, in a green costume festooned with diamond-shaped points, complete with a green balaclava helmet with floppy ears. There is a photo from which a podgy, extremely solemn and distinctly un-elf three-year-old John glares at you. The group were supposed to dance a polka, but having emerged on to the stage, John stared at the audience, not budging an inch, mesmerized that all his elders were gazing upon him – 'Dance, John, dance', the dancing mistress hissed from the wings, all too audible to the audience. John gave a single hop and the audience roared. 'Dance, John, dance,' she shrieked, to no avail. All the other elves polka-ing vigorously around the stage were totally ignored as the eyes of the audience fixed on John, who eventually managed a third and final hop and received a rapturous ovation. John's dancing career, such that it was, staggered on until it ended ten years later, at a rather superior birthday party where John chose the most beautiful girl in the room as his dance partner, surprisingly neglected by the other boys. After spending seemingly hours trying to engage this nymph in conversation, he eventually realized she was deaf and mute. It was an age that sadly shunned or even mocked those with such disabilities, in stark contrast to our more inclusive society – the deaf and mute brother of the groom in *Four Weddings and a Funeral* is no longer shunned, but steals the show.

The novelist Graham Greene wrote that there is always one moment in childhood when a door opens and lets the future in. Those two incidents flag up a future where John is to be decked in strange exotic costumes, gilt-embroidered copes and mitres and rochets and chimeres, more Middle Earth than contemporary twentieth century. A future where we also have awkward John not fitting in, going against the crowd, yet stealing the show – he was once at a World Council of Churches gathering in Zambia, when all the delegates were instructed to raise their hands in solidarity with exploited black nations. 'I was the only one who didn't,' John admitted to me afterwards. 'You must realize I'm not a waving my hands in the air sort of guy!' And I recall myriad painful conversations, when John's silent stare scrambled my brain and rendered me mute.

John's early life was intensely jolly, shades of Richmal Crompton's creation *Just William*. This was John's favourite boyhood read, not because it was fiction but probably because it reflected life as he knew it. Calverton House in Stony Stratford, formerly a Victorian vicarage, had been converted into a GP's house with a separate surgery and a night-time bell for patients who had no phone. John's father's predecessor Dr Gooch had installed a German field gun in the drive to discourage veteran night patients bothering him with their shell shock. Though John was intrigued by this contraption and loved to play on it, his father gifted it to the recreation ground. Cash-strapped – he complained that profligate Poppy seemed to think money was delivered along with the morning milk – Arthur wanted to encourage rather than discourage patients, especially solvent ones. His most bizarre patient was a much-visited hypochondriac, a wealthy girlfriend of King Zog of Albania, who sang at charity concerts in the local cinema. She was assisted by a man playing the saw off stage, who provided a mechanical substitute to cover for otherwise elusive top notes.

The spacious grounds and gardens boasted a tennis court, stables, a chicken run and a sty, with a succession of sows named Susan after a portly aunt. Two fields and water meadows sloped down to the River Ouse, close to an aqueduct, with a boathouse and a deep pool perfect for swimming. When it came to inviting people to join his swimming parties, the sky was clearly the limit:

Dear God
If you feel lonely up in the sky would you like to come down and stay with us, you could sleep in the spier-room [*sic*], and you could bathe with us, and I think you would enjoy yourself.
Love from John

The postman recognized John's eight-year-old handwriting: rather than massively diverting his round to deliver to the Almighty, he cannily returned the letter to John's father.

In our conversations in 2006, John shared a random collection of his first memories, inevitably fleeting. In the year of his death, there was a film due to be released about the doomed Airship R101. Back in October 1930, three-year-old John was absolutely fascinated as the Airship R101 passed over their house, observing its via dolorosa immediately prior to its tragic crash in Paris. His parents' warning not to draw attention to a guest's wooden leg went unheeded by future physiologist John, who spent the visit crawling on the carpet, angling himself to look up the highly embarrassed amputee's trousers. John inherited his father's skill with carpentry, making imaginative models in his father's workshop with Meccano and plywood. John and sister Pam played well together, riding a couple of ancient horses on permanent loan from a priest at Pam's Roman Catholic school, Thornton College. When war loomed, they were sternly instructed to leap from the saddle and hide in hedges and ditches should a Nazi Messerschmitt blot their carefree horizon. Their father equipped them with his ancient shotgun so John could protect his sister from being ravished by a Nazi parachutist; but with no Huns forthcoming, they had to resort to shooting (but, more often than not, missing) squirrels and other vermin. The shotgun was retained and used by Rosalie Habgood at dusk to shoot pesky squirrels and crows in the grounds at Bishopthorpe Palace. Her son, Adrian, mercifully oblivious that one day he would be Principal Forensic Officer with the West Yorkshire Police, gamely drove their 2CV with the sunroof open while his mother stood vertical, taking potshots. I understand she once narrowly missed two of the previous chaplain's lads, within inches of being prematurely dispatched to meet their Maker for the heinous sin of skulking in some rhododendron bushes.

When John was five, the family bought their first Eccles caravan, styled like a cottage made of thin walls of plywood with quaint leaded windows, set on four wheels with little, if any, suspension. The caravan was pulled by a continuously overheating bull-nosed Morris, not surprising when it had to haul the family, the caravan, deckchairs, a large tent, a lavatory tent, a table, the family labrador, Barbara the au pair and Winifred the portly cook. It seems they just showed up and persuaded farmers to loan them a corner in a field. Venues included Avebury Ring, where one of the ancient stones was used as a dinner table, Happisburgh on the Norfolk coast and Charmouth. While their parents fished for trout, John and Pam examined fossils, learnt to swim, and also to sprint when a bull inconveniently interrupted their picnic. The family, including their labrador, visited a destroyer moored at Lyme Regis, and in 1936 viewed the *SS Queen Mary* passing by at Southampton. This was when John realized he needed glasses since he couldn't even see the liner in front of his face. The Second World War put an end to their jaunts by the coast and, following an appeal, the Eccles caravan, shaved of contents, cooks and au pairs, was donated to Monty's North African campaign, no doubt striking terror into Rommel's heart.

Clearly, family life was deliriously happy. John described his father as 'quiet, reserved, with the tiniest handwriting, yet funny and good with children – particularly sick ones'. Poppy, his mother, was great fun and made every party go with a swing. And there were a lot of parties, teaming up with 'Fatty Payne', their High Church vicar, to organize flag days for wounded old soldiers, with collecting boxes strapped to the back of the aforementioned pet labrador, as well as the garden at Calverton House being used for numerous fetes, fire-brigade displays and clay-pigeon shoots. These activities morphed in the war to Arthur serving in the Home Guard and Poppy joining the WVS and staffing a mobile canteen. She provided convoys, snaking through the town, with meals of such five-star quality that soon it seemed every single convoy in the British and American army diverted via Stony Stratford. John enthusiastically staged a wartime version of 'The Sorcerer's Apprentice', continually toing and froing through the town with his wheelbarrow, overflowing with pigswill for the journey home, then brimming with pork joints and vegetables on return to the canteen.

Wartime brought a flurry of evacuees and guests at Calverton House, hush-hush employees at nearby Bletchley Park among them, including F. L. Lucas, a Classics don from King's, Cambridge, and expert in German linguistics. He headed up the intelligence sector at Bletchley, but infuriated Poppy because of his eccentric habit of dining in his slippers. Their attic, shades of *'Allo 'Allo*, secretly housed a certain Commander Cooper, a genius who devised a system of radio beams to guide bombers to their targets. Pam did her bit working at Bletchley, plotting U-boat positions, while sadly bereaved of two boyfriends killed on active service. To help her recovery, after the war John accompanied Pam to the Alps for his first holiday abroad. The holiday was cheap, provided by a fierce aunt who ran a camp combining fundamentalist evangelism with bracing mountain air. John and Pam skived the Bible classes and skied instead, with John keeping up a hilarious travelogue worthy of Bill Bryson.

John's parents not surprisingly were exhausted by all these wartime activities, with Arthur retiring in 1947, too old a dog to learn NHS new tricks. Poppy was always eccentric, frequently omitting entirely words she didn't understand when lecturing mothers at the Infant Welfare Centre, also getting words muddled, such as appealing for employment for de-capitated (incapacitated) soldiers, exclaiming that a local mother had given birth to quadrupeds, and describing someone as a bit of a deep horse. Occasionally she could hit the nail on the head, as in this hilarious epitaph: 'He had no enemies, but his friends disliked him intensely.' Over the years she became more and more eccentric, developing an erratic ob-session with fishcakes, which she purchased in season and out of season. Dementia took its toll, and she died in a care home in Basingstoke in 1968. I guess her decline inculcated in John an acute sensitivity to those, high and low, who don't present in any normal way, making him determined to see the golden person behind the craziness. Set on salvaging some-thing positive from the utterly tragic, John used most of the money she left him to build a hard court for his students at Queen's, Birmingham, in her memory. She had been a devotee of the tennis courts at Calverton, although John's service never rose to beyond that of ballboy.

Academic prowess was John's strong suit. His education began along with Pam at a local infant school, under the guidance of three Misses Stockings, two of whom actually taught while the third, described by John as the oldest and ugliest sister, hovered menacingly. 'There was no play, no gimmicks, you just sat at your desk and did as you were told, with the syllabus focusing on reading, writing, grammar, arithmetic, history, geography, drawing, French, Latin and Scripture.' Their method was clearly successful, because when John moved to board at Hill Brow prep school in Eastbourne, in the autumn of 1935, he was plunged into a Scripture test where he proved to be the only boy who could name all

12 of Jesus' apostles. 'One up for Miss Stocking, but not a good start for a new boy,' John wryly commented.

Eastbourne was thronged with prep schools, with crocodiles of school children criss-crossing Beachy Head on their Sunday walks, seemingly oblivious to the fatal drop. Fifty-five boys were taught by ten full- or part-time staff, who criticized shy John for not reading enough and expressing himself uninterestingly. Despite this, John soon proved himself the brightest, academically two years ahead of his contemporaries. Since the post of head boy was awarded to the most academic pupil, John achieved the accolade two years running, with the school flag flying on his birthday, embarrassed by his mother presenting prizes on two consecutive speech days.

John found that his intelligence, coupled with having to exercise a considerable disciplinary role over boys his senior, isolated him, making him deeply miss home: 'During the holidays, the thought of the journey to London, the final lunch at the Cafe Royal and the 3.45 p.m. school train to Eastbourne, hung like a black cloud growing ever closer.' Hill Brow's headmaster, F. J. H. Matthews, wrote to John's father on 1 August 1939, admiring his conduct as Head Boy but concerned that John was worried and losing weight:

> It has seemed to me that some of the older, though junior, boys have not taken too kindly to his being over them. I think, too, the exercise of a little more tact on his part will make his path smoother.

John enjoyed the academic work, however, and indulged his hobbies, which included secreting a huge acid-filled accumulator in his tuck locker to power his Meccano motor.

With the advent of war, Eastbourne was on the front line, so John was moved to a school nearer home, the Knoll at Woburn Sands. Mr John Zair, the elderly head, taught John maths, and curiously bridge, with Mrs Zair organizing parties for John and other boys on a Sunday evening. The deputy head, Noel King, a tall, aesthetic man with a monocle and a hot temper, taught English, Latin and Greek, criticizing 12-year-old John for producing translations from Greek into English that were 'too childish'.

His excursions into sex education, which were conducted on a one-to-one basis, were, to say the least, unconventional. Mine took place sun-bathing naked on the grass beside the swimming pool, behind locked gates, and was concentrated on anatomy and the changes to be expected therein. Noel King clearly enjoyed it. Nobody came to much harm, however, and I learnt more from him than Mr Zair, whose only piece of advice, delivered with much embarrassment, was to fix an empty cotton reel on to the back of one's pyjamas to prevent nocturnal emissions.

Mr Zair had written to John's father wondering whether 'you would like me to speak to him on sexual matters, or whether, being a doctor, you would like to do this yourself'. The headmaster was more forthcoming in his high assessment of John: 'Combines modesty and seriousness of purpose with a good sense of humour. His artistic and mathematical leaning gives him a good mental balance. He is a most delightful boy to teach – he is not only very appreciative but shows it.'

The French master was a member of the Home Guard, and for most of his lessons in 1940 he brought the platoon's only Bren gun into class, teaching the boys how to strip it down, clean and reassemble it. The drawing master proved the best of a strange bunch, awarding John with a paint box and sable brushes, which he used throughout his life.

There was a bit of a muddle with his entrance exams for Eton in 1941, when John missed the Greek exam entirely, ruling out a scholarship. Without that scholarship, his father could not afford Eton's extortionate fees. However, one of the housemasters, Charles Mayes, also head of science, impressed by John's scientific and mathematical prowess, came to the rescue, and in collaboration with his house's dame (matron), a distant relation of the Habgoods, offered a reduced fee. Self-deprecatingly, John claimed he was only let in to beef up a house that had a dim academic reputation. The drawing master's gnomic comment on John's final cramped report from the Knoll speaks mountains: 'The pleasure which his work has given me cannot be adequately expressed in the space at my disposal.'

3

Eton John

In 1994 I accompanied John Habgood for a confirmation at Grove Hill in a rough part of Middlesbrough, so rough that the church had to employ bouncers to guard any parked cars to make sure they still had four wheels on their owner's return. The bouncers jeered at the Archbishop and me in our cassocks, 'Who's got a pretty party dress on, then?' John Habgood remained aloof and oblivious. The service went without hitch or further heckles, but at the end, as we were processing down the aisle, a scruffy urchin playing at his mother's feet looked open-mouthed as the Archbishop passed by, decked in a golden cope and mitre, carrying an ornate, silver crosier. 'Look, Mummy, a king!' he exclaimed. On the drive back to Bishopthorpe I broke the usual silence and repeated the child's comments, expecting the humble Archbishop to find them amusing. 'But he is absolutely right,' he replied, his face deadly serious, without the hint of a smile, 'I am.'

'Those who think themselves worthy of great things are worthy of great things,' claimed Aristotle. I guess Eton, hailed as a junior club for the influential-elect, bestowed on John Habgood an effortless and benign sense of entitlement. He once said that the main advantage of going to Eton meant you didn't have to spend the rest of your life worrying about or thinking up excuses why you hadn't gone to Eton. More seriously, he claimed the College gave him both the self-confidence and the tools to lead, without thrashing about wondering whether he should be in charge in the first place. The present Archbishop of Canterbury, Justin Welby, himself attended Eton and kindly shared his own very perceptive reflections on the place. He feels Eton's sense of entitlement, carrying the concomitant risk of innate snobbery, had a dark side, a game of the highest stakes from which some never recovered. He recalls both those who rose to the top and clearly felt they were worth being there, and also those whose lives were destroyed by a sense of failure or bullying. That John was able to shine rather than be consumed is highly significant.

Sense of entitlement notwithstanding, even Eton wasn't spared the deprivations of wartime, and John's letters home caught the austerity. Long leaves (vacations) were abolished; phones were disconnected, so boys could only write and receive letters from home; petrol rationing severely curtailed parental visits; and a night curfew meant a day-return home by train was hardly possible. Towards the end of the war, the College was in the front line for V1/V2 rockets – watchers on the chapel roof would ring a bell when they saw a rocket on its way, and pupils would dive under desks until a mercifully distant explosion signalled the all-clear. One rocket nearly took out the future Primate of England, when it exploded on the racecourse only hundreds of yards away from John, rowing upstream from Windsor. Fortunately John was low beneath the river bank, which shielded him from the bomb blast but not from the loud bang, which temporarily deafened him.

With clothes' rationing, there was a flourishing trade in cast-offs. Most suits had to be hired from a local tailor, with John reprising his wheelbarrow skills from Stony Stratford and on occasion pushing huge handcarts piled high with suits, taking them to be cleaned. The compulsory Eton white ties had to be made out of folded paper. Each pupil had their own room, heated by a coal fire, but rationing limited the coal to one small scuttle per week. 'It is very cold, like the North Pole,' John complained in one of his first letters home – and that was in balmy October! While in the Lower School, John's duties as a fag kept him warm, sprinting to and from the tuck shop delivering rafts (slices of fried bread) for the privileged members of the Library.

In another letter, he described how he had returned to his chilly room muddy and freezing, having come 150 out of 300 in a three-mile steeplechase across Windsor Great Park, which included four water jumps, all too wide to leap, with muddy water in the final one, four-feet deep. Feeling hopeless at games, he hit on the ruse of being a 'wet bob', filling his time rowing on the river. Often he rowed in a single rigger, going at his own pace, spending most of the time resting under a riverside willow.

Occasionally he had to show willing, rowing in a fours or eights, even winning a minor cap. He actually enjoyed playing Eton Fives, partnering with future Home Secretary Douglas Hurd, who caned fags for the heinous sin of 'showing insufficient enthusiasm'. Surprisingly, John enjoyed the army corps, dressing in First World War uniforms, going on manoeuvres, marching through Great Windsor Park on field days behind a real army band. 'I boiled in my uniform,' he wrote home, 'my equipment weighed a ton!'

John, along with 40 other pupils, was in Charles Mayes' House, sited on the edge of Eton's grounds, which had a reputation for being dim. In those days pupils were often assigned their future house at birth, through their families' close relationship with the housemaster. Some houses had the reputation for being snobbish, others majored in games, some were tough, others were vulgar, some were civilized, one or two (at their wealthy housemaster's personal expense) were well fed. Mayes' House was dank and depressing, its boys scruffy: 'If a boy was caught smoking or cheating in Trials, it was most likely to be one of Mr Mayes' boys.' In a college where proficiency in Greek reigned supreme, and was the marker of how bright a pupil was, science was the Cinderella of the curriculum; Charles Mayes was head of science, making his house seem even more peripheral.

When he went up to Eton in 1941, John cut a gangling figure, his tailcoat hanging upon his slightly drooping shoulders like a loosely limbed scarecrow. Given the social disadvantages of Mayes House, with John describing the other boys as 'quite a rough lot', he seemed like a fish that had swum into the wrong pool. Yet all in the house and college soon knew and liked him, finding him pleasant and friendly. Helping the bullies with their homework won them round, with the worst bully inviting John back to his home for an illicit puff of Turkish cigarettes. In a frank memoir written for his family, John reassures them that nothing else illicit ever happened: 'Despite what is often said about Public Schools, there was very little overt sex as far as I was aware. Much of the time we were cold, hungry and tired after spending many nights in air-raid shelters, so perhaps we were just not up to it!'

Quite a few doddery Mr Chips had to be recalled from retirement, covering for colleagues serving in the armed forces, which John felt lowered the standard of teaching. But John got on very well with Charles Mayes, who repeatedly enthused about John in reports sent to Dr Habgood (addressed as 'Dear Habgood') after each Half (Eton-speak for 'term').

I didn't see much of him this Half, since he was on the river and I on the cricket field, but I notice he is working hard, reading in his room with his light burning late at night. A natural, inquisitive student.

During his time at Eton, Archbishop Justin Welby was housed in South Lawn, which he suspects may have been the same building as Mayes' House. In his experience, Eton either gave students the opportunity to do very little and be very undistinguished, or, if they wanted to, have some of the best teaching and educational opportunities going. Archbishop Welby concludes that for John Habgood to be at the latter end reflects a strong character of self-discipline and determination in order to stand out in such a crowd.

Working late into the night was a habit that persisted into his years as Archbishop. I recall him toiling night after night in his study perched high above the Ouse at Bishopthorpe. He always finished promptly at 9.30 p.m., turning off all the office lights, oblivious that he was casting me in my study into darkness. I was forced to fumble along pitch-black corridors, feeling my way around sundry portraits of previous archbishops, with scary ones like Richard Scrope and Cardinal Wolsey proving unwitting signposts to the exit. I knew I had nearly made good my escape when I chanced upon a large black-and-white photo of the 1958 Lambeth Conference, tucked in by the side entrance. In the gloom, this throng of mostly white bishops from across the Anglican Communion looked particularly stern. They had just voted in favour of artificial contraception, and were no doubt terror-struck that when they returned to their sees, their fecund wives would now be demanding sex on tap. In his final months as Archbishop, John allowed himself the luxury of finishing at 9 p.m., when he descended into the palace's private quarters to share hot chocolate and a dark smile with Rosalie.

John was soon winning Trial (yearly exam) prizes in physics, maths and chemistry, with glowing reports going into great detail about John's various approaches to solving differential equations and mastering calculus and optics. 'No Trials this Half, so he couldn't obtain his usual distinction,' Mayes crisply comments.

A patriotic history teacher, clearly too wedded to an infallible British Empire, complains that one of John's radical essays 'contained several bad exaggerations on allied mistakes in the Great War'. In one report, towards the end of John's time in Upper School (Year 11 in new money), Mayes presses John's father to decide whether John's future is to be medicine or science – science clearly won the day. By the end of his time at Eton, John won the coveted Oppidan prize for the best non-scholar, and equally coveted Mosely prize for physics and chemistry. Mind you, the classes were small, five in the chemistry class and just three in the physics class. Another contender for the Mosely prize, Gordon Whitby, who went on to be Professor of Clinical Chemistry at Edinburgh University, said of John, 'Though junior to me, he had a better understanding of physics. I was, perhaps, a little afraid of him.' John applied to read natural sciences at King's College, Cambridge, but oddly his prowess did not win him a scholarship. However, he was awarded a recently created (and more generous) state bursary, designed to encourage research into topics such as radar, which would help to win the war, and the peace.

That war inevitably loomed, with John serving in the Home Guard, fire-watching as well as doing war work that ranged from potato-digging to gluing large pieces of wood together to create gliders to be used in the D-Day landings. Several days each week, Mrs Mayes, much despised by the rest of the staff for 'being common', quietly donned overalls and worked in a nearby munitions factory. Just once, in a letter to Dr Habgood at the end of 1944, Charles Mayes lets the impassive facade of the professional schoolmaster slip to reveal an anguished father talking to another anguished father about the high price wielded by war:

> News from Italy received on Christmas Day makes it highly probable that Andrew, our son, is a prisoner, but we do not know how badly he is wounded. He had to be left behind enemy lines, though his patrol stayed with him and tried to bandage him up after he had ordered them to go back and leave him.

During wartime the chapel windows were boarded up, their stained glass removed for safekeeping. Despite the gloom, John on the whole enjoyed the services there, as he also enjoyed Charles Mayes reading C. S. Lewis's *Screwtape Letters* to the boys in his house, albeit a somewhat curious bedtime story. However, the teaching of divinity was poor compared to science, arresting John's spiritual development, until one bath time John decided that the God he had invited to bathe with him in the stream at the bottom of Calverton House's garden ten years before would never turn up, because he no longer existed and Christianity was not true.

In conversation in 2005 I pushed John for more detail:

As I recall it, the whole process was primarily intellectual rather than emotional or moral. I don't think I really changed much as a person, and certainly my atheist phase did not involve any dramatic change in lifestyle. My rejection of religion had nothing to do with the desire to rebel, but everything to do with its perceived implausibility. I was confirmed at Eton, and took it very seriously. But I had no help in integrating what I was taught with what I was learning as a science specialist. In confirmation class, for instance, I was told that the beauty of the sunset was proof of the existence of God. In chemistry we were shown how to create sunsets by shining a light through a tank of water in which a chemical was slowly being precipitated. In divinity the Synoptic Problem (the literary relationship between the Gospels) got the full treatment, but at the expense of understanding how and why the Gospels could still speak to us. In short, the teaching was bad, so one evening I decided it was all nonsense. One bad effect of this decision was to give me a sense of intellectual superiority, reinforced when I moved to Cambridge. Most of the smart people in King's seemed to be atheists, something ex-schoolboys among a crowd of war veterans could use to their advantage. Yet I was doing little more than fooling around on the edge of things, dismissing a Bible I had hardly read, and relying on arguments which had not hitherto really been challenged.

John began at Eton when Nazi invasion of Britain's shores seemed well-nigh certain; four years later the Nazis had been vanquished and Britain and Europe faced a new and promising dawn, of which John was a part. In his final Eton report, Charles Mayes made a telling observation about John's time commanding the house squad of Eton's army corps: 'To win the willing co-operation of every member of the section and command them as he did showed a capacity for leadership of a very high order.'

The final word on Eton goes to Archbishop Welby: 'When I was at Cambridge, the boatman at the University Boat Club commented that Old Etonians came in two forms, "proper gentlemen who I'd trust anywhere, or complete bastards".'

4

King's John

Autumn 1945 was the season when heroes returned. Having been seconded to break codes of fiendish complexity in Bletchley, King's College fellows came back to Cambridge, magi no longer at ease in the old dispensation, eager to crack the codes of life rather than eulogize the status quo. Then there were sixth-formers, anachronistically in their mid-twenties, mostly winners of scholarships and exhibitions, who had had their entrance deferred while they served in the armed forces. Then there were men who had been selected by the armed forces to pursue a truncated 'war degree', allowed to proceed to graduation in six rather than the statutory nine terms. To complete this heady mix, there were real schoolboys like John Habgood, who came up straight from Eton with a state studentship, an award that brought two major benefits: it bypassed having to spend another year at Eton to retake the scholarship exams; and since the studentship aimed to channel bright young things into scientific research, it exempted John from National Service.

John's director of studies, Dr Stockdale, encouraged him to read physiology as well as the standard maths, physics and chemistry. 'I had no idea what physiology was, had done no biology at school, but I meekly complied and I have blessed him ever since.' Thereafter John's time was saturated with lectures, practicals and supervisions, with the immense privilege of one-to-one sessions with world-class experts in their field. A letter sent home in October 1945 thanks his parents for the gift of a bicycle, on which he hurtles with hundreds of others from lecture to lecture, a terrifying academic peloton hourly staging its Tour de Cambridge.

John gained a First in the prelim examinations taken after his first year. He kept all the papers he sat, marked with the questions he attempted. They came across to me, with a similar background in natural sciences, as fascinating, very doable with practical applications, though

22

pitched somewhere between Advanced and Special level. I guess their aim was to consolidate and refresh sixth-form work, which understandably had been kicked into touch when Japanese warriors were screaming at you in Borneo's jungles.

Whatever, the future Primate of England has to find the focal length of two lenses, calibrate a voltmeter and ammeter, design a dynamo from scratch, synthesize benzene and calculate the range of a shell. Finally, in physiology he chooses an organ, sketching considerable variations in its activity, and discusses the effect of the nervous system on digestion – no doubt 27 fraught examination hours in the spring of 1946 gave him ample evidence of the latter.

What we do have evidence of is a mindset being established here. Faced by a range of tricky scientific problems, John coolly, calmly and confidently works through to a solution. This can-do attitude he applied to equally tricky and wide-ranging problems in the Church, firmly believing that there was nothing in all creation, even a muddled General Synod, that couldn't be fixed. Not for nothing was his nickname 'the Saviour'.

Dr Stockdale declared John had reached his ceiling in maths. So, heeding his advice, he dropped it for Part I, something he spent the rest of his life regretting. Whenever the Archbishop presided at a church service outside the York Diocese, I led him in procession with a tall primatial cross, taking care to avoid colliding with low arches and ceilings. I once clonked into a sanctuary lamp, which swung accusingly, like the pendulum of a grandfather clock, for the rest of the service. Afterwards I apologized to the Archbishop for my clumsiness. 'Think nothing of it,' he grinned. 'I was fascinated how regular the swing was, and calculated the acceleration due to gravity while the vicar was boring the rest of the congregation with the notices.' You can calculate the acceleration due to gravity by multiplying the length of a pendulum by four times pi squared and dividing it by the square of the time it takes for a complete swing. Literally rocket science. Amazing that the maths John had studied over 40 years before still sprang fresh to mind.

Dropping maths notwithstanding, John achieved another First, as well as being awarded an exhibition, in the Part I exams completed in 1947. Again the selected questions seem doable, if wide-ranging, although strangely, as in 1946, there are no questions on subatomic particles, nuclear fusion or fission or Einstein's general and special theories of relativity. Perhaps all is still in denial after the horrors of Hiroshima.

Such denials happened. Years later when John was Vice-Principal at Westcott House he was approached by his former King's mentor, Sir Bryan Matthews, who had made his name in the field of electrophysiology, researching into the physiological effects of high-altitude flight. Matthews was disturbed by Sputnik's launch in October 1957, in that he couldn't believe such an achievement was possible outside Cambridge, let alone outside the 'free world'. Although the satellite orbited the earth for three weeks, and was tracked by every schoolboy aspiring to be a physicist, Matthews claimed the whole thing was a Soviet hoax, suspecting that it was nothing more than a series of intercontinental missiles fired by a powerful canon.

Back in Part I in 1947, rather than splitting the atom, John has to content himself calculating the speed of colliding billiard balls, sketching interference patterns caused when light passes through a narrow slit, measuring the velocity of light, synthesizing ammonia and nitric acid, calculating the terminal (!) velocity of a parachutist, outlining the theory of the periodic table and charting 'the effect of sugar on urine in man' – clearly Cambridge women had yet to piss. He spends four hours blowing bubbles, investigating the relationship between the diameter of the pipe and durability of the bubble. For the three-hour essay paper he chooses the title 'Signs of Life', little realizing that he is going to spend 40 years seeking them amid the deadness of the Church of England.

For his final year, John majored entirely on physiology, and again was awarded a First, along with a major scholarship and research studentship. He answered questions on the brain, the ovaries, hormones, the retina, sound perception and the nerves, selecting the title for his three-hour essay, 'The normal of biology is the individual normal and not the statistical normal.' He wisely dismissed the baffling alternative: 'Aristotle dissected fishes with Plato's thoughts in his head.' Chillingly his anatomy tutor wrote to him apologizing that no thorax could be found for dissection, but offered him a brain or a foetus instead. John chose the latter, only to be utterly sickened by the sight, agonizing over a mother's grief for her unborn child.

In 1948, Cambridge physiology was leading the world, and John joined a select team headed up by Lord Adrian and Sir Bryan Matthews and was supervised by Dr Feldberg, a German Jewish refugee, who had made groundbreaking discoveries about chemical transmitters released by damaged nerves. The title of John's PhD was 'Hyperalgesia – an Electrophysiological approach', investigating why the tissue surrounding a wound, but not involved in the original trauma, nevertheless became sore.

His basic technique was to apply a shock to one nerve and measure the impulse on an adjacent nerve, for which he had to manufacture his own apparatus. He salvaged a bomb aimer from an aircraft dump and converted its beautiful brass fittings and gears into a cathode ray oscilloscope. He also converted a wind-up gramophone into a camera with a moving roll of film, which recorded tiny flickers of light reflected from a moving coil, connected to an amplifier, wired up to a frog's leg. The apparatus was highly unreliable, and to make matters worse the frog's leg sometimes acted as a rectifier and picked up *Music While You Work* from the BBC's Light Programme. Following endless frustrations, John gained sufficient results to earn his PhD, with two papers published in the *Journal of Physiology*, with the catchy title, 'Sensitisation of the sensory receptors in the frog's skin', and, intriguingly, 'Antidromic impulses in the dorsal roots'.

John was granted a vivisection licence, experimenting on frogs, rats and cats. The licence was strictly regulated by the Home Office, with an annual return required giving details of:

a. experiments on dogs, cats, horses and other animals without anaesthesia;
b. experiments begun under anaesthesia;
c. experiments wholly under anaesthesia; and
d. demonstrations before students.

The vivisection licence was akin to a DVLA licence telling you what you could and couldn't drive, with categories of licence for each activity, ranging A–F and AA–FF. In April 1950, John wrote an article on brains for *The Pilgrim Newsletter* (published by Scripture Union), exploring the interface between science and religion. He described an experiment where he severed cats' spinal cords in several places and measured the effects, which included the chilling phrase, 'If one merely cuts off the cat's head . . .'. Later in the article he informs us that 'a frog may be jumping about again a few minutes after its head has been removed, whilst a cat may need several hours before its reflexes even begin to return'. It all seems fiendishly cruel to modern sensitivities. Yet in a Europe reeling from Auschwitz, with medical science desperate to ease the agony of horrifically wounded servicemen and bombed civilians, cutting up the odd stray cat back then seemed a necessary means to a crucial end.

Nevertheless, it haunted John as much as the foetus he had dissected – 'The vivisection of rabbits and cats sickened me' – with John preferring to use himself as a human guinea pig rather than experiment on dumb animals. We once visited a sixth form in Mirfield, and John nonchalantly stood at the front of the biology class, decked in a purple cassock. He informed the startled pupils how he once had consumed nothing but oatmeal and water for a fortnight, carefully measuring *all* his excreta to see how much was absorbed. Their jaw dropped further as he outlined another experiment, which involved eating a pound of salt to see the effects on his blood pressure. The problem was he hadn't really explained that all this was when he was a former scientist back in the 1940s, with the sixth-formers incorrectly assuming that this was the routine self-denial and mortification expected of all modern bishops.

A not untypical diary entry from July 1950 makes poignant reading: 'Did experiments on my arm, not very successful attempt to anaesthetize nerve. Found no change of threshold, but could not get good hyperalgesia – too painful. I don't think I added much to the sum of knowledge.' But mortification of the flesh and stigmata notwithstanding, I find it striking that John spent his pre-ordained years focusing on the nature of a wound.

In later years, John was a great admirer of the playwright Dennis Potter. While the tabloids were fulminating about Potter's 1980s' TV series *The Singing Detective*, including the infamous heaving buttocks scene in the Forest of Dean, John boldly declared the series as nothing less than a magnificent tale of fall and redemption. Nearing death, Potter was interviewed by Melvyn Bragg, who sneered at his faith as nothing but a bandage around the wound. 'No,' Potter replied unfazed, 'it is the wound; faith is the wound.' John often quoted from that interview, as if looking into the wound for all those years wasn't so much a distraction from his call to ordination but, rather, the very essence of it.

John's heady time as a Cambridge scientist had its lighter moments. Rationing was severe, with even bread being rationed in 1946, although the Archbishop of Canterbury twisted the government's arm to give extra bread units to students. John cooked his meagre weekly bacon ration every morning on the gas ring in his rooms, just to inhale the aroma, only consuming the cooked bacon at the end of the week. Pigeon stew was the staple diet in hall, with the strong suspicion that they had been culled from King's College chapel's famous roof. John enjoyed the cheap but lavish helpings of cottage pie served at the British Restaurant; for a time he lodged with a widow and her young daughter in Silver Street, able to resist the daughter's charms but succumbing to the charms of her mother's treacle pudding.

He also lodged with the Clarks, a newly married couple, who nicknamed him Happy, highly impressed by his exquisite table manners, not least that he only accepted second helpings at the third time of asking: 'Well, perhaps I will after all.' Robert Clark was an eccentric chemist, who, when he wasn't experimenting with mind-altering drugs, arranged an array of wire netting just below his bedroom ceiling. He had the habit of powering up the mesh to tens of thousands of volts, which theoretically neutralized ions in highly charged clouds to head off thunderstorms. While the contraption must have given an undoubted frisson to the newly-weds' sex life, John was dubious about its effectiveness, not least because of the significant risk that the apparatus itself could produce the very lightning strike that it was designed to prevent. If only he had been more enthusiastic and in a parallel universe installed it beneath York Minster's transept roof, he might have stayed the hand of God and averted the 1984 fire. While lodging with the Clarks he joined the life class in the art department of the nearby technical college; in his relaxed retirement he candidly admitted to me, with a certain twinkle in his eye, that it was more to explore the female form than artistic technique.

During his first year as a research student, John was allocated a room in Chetwynd Court in King's. He writes:

The adjacent room had been converted into a bathroom with three baths, and each evening the 'Chetwynd Bath Club' met for the kind of conversations which are only possible when one has nothing left to hide. I was frequently there, since there was not much chance of sleeping while others were bathing. We were a very mixed bunch, and talked about everything under the sun. It almost made up for missing National Service.

During that year John kept a lion in his room, a large stuffed one originally bought by his half-sister Bunny. She had got carried away at a sale, but had to pass it on to John because they found it frightened her GP husband's patients, sending their blood pressure and pulse sky high. No doubt it had a similar effect on the natural science students and medics John supervised from Downing and Girton Colleges.

John clearly enjoyed teaching. He was able to explain difficult concepts clearly and simply, and in 1950 the lucrative post of University Demonstrator was created for him in the small department of pharmacology, a wing of the physiology department. Other than realizing that few drugs around at the time were actually useful, John knew little of the subject that he suddenly had to teach unruly medics before and after their hospital placements: one lecture on the dangers of nicotine ended with him being showered with cigarettes by unconvinced medics.

John was unsuccessful in being elected to a prestigious fellowship at King's in 1951, which was won by Gordon Whitby (who had studied physics with John at Eton) in what the Provost of King's described as a very strong field. In the autumn of 1951, John explored a secondment in Sweden with the distinguished physiologist Yngve Zotterman, but on advice from the Provost, resisted the offer, fearing his absence from Cambridge would impair his chances of a second shot at a fellowship. John also resisted the offer of a senior lectureship in physiology at the University of Malaya, a post that head of department Professor Glaser described as *not* a dead end, combining work with travel – Glaser had previously supervised John's fortnight diet consisting solely of oatmeal.

The Professor wasn't surprised that John turned him down, suspecting there was another star on his horizon: 'I knew since you took part in the oatmeal experiment that your inclinations lay in that direction, and I am not going to grumble about the loss to Physiology or say much about the obvious gain to the Church.'

Resisting any move from Cambridge was a wise decision, because in April 1952 John was elected fellow, writing the following letter of acceptance to the Provost:

I feel it is a great honour and responsibility to be elected to such a position, and despite my ultimate intentions, there is, in a sense, nothing I would like to do more than to stay on at King's – but then who wouldn't wish to do the same? In fact, however, I am making plans to go to a Theological College at the end of 1953, and I am glad of your assurance that I can do this with your blessing. I feel I shall be acting in accordance with my promise in trying to bring something of the traditions of the college to a wider audience.

The Church? Theological college? What had happened to cause such a seismic shift in direction?

5

Called John

For 30 years I have walked alongside those whose deepening faith drives them to consider a massive change in their life's direction. My strapline is that 95 per cent of those people have been disturbed by God, 5 per cent by God-knows-what! Their call is usually inchoate and I find them very difficult to read, because God is very difficult to read. They hold together all sorts of conflicting emotions, simultaneously idealistic and delusional, self-sacrificial and self-promotional, bewildered and certain, prayerful and sanctimonious, humble and ambitious.

Former Archbishop of Canterbury Rowan Williams talks about true vocation being a process where all our facades and veneers are stripped off to be our true selves before Christ. As Director of Ordinands I used to look from a candidate to the crucifix on my study wall and see how much it jarred. In my book the best priests give space and grace to notice the Christ crucified under their noses. Once my secretary spilled boiling-hot coffee on my lap, and the ordinand I was interviewing didn't even notice, prattling on about how marvellous he was. Another time, I asked a vicar how he would feel about being visited in hospital by a young man he was encouraging to be ordained. 'I could only cope with him if I was well,' was his revealing reply. On one retreat, one of our ordinands discovered the body of the retreat house warden, who had tragically committed suicide, causing the retreat's focus to have a cosmic shift. I was highly concerned that some would-be ordinands were unmoved by the sudden death, pestering me about their draughty college rooms or inadequate grants. Many would-be ordinands became won't-be ordinands that day.

John Habgood was clearly brought up to be 'good', with his whole family one way or another involved in public service. They were happy, united and morally serious, driven by a strong desire to be constructive and build a worthwhile society in the face and aftermath of a devastating war. John claimed that his move from physiology to faith was seamless and obvious, and that he didn't really change much as a person. The 'good' scientist simply became a 'good' priest; the man who had spent years puzzling over how frogs' nerves worked decided he would rather get beneath the skin of humankind and soothe troubled souls. However, I sensed a clunk of gears that would make even a learner-driver wince; what was going on?

In November 1946, bored by weekly bridge matches and their interminable post-mortems, he instead accepted an invitation to a party for Old Etonians, which was addressed by ex-Guards Major Bill Batt, who was helping run an evangelical mission to the university. John was struck by his sincerity and absolute certainty while simultaneously bemused by his habit of addressing God as if he were his commanding officer. The next night he went along with Major Bill to a mission service at Great St Mary's, powerfully addressed by Donald Barnhouse, a Presbyterian minister from Pennsylvania. This was followed by two 90-minute private sessions with Dr Barnhouse.

> My intellectual criticisms were met with plausible answers, delivered with a degree of conviction which in retrospect I can see made them seem more plausible than they were. I am not aware of having met real belief of this intensity before, and its effect on me was to make me feel I had been fooling around on the edge of things, so I allowed myself to be taught. There followed a rich and exciting period in which I discovered the Bible, prayer and church involvement.

The Cambridge Inter Collegiate Christian Union (CICCU) were superb in their follow up, drawing John into a busy round of prayer meetings, Bible studies, lectures, as well as Keswick conventions and young people's camps, ranging from an impromptu sail on the Norfolk Broads (where John cooked rather than skippered), to an annual camp and beach mission at Criccieth on North Wales' Lleyn Peninsular.

Within a short time he was teaching rather than being taught, producing regular well-written articles in publications such as *The Pilgrim Newsletter*. These had the same benign air as his bishop's letters in Durham and York, arresting if slightly superior pronouncements on almost every walk of life, disarming critics of various hues with a pithy phrase, using biblical material with a light touch, his weapon a rapier rather than a blunderbuss.

John stressed that his conversion led to embracing life in all its fullness, an eager discovery of Shakespeare, T. S. Eliot, Dorothy L. Sayers, poetry, theatre, music, literature, and a heightened engagement with the world and a new social order, as championed by William Temple. His faith too had a certain breadth, attending Holy Trinity, where he served on the PCC, and was influenced by Stanley Betts, its vicar, a more open Evangelical and less hard-line than some of the CICCU stalwarts. John increasingly played the pastor rather than the tutor, listening attentively to the personal problems and worries that students shared with him and pointing them to a solution. He regularly ate in a restaurant in Hills Road, chatting to another regular diner who was dying of cancer, counselling her unto death. He also attended St Bene't's, run by Franciscans, with long conversations with its parish priest, Brother Michael Fisher (later to be Bishop of St Germans), who became John's confessor. Fr Harry Williams, Vice-Principal of Westcott House and Mirfield monk, gave helpful and relaxed spiritual direction which broadened him.

This broadening was clearly deemed unsound by some in CICCU, to which John gave a counter-blast with a fiercely argued 15-page open letter. It was driven by a Saturday night Bible study where a country parson had unwisely taken on Darwin, dismissing him and all he stood for because he looked like the very monkey he claimed to have evolved from. The gathering had laughed with rather than at the inept speaker, and John had been offended by the paucity of their intellect. They were kind to laugh, because it was a very old joke; Bishop of Oxford (Soapy) Sam Wilberforce had once jibed at Huxley over whether it was on his mother's side or his father's side that an ape featured in their family tree.

The thing is, in my experience those Saturday night CICCU gatherings were always like that. Warm and friendly gatherings of like-minded individuals, with the speakers, onside with their audience, their prejudices and their God, using personal anecdote and humour to domesticate the Bible and theology and deliver bite-size and occasionally challenging reflections. I remember one mirthful guy speculating how many ranks there would be in the 12 legions of angels Jesus could have summoned at Gethsemane. I have used a similar technique, musing on the Galilean police stopping a wedding guest wending his chariot home after consuming 180 gallons of wine at Cana: ' "'Allo, 'Allo, 'Allo" – or rather, "Shalom, Shalom, Shalom" – been drinking with Jesus have we, sir?' Not a lot of intellectual rigour, but it gets people laughing, opening them up for my killer punch.

Okay, it's all a literary construct and a bit of a false game, but just one game among many. Morse, Miss Marple, Hercule Poirot, Nordic Noir all have their conventional if far-fetched plots, which pass the time but also have a moral punch. James Herriot and *All Creatures Great and Small* consists of predictable characters and storylines, canny Yorkshire farmers, beautiful scenery, loveable animals, with inept, clumsy Mr Herriot surprisingly turning their Good Fridays into Easter. Reality wasn't quite like that: James's doe-eyed wife Helen in real life proved to be a woman not to mess with; the loveable if eccentric Siegfried in real life took against James, forcing an out-of-court settlement. Whatever, Herriot's marvellous books and TV series spawned a warm glow on Sunday evenings, and turned veterinary medicine from being the Cinderella of subjects to being the belle of the academic ball.

John frequently noted in *The Pilgrim Newsletter* how his own scientific world played games, turning a blind eye to the torture of helpless animals, as well as passing dismissive comment on religious systems about which it knew nothing. Nevertheless, John's critique of CICCU is scathing, most concerned that the heady faith they encourage often grows cold once their adherents leave Cambridge. He accuses them of having a closed mind; being a citadel of belief beyond the range of ordinary criticism; teaching others but not learning from them; giving in to the temptation to produce a spiritual Bradshaw's; clinging tenaciously to a system of philosophy accepted blindly and thoughtlessly, confined into a little pen of fixed belief and attitude; reducing the process of entering the kingdom of heaven to merely knowing the correct password; and claiming all social problems can be solved by conversion or, failing that, the Second Coming. John briefly breaks off from this diatribe to express admiration for CICCU members' boldness, zeal, devotion and self-sacrifice, but concludes that it is better to be honest than fervent. He calls CICCU to a fivefold reform: to realize that evangelism is not the most important Christian activity; to contribute to, rather than brief against, the intellectual councils of the

University; to be more catholic in its meetings; to be humble; and to be-friend rather than alienate other Christians, including not calling John's beloved King's College chapel the devil's masterpiece!

Clearly something must have upset him! There is a love angle, in that he had had an intense romantic relationship with Lorna, a music teacher who had also served on Holy Trinity PCC. On one of their long country walks she surprised John by confessing she loved another, coincidentally an Old Etonian senior to John, who too had been in Mayes' House. In the end, her relationship with both Old Etonians came to nothing. 'Though distressing at the time,' John concludes, with characteristic understate-ment, 'it made it easier to settle down in theological college where wives and girlfriends were treated as if they did not exist.' Such as Cuddesdon College, which then required any wives not to live within a 50-mile radius of the college, presumably to prevent ordinands popping home for a spot of 'afternoon delight'. But John's cool assessment notwithstanding, I do wonder if being spurned by Lorna soured him against the evangeli-cal tenets that fired her.

Or maybe he felt he'd been abused, a shy, tender 19-year-old being hectored for three hours by a US evangelist, more Orwell's 1984 than 1946 Cambridge. Maybe, as he pushed forward the frontiers of know-ledge in the laboratory, he had yearned for a safe haven, where he could be told what to do rather than have to discover it, only then to resent that haven and resent himself for giving in to it. Maybe fundamentalist Christianity offered him solid ground in the midst of the uncertainties and horrors of war and a broken post-war Europe, only to realize that God was in the wound, impaled on those crosses rather than an escape from them.

The Revd Professor John Polkinghorne, champion of the interface between science and religion, coincided with John at Cambridge and CICCU. He described John cutting a lonely figure in CICCU, an intellec-tual trophy rather than an influence, with a cool reputation of someone who would hardly be described as clubbable. John heard a rumour that he had failed to be elected fellow in 1951 because King's feared, as an Evangelical, he would not be intellectually up to it; maybe distancing himself from CICCU so ruthlessly reasserted his academic credentials, clearing his path for a career both in academia and in the Church.

Whatever, CICCU fired John's faith and sprung him upon the Church and world. He chose to train for ordained ministry at Cuddesdon College. He defended his choice to a dubious Major Batt, that it would offer him spiritual discipline and academic freedom, a pause in a rural wilderness prior to a busy ministry. The then principal, Kenneth Riches, had invited John to visit the place in October 1951 and simply meet the kind of people who came to Cuddesdon and check he would not be irritated by the quite small and trivial things that filled their day. In April 1952 John attended a selection conference chaired by Hedley Burrows, Dean of Hereford, who had forgotten to bring his false teeth to the conference. Despite his previously lampooning CICCU, John reverted to defending a biblical literalism when interviewed by the chairman, only to be dismissed with a gummy, 'Oh, you shoon will move on from all that shilly shtuff.'

Having been recommended for training, John explored the possibility of being ordained and continuing as a don at King's, but opted instead for a parochial role. Over the summer, John congratulated Riches on being made Bishop of Dorchester – 'Does one congratulate bishops?' he muses in his letter. He opted to begin at Cuddesdon on 31 January 1953, the start of the Lent term, when he felt able to leave King's without letting down anyone too badly.

The new principal, Edward Knapp-Fisher, tried to postpone John's start to the autumn of 1953, wanting to do away with a practice that had spilled over from the war, when men came and went at various times of the year when not preoccupied with war work. John was having none of it: an offer and promise had been made by the former principal, which his successor was duty-bound to honour. John described Knapp-Fisher as a great man of prayer who majored on the Anglican church fathers, a buttoned-up and stern disciplinarian. However stern, on the issue of John's start date Knapp-Fisher relented, his correspondence coming across as somewhat brittle, while also reflecting a sense of awe concerning Cuddesdon's newest recruit.

So on 31 January 1953, John began, no doubt honouring the terse instruction, not dissimilar to termly notices served by his old prep school in Eastbourne, to bring sheets, pillowcases, towels, gown and (if possible) cassock and surplice. Except this time there was no school train, shades of the Hogwart's Express, departing from Waterloo at 3.45 p.m., since remote Cuddesdon was miles from any station. John had to make his own way there, on a two-cylinder motorbike, which enabled pilgrimages to Blackwell's when life at Cuddesdon became too much to bear.

John's fellowship at King's continued while he was pursuing a valid course of study, so the motorbike was handy for flitting between Oxford and Cambridge. Before Christmas 1952, John wrote tellingly to the Provost, who wasn't the only one to be baffled by John's change of direction:

I hope that my visits to King's in the future will not be too infrequent, but since this is the first real break I have had with the college for a long time, I wanted to mark it in some special way. As you yourself once said 'One never leaves King's,' and that I am sure is true, if only in a spiritual sense. But perhaps it is truer to say 'King's never leaves you': once a Kingsman, always a Kingsman. So, in spite of your fears, I don't think that dreadful place Cuddesdon will do too much damage to me, and at any rate I shall be returning to you from time to time for corrective treatment! I must again apologise for leaving so soon, and for any inconvenience it may have caused. My only excuse is one can't really do a job properly, when one's heart is somewhere else.

A last word from Charles Mayes, his housemaster at Eton, whose letter to John of June 1952, congratulating him on his fellowship, had a sting in its tail:

You are likely to have a difficult decision to make when the time comes, if your research is beckoning you on; for it is easier for a scientist to be an active Churchman, than for the parish priest to pursue scientific research.

6

Cloistered John

Cuddesdon College was founded in 1854 by the aforementioned Samuel Wilberforce, bishop of Oxford. It was an age when it was the fashion for diocesan bishops to gather around them those approaching ordination, invariably Oxbridge graduates, to supplement previous study with an intensive period of spiritual discipline and prayer in a quasi-monastic setting. The saintly Edward King was an early principal. He set a Tractarian stamp and rigour on a place which soon proved to be happy in its skin, able to take on board the radical challenges of evolution and critical biblical scholarship that polarized the Church in the late nineteenth century. During King's time a potential candidate came for a day's visit, beginning with a breakfast in silence, at which all the students gathered, sporting pious looks as well as their black cassocks. King, realizing how daunted the candidate must have felt, leant across and whispered, 'Don't worry, we ain't as good as we looks!'

The college was buried deep in the Oxford countryside, eight long miles from Oxford, based in a pretty tiny village that originally housed workers in the bishop's palace and estate. By the 1950s it was ostensibly an independent institution, though regulated and inspected by the Church of England, drawing ordinands from across the UK, who either funded themselves (as John did with his fellowship from King's) or drew on limited diocesan or local authority grants. The ordinands were mostly single, in their early twenties – John would be one of the older men at 25. The lifestyle was deliberately frugal, so maintenance costs were low. My father attended Lichfield Theological College in 1960, with a grant from his sponsoring diocese of just £100 per annum, which had to house and feed him, my mother and me. Years later I discovered some correspondence in his personal file, proposing to double the grant. A mean archdeacon declined the proposal, noting, 'A little holy poverty will do them good.' At least Lichfield allowed an ordinand's family to live within walking distance.

John quickly realized the teaching at Cuddesdon was far from brilliant, but he enjoyed the worship, which alternated between the college chapel and the ancient and freezing village church, and found he had time galore to pray and read, as well as completing the prescribed General Ordination Examination in Christian doctrine, worship and ethics, church history and the Old and New Testament. Eighteen months didn't afford enough time to take a formal theology degree, which might seem to place John at a disadvantage in terms of future possibilities within the Church. When John was appointed Vice-Principal of Westcott House in 1956, a couple of council members expressed reservations that he had no formal theological qualifications. David Jenkins, controversial Bishop of Durham and former Professor of Theology at Leeds, rated John as α/β, a collator and co-ordinator of thought rather than an original thinker: 'He is not a theologian and does not think theologically. He is reserved, but what is behind that reservedness – much or anything?'

It all seems a bit snobby. I agree with my former tutor, the Franciscan Barnabas Lindars, Rylands Professor of Biblical Exegesis and Criticism at Manchester University, who reckoned that theology wasn't like any other subject, where a three-year degree could equip you for life. Rather, theological knowledge and expertise accumulated, only coming to a head of steam after decades of reading, thinking and connecting. John immersed himself in all that and, contra David Jenkins, always had a fresh take and something original to say.

Certainly he was a very disciplined and widely read autodidact, with an amazing reading speed. We were once reading the same book during a retreat, *The Christlike God* (1993), by John V. Taylor, Bishop of Winchester. It was highly original and bracing, but by no means an easy read. I was managing my usual reading speed for theological tomes of 30 pages per hour, but I clocked John's speed at 90. I wondered whether he had skimmed over some of the more tricky paragraphs, but when we happened to discuss the book later, John had a grasp of the detail that was nothing less than forensic.

And back in the 1950s, reading yourself in was a common practice. People such as Robert Runcie had read Greats at Oxford, and then, with no theological qualifications, held down posts such as vice-principal and principal of Oxbridge theological colleges, as well as serving as Dean of Trinity Hall, Cambridge, and ultimately going all the way to Canterbury. We did a Gilbert and Sullivan-esque skit about Runcie when I was at theological college, with the refrain:

Some said I should read Theology,
but why, when without it I get Canterbury?
I knew so little Theology,
that now I am the ruler of the C of E!

Our principal banned us from performing the skit at the eleventh hour.

At Cuddesdon the handful of villagers were undoubtedly over-pastored by eager ordinands and less eager staff, but John struck up a good relationship with a young woman who had been severely paralysed by a stroke, whom he took for long walks in her wheelchair. 'She was marvellously courageous, and interesting to talk to, as over the years she had been looked after by many ordinands, and was quite shrewd in summing them up.' She called her paralysed arm and leg Charles and Arabella, because they had (or rather didn't have) a life of their own. Once ordained, John wrote children's magazine stories about two children named Charles and Arabella, which he used to send to her to keep in contact.

Another confidante was an ordinand called Nick Stacey, a sparkling former naval officer, who unlike John was extrovert and athletic, a sprinter in the Helsinki Olympics. The two opposites attracted each other and sparked each other's imaginations. Stacey described John as quiet, with a rather dry sense of humour, born wise and cautious, always calm, reasonable and self-disciplined, with a maturity beyond his years.

There are some priests, one always feels, who would go to bed in their cassocks if left to themselves. John was not in this category, but I never really knew him to let his hair down, partly because of his shyness.

Stacey was in awe of John's enormous integrity and a quiet purposefulness, which, coupled with his outstanding intellect, made him a credible and respected figure in the college. While at the college, Stacey enlisted John to launch a scheme to take orphaned boys on outings, which enabled John to enjoy his first ride on the footplate of a steam engine. Stacey and John went to hear Billy Graham at his infamous crusade at Harringay, and dared each other to go forward; they did, and were duly counselled. John observed that 'only fundamentalists could put on a show like that. The success of Graham's campaign is that he can use the Bible in a way that many of us would think was dishonest.'

John found Cuddesdon over-churchy and fussy, with a diary entry from 1953 expressing his fury at having to act as candle-bearer at Solemn Evensong. The preacher happened to be Mervyn Stockwood, then Vicar of Great St Mary's, soon to be appointed Bishop of Southwark, and his radical message, telling it as it was, fired John. Most of the other preachers were dull, advocating an outdated ecclesiology and theology that seemed oblivious to the needs of a generation traumatized by two world wars. Twenty-five years later, when I trained it was much the same: tedious talks and sermons delivered by ancient guys, akin to those isolated Japanese troops who were discovered in the depths of Borneo's jungles in the 1960s and 1970s , who hadn't realised the Second World War had ended, fighting battles in a skirmish that had long since passed.

John channelled his frustrations with theological college into satire, as evidenced by spoof tracts such as 'The Church of England Society for the Promotion of Interplanetary Travel', or his 'Application for permission to be ill for the Cuddesdon Health Service'. John was later to write this when Vice-Principal of Westcott: 'The Church is a horrible human institution, and the only justification for it is that occasionally God shines through, and beyond the ghastly clothes and the rest of it, one discovers a love that surprises one.'

As so often happens with ordinands, John was fashioned not so much by the college as by the placements it sprung. He sought out one at Goodmayes Mental Hospital in Romford, to experience the practical side of his psychological and neurophysiological studies, with the following recommendation by a doctor in London, who clearly rated John highly:

This is a very solid, reliable chap with no trace of eccentricity. He seems to have concluded that it would be good to know something about mental disorders before taking up parish work. If you could use him you will find him energetic, not a bit 'ritzy' and not in any way inclined to throw his weight around.

These were the days of locked wards and burnt-out people with schizophrenia. John worked for three weeks as an orderly, paid £7 per week, mostly cutting very disorientated patients' toenails, describing the experience as 'a lesson in facing utter degradation'. Once again a case of looking into the wound.

A happier secondment took place in the dry summer of 1953, when John and two other Cuddesdon students joined the Bishop of Whitby for a walking mission around the Pickering deanery, taking their cue from Luke 14.15–23, the Invitation to the great feast. From 23 June to 5 July they walked through each of the 12 parishes and most of the villages in the deanery. They held a formal outdoor mission service in the evening, seasoned with pithy phrases like, 'We beseech you that ye walk worthy of the vocation wherewith ye are called.' Four traditional hymns (including 'Rise up, O *men* of God') were followed by a challenging sermon and then a call to love the Church and dedicate afresh their lives in Christ's service. They stayed overnight with parishioners, then held a Eucharist in the parish church the next morning before setting out to the next village, having sent its vicar a postcard the previous day, alerting him to their impending visitation.

The deanery centres on the market town of Pickering at the southern foot of the stunning North York Moors, rising to places like Lastingham, home of Saints Cedd and Chad – John was deeply moved by its numinous ancient crypt, which transported him back to a seventh century packed to the brim with northern saints. But John also paused in homage in the high moorland villages that straddled the North York Moors railway, marvelling at steam train after steam train huffing and puffing as it snaked up the moors towards Whitby. John snaked up another moor to Wydale Hall, run by Anglican nuns. Many of them were also former scientists, teachers at the girls' school at the mother house of the Order of the Holy Paraclete (OHP) in Whitby. John suddenly had to crank himself up a gear, conversing about the intricacies of physics and maths rather than puzzling over passing remarks from dour farmers, such as, 'Ee, ain't all this sunshine grand, lad? Si thee, we'll have t' harvest in afore Llamas-tide if we crack on!' John commented, 'I don't think we made many converts, but it was a good introduction to impromptu preaching, as well as Yorkshire.' Their tour de force concluded with an open-air service in the ruins of the Cistercian Rievaulx Abbey; afterwards the Bishop wrote to John, thanking him 'for being such a happy pilgrim'.

Soon after John had been made Archbishop of York he revisited the deanery and addressed local clergy, reminiscing about his visit 30 years earlier to this land of lost content. 'I remember there was this stick-in-the mud called Inder who was Vicar of Sinnington,' he jested. 'Still here, your Grace, still here!' came a booming voice from the back of the room. In 1993, at the tender age of 78, the redoubtable Robert Inder wrote to the Archbishop, informing him he was going to marry his housekeeper of several years. 'But not for sexual purposes,' he stressed, lest there be any doubt.

John, hoping to serve both as a parish priest and university chaplain, explored possibilities in London. Holy Trinity, Prince Consort Road, next to Imperial College, seemed ideal, but the post there failed to materialize due to a lack of suitable training incumbent, so he accepted an assistant curacy just up the road at St Mary Abbots, Kensington.

He was duly ordained deacon by the Bishop of London in St Paul's Cathedral on Trinity Sunday, 13 June 1954. There is a collection of letters wishing John well, including one from the Bishop of Whitby, encouraging John to consider focusing on a healing ministry, which drew on his medical skills. John was to be ordained alongside Simon Burrows, son of Hedley Burrows, the toothless Dean of Hereford, who had chaired John's selection conference. Hedley wrote, assuring him he would be remembering him on Trinity Sunday rather specially, that it had been a great joy to get to know him, and that he would have a ministry of high importance to many people in the years to come.

But the most moving letter was a simple one, written by John's father on the eve of his ordination:

My dear John,
You are constantly in our thoughts and prayers this week-end and we want you to feel sure of our loving interest and approval of the step you are taking.

You have all your life been a joy to us and an influence in the house which has affected our lives more than perhaps you realise.

We thank God for giving us John and feel sure you will find happiness in your new life.

All our love,

Mummy and Daddy

7

Kensington John

St Mary Abbots, Kensington, was one of those grand London parishes, harking back to Victorian times, with three churches, served by a despot of a vicar and six curates, who also acted as honorary chaplains at a London University college. The parish church had been bombed and fitted with a temporary corrugated iron roof, which made for bad acoustics. Its vicar, Stanley Eley, was a small man with an extremely loud voice, who refused to have an amplification system, and so taught all his curates to throw their voices. John thought he'd caught the knack of voice projection, but from the number of complaints I received as his chaplain about him being softly spoken, he clearly hadn't; I was too much in awe of him to pass the complaints on. Eley went on to be Bishop of Gibraltar, presumably barking the gospel across the Straits to convert heathen Africans gathered on the distant shore.

The parish ranged from a royal presence in Kensington Palace to the slums in Campden Hill, with young executives housed in tiny flats. John was expected to do door-to-door visiting in a borough brimful of the great and the good, which now sports no less than 177 blue plaques. During John's time he could have chanced upon a heady cocktail consisting of Winston Churchill, T. S. Eliot, Sir Alexander Fleming, Hugh Greene, Tony Hancock, A. A. Milne, Christabel Pankhurst and Sir Malcolm Sargent. He recalls accidentally visiting the Vietnamese Embassy, as well as unintentionally calling on sex-kitten Mai Zetterling, the famous Swedish actress who answered the door of her flat dressed in a flimsy negligee. The latter experience may have influenced a curious lecture he gave to junior clergy at Bishopthorpe in 1994, about the appropriate time to visit women. He instructed them that the safest time to visit women was during the morning, when they would be too busy with their household tasks to contemplate any naughtiness with the curate. He counselled avoiding afternoons, a more leisurely time when the female libido was roused to dangerous levels. 'And never ever visit a woman in the evening,' he sternly concluded, waving his finger as if sex was a foregone conclusion with any lone female you happened upon after dark. He seemed strangely oblivious to the fact that nearly half of his audience actually consisted of women clergy.

A normal Sunday in just one of the churches, whose formidable list of sidesmen included generals and admirals, consisted of 7 a.m., 8 a.m. and 12.30 p.m. Holy Communions, a 10 a.m. Sung Eucharist followed by 11.30 a.m. Royal Mattins (compared to normal Mattins when only the Lord Almighty is present), a 3 p.m. Children's Service, 4 p.m. Baptisms, a 6.30 p.m. Choral Evensong and then a youth club and discussion group. Monica Libby, a youthful member of the congregation at that time, recalls John being a young priest who was very serious, well above them in intellectual ability. At first she feared his sermons were well above her, but she grew to find them stimulating, particularly grateful he had introduced her to Dostoyevsky. More than 50 attended his discussion group, with John mingling easily with the youngsters over refreshments, following a talk by arresting speakers. John also organized outdoor services for children in Holland Park – there is a photo of him standing proud on a park bench, addressing rapt children seated cross-legged on the grass. Penelope Hawkes, another former parishioner, remembers John's frequent visits by bicycle to her dying father, who enjoyed long conversations about their Cambridge days.

In 1955 John was also given charge of Christchurch, Victoria Road, known as 'the village church' – the former curate had been persuaded to retire, and when John discovered a stash of empty whiskey bottles under the altar he realized the reason why. He also served as chaplain of Mary Abbots Hospital. Before Easter that year, there were 22 slots advertised when clergy would be available to hear confessions.

Given all these responsibilities, John was clearly very irked to be summoned by the vicar for a severe dressing down on Christmas Eve 1955. It seemed that John had walked past a leading parishioner in Kensington High Street without acknowledging him whatsoever. 'Stupid man,' John commented, clearly still sore after half a century. 'Didn't he realize I was thinking?' There are a lot of episodes like this, where John's single-minded focus holds sway, and people simply don't appear on his screen. Early one morning a student at Queen's bumped into John in the grounds. 'Good morning, Principal.' No response. 'Good morning, Principal,' he repeated, turning up the volume. No response. 'Good morning, Principal,' he almost shouted, for the third time of asking. 'I'm praying,' came the dismissive reply. We once went to a confirmation at Hessle, near Hull, and arrived in torrential rain. Despite the deluge, the two dear churchwardens had stood for ages on the kerb, waiting to greet us. Purple-cassocked John strode out of the car, without exchanging a word with them.

Doreen Eley, the vicar's wife, is less critical than her husband, and contributes to the considerable postbag eulogizing John's preaching:

I write to tell you how much I appreciated the 3 hours devotion you took today, and to thank you for a most moving and spiritual approach. As Stanley will tell you, I fear I am usually somewhat critical of sermons and the like, and I have 'sat under' many priests on many Good Fridays, but I never remember anything as excellent as your addresses today. May God continue to bless you.

The monthly parish magazine contains children's stories penned by John, including one about a boy called John (!) who wanted to be king, fantasizing about all sorts of power and privilege before finally modelling himself on King Jesus who rode on a donkey. Charles and Arabella (named after his Cuddesdon contact's paralysed limbs) get into terrible scrapes. A spat develops while serious-minded Charles writes an essay and girlie Arabella knits a tea-cosy, degenerating into hurtling ink bottles and decorations ruined. Their behaviour is so improved the next day that their father dubs it Good Friday, and then explains the original Good Friday, when Jesus refused to retaliate to spite and insults, and never ever threw ink. Charles far prefers reading sci-fi about spacemen to being bored by the Bible – clearly more a portrait of the artist than the sitter – nevertheless leading to a long lecture on the Scriptures by his form master, who is surprisingly astute on biblical studies:

The Bible is not a supernatural document which fell down from heaven, but a book written by fallible human beings in particular historical situations, whose very oddities and incongruities have their indispensable place, because they respond to the real complexities of human experience. It is the story of everyman, one which we can live ourselves into, and so find the meanings of our own lives.

Lest this goes over Charles' head, he is reassured that the Bible is like a London A–Z, guiding him through the myriad streets of life.

There are two moments when you feel the hand of history is on John's shoulder. John writes a parish magazine article describing the centenary at Cuddesdon in August 1954, when 'black clergy, white clergy, clergy of every conceivable shape and size thronged the lawns, gossiped interminably and gave thanks for all that Cuddesdon meant to them'. There is a photo of the Archbishops of Canterbury and York, in a procession led by crucifer John, standing taller than both.

> Geoffrey Fisher encouraged all to be thankful without being sentimental. Archbishop of York, Cyril Garbett, describing himself as a venerable antiquity, explained in detail how he might have used the opportunity to attract young men to the vigorous life of the Northern Province. 'But,' he added, 'I will not say a word about it.' Can there be any higher recommendation of a Cuddesdon training in ecclesiastical diplomacy?

Thus concludes John, fourth in line to Ebor's throne.

John initially lodged near Olympia, but tiring of cycling two miles into Kensington and back several times a day, he responded to a notice in a local newspaper, advertising a spare room in a basement flat just yards from Kensington Parish Church. John was an unwitting fly who innocently walked into a very complex web. The flat was occupied by a widow, Iris Marjorie (Madré) Owen, her Aunt G, elderly and weak after a stroke, and Madré's daughter, Faith, who had been brain-damaged at birth. Shy John, yearning for solitude for his sermon preparations and studies, was alarmed by a stream of visitors to the flat, the most frequent being one Michael Ramsey, then Bishop of Durham. It transpired that Mrs Owen's late husband, Leslie, had been Warden of Lincoln

Theological College when Michael served as his sub-warden. Then Leslie was Bishop of Jarrow when Michael was professor at Durham, living just next door but one. Joan, Leslie's secretary and chauffeur (who had learnt to drive as she had learnt to type, by trial and error), then married Michael in 1942. Faith Owen was her only bridesmaid, flanked by Eric Abbott, Michael's best man and future Dean of Westminster – in the 1950s another frequent visitor to Madré's extremely accommodating basement flat.

In 1944, Leslie had been appointed Bishop of the newly created see of Maidstone and Bishop to the Forces, to assist the Archbishop of Canterbury in his care of chaplains to the armed forces. He was one of the few who narrowly survived when a flying bomb hit the Guards' Chapel in London in 1944. He died soon after being translated to Lincoln in 1946, probably as a result of lung damage from the dust he had inhaled from the bomb blast.

Mrs Owen had long conversations with John, bringing him up to speed with immensely complex Church of England politics, in which she was very well versed. Her father, Walter Lawrance, had been Archdeacon of St Albans and then became the first Dean of St Alban's Abbey after St Albans was made a diocese, restoring the Abbey and increasing its congregation tenfold. Madré, born in 1889, had assisted her father with parish work, but following his death in 1914 served as a nurse for the war wounded until 1919, returning to the Abbey to marry Leslie in 1920.

For five years after John left Kensington she had a long, intense and very intimate correspondence with him, amazing letters, which John kept. In them she plays a surrogate mother (Madré is Spanish for mother) advising John not to take himself too seriously; warning him that he has matured too quickly; acknowledging that John found it hard to accept guidance; correcting a second version of a Westcott compline sermon, having rejected the first; sending John a pot tortoise to remind him to go slow, assuring him that tranquillity will triumph over turmoil; begging him to take time off, and to abstain from work rather than food. She also treats him as her protégé, advising him to talk things through with superiors he finds infuriating; quoting Attic Greek (correctly, complete with accents); exploring mysticism – 'I can't do without Kierkegaard!'; unravelling church politics, secretive stuff with coded phrases, and disguising key players by using their initials only, tetragrammatons for 1950s' gods – more Bletchley than Kensington. She flatters him, with sentiments such as 'I want you so much . . ', 'if you were only here to laugh with me . . ', 'your wisdom is so often needed . . ', 'the love I have for you must inevitably have the cross right in the middle of it . . ', 'what a wonderful sense of peace you bring', signing off one letter with 'I am, since I have been since our first meeting, your loving Madré'. Then there is the mundane: washing lines breaking over the bath and drenching the laundry; thanking John for installing a rope and pulley in the bathroom so she could haul herself out of the bath when she was laid low with phlebitis; visiting clergy who sternly counsel against receiving communion by intinction; a fall-out with the vicar who libels her in the parish magazine for scheming and manipulating the congregation; seeking advice about a girl who had just come down from Girton and had a terrible crush on Ken Carey, Westcott House's Principal. She even writes asking whether she should switch off her new TV during a thunderstorm; presumably by the time busy John had replied, the storm had passed. Given the tone of all this correspondence, their conversation in the flesh during John's Kensington days must have been electrifying.

She was unafraid of being a severe critic, and taught John much about the rights and wrongs of preaching and leading worship. She shared with her late husband a deep spirituality, which Leslie had used, along with a small group of like-minded clerics, to forge the very selection system and formation that John had just undergone. It could be summed up by having the nerve and verve to 'pray theologically', to have an insightful and informed conversation with God that involved both speaking and listening. For four years at Bishopthorpe I listened to John pray, words that sounded as if they had been weighed up and crafted over a long period: my heart burned within me as I walked on his road. On Mrs Owen's bedroom wall was a large framed picture, containing the single illuminated word, 'Eternity'. John comments:

> It was the focus of her room, as it was the focus of her life. And I have never ceased to be grateful for the experience of living with someone who knew and was living in eternity, whose mind and heart had ascended with the ascended Christ.

Michael Ramsey was very much part of Leslie Owen's set. 'Michael is quite wonderfully transformed since going to York,' Madré writes after he was appointed Archbishop. 'Michael came to see us during the Church Assembly,' she remarks, *en passant* in another letter, concluding with the classic, 'No, Michael is *not* meant for TV.' Few can forget those grainy TV pictures of Michael Ramsey tottering beside the Queen at her Coronation. Madré and Michael go back to Lincoln days, although back then she found him a very odd young man, at times near mental breakdown. There were times when she would find him lying on his bed, incoherent, seemingly incapable of doing anything. Once he and Leslie were divided over a theological conundrum; while in a tea shop, Michael hit on a solution, but waved his hands around so enthusiastically that the waitress refused to serve him. Yet Ramsey's time at Lincoln produced his classic, *The Gospel and the Catholic Church* (1936), with its own buzzword: 'Glory'.

Those lengthy and intense Kensington conversations clearly rubbed off on John, affirming his own innate sense of wonder in the glory of the created world and creatures that inhabited it, as well as in his own acts of creation on the easel or woodwork bench, or simply mending a broken machine and wondering at the workmanship revealed. Certainly those Kensington conversations fired a lifelong devotion to Michael Ramsey. When John moved to York, he had his portrait painted by George Bruce. Bruce significantly had also painted Ramsey's portraits for Durham, York and Canterbury, inhabiting his holy subject, adoring him, even travelling with him for parish visits. It must have made for an interesting arrival: a driver, a chaplain, an archbishop – and an artist! When the Ramseys became too frail to live on their own, John and Rosalie did a flat up for them within Bishopthorpe Palace, with Michael starting each day worshipping in Bishopthorpe Palace chapel, followed by long conversations about diocesan clergy whom Michael vividly remembered from 30 years before. St Anselm, a previous Archbishop of Canterbury, undergirded the ministry of both men:

Come now, little man, put aside your business for a while, take refuge for a little from your tumultuous thoughts, cast off your cares and let your burdensome distractions wait. Take some leisure for God; rest awhile in him. Enter into the chamber of your mind; put out everything except God and whatever helps you to seek him. Say now to God with all your heart: 'I seek thy face, O Lord, thy face I seek.'

Another member of Leslie Owen's set was Ken Carey, Principal of Westcott House, confirmed bachelor though pin-up boy for Girton maidens. On 12 March 1956 he sent John a four-page handwritten letter, speculating that Robert Runcie, his vice-principal, might leave in the next 12 months, and wondering whether, in that eventuality, John would be willing to replace him. Carey's expectations for the post-holder were modest, that he should be a scholar and a recognized High Churchman. It was all written in the strictest confidence, with neither Robert Runcie nor Stanley Eley privy to the offer. Carey does suggest, however, that John discusses the possibility with Madré Owen, who presumably had promoted John's cause. John had a rendezvous with Carey in the King's Cross Hotel over lunch, when the offer was made, subject to Robert Runcie's departure and the Westcott Council's approval. The quasi-interview clearly went well, although John thought he had blown his chances when he ordered treacle pudding for dessert, on a Friday of all days, a day of abstinence.

Robert Runcie was appointed Dean of Trinity Hall, where he wooed the Master's daughter, Westcott House's Council eventually approved John's appointment and the offer was accepted, prompting an acerbic magazine letter from the stentorian Canon Eley.

I know you will all share my regret . . . that John Habgood has been appointed Vice-Principal of Westcott House, one of the two theological colleges in Cambridge. His gifts and his past association with Cambridge made his choice for this work a natural one, but both he and I wish it had not come quite so soon. In the two years he has been with us he has made an excellent start in his ministry, and given a very definite contribution to the life of the parish. He will be greatly missed by his many friends here.

Tellingly, the same magazine advertised a talk on 3 June by the vicar on 'Temptation', and a talk on 24 June by John Habgood on 'Dreams'; John's dream of synthesizing faith and academia was about to be realized.

8

Westcott John

John's appointment to the post of vice-principal did not go quite as smoothly as Ken Carey planned, in that he wasn't really at liberty to offer the job in the first place. With reservations about John's lack of theological qualifications, Westcott House Council considered two other candidates. Carey robustly defended his choice: someone with a first-class pedigree in one subject is likely to be a first-class thinker across the board; and while John was not a theologian as such, he had a proven record of thinking theologically.

Carey managed to win the day and John joined the staff at Westcott House in October 1956. He was to teach Old Testament, early church history, liturgy and ethics, with the Chaplain teaching New Testament and doctrine and the Principal teaching prayer and pastoralia.

Getting up to speed with four specialist areas was obviously a considerable challenge, which was further complicated in the first weeks by the House cook walking out and several French priests walking in, and one ordinand dying of lung cancer. Fortunately most of the work was teaching 'not so bright beginners' (John's phrase). He was particularly scathing about a large and thick tenor, whose son surprisingly went on to be Bishop of Winchester. Otherwise John simply had to fill in the gaps for students who either had graduated in theology already or were completing the Cambridge theology tripos and therefore were supervised by divinity faculty staff.

Considering they worked and lived closely together in the House, there are a surprising number of long letters from Carey to John during their five years in harness. Usually Carey is handing over the reins prior to some grand tour. 'Tell the boys how very grateful I am for the cards and presents,' he instructs John on New Year's Eve 1959. 'Carey's boys' were young ordinands who found particular favour.

The subject material of his letters to John is wide-ranging, including pastoral care and discipline of individual ordinands, covering the teaching syllabus and liturgy, or gossip about church appointments, culminating in Carey's appointment as Bishop of Edinburgh. The tone is very affectionate, with Carey clearly in awe of John's administrative gifts and intellect, agreeing with Madré's lavish assessment of him, 'If any man was sent from God whose name was John, it was you.' Carey often resorted to the imagery of A. A. Milne, declaring himself a bear of little brain, although John felt he knew far more theology than he let on. Any major decision or crisis Carey inevitably runs past Madré, including his disappointment that he was passed over to be Dean of Westminster when Eric Abbott was appointed. 'Ken writes how devoted he is to you – Bless you for helping him at this time,' Madré writes.

John inherited a green Hillman from his father, and broadened the outlook of ordinands from a lowly background by taking three of them on camping holidays on the Continent. In 1957 they went to Lourdes, in 1959 to Rome, Assisi and Florence, usually camping in fields by a river, with ablutions in the river or behind a hedge. John was always very relaxed about bodily functions. Once on a long trip to the Cumbrian coast, he suddenly ordered our driver to pull in at a lay-by by Bassenthwaite Water, so he could relieve himself behind a tree. A woman in a Metro pulled into the same lay-by, but I stood against the driver's door engaging her in conversation, effectively preventing her from getting out of her car until the purple-cassocked Archbishop returned from his excursion; God knows what she thought we were up to.

Clearly John's time and correspondence with Madré relaxed him, encouraging him not to take life and himself too seriously. Madré only wished the curate who succeeded John as her lodger took life a little more seriously, complaining that he never went visiting, donning his pyjamas and taking to his bed each afternoon, his room a total mess. He is so laid back he manages to miss his first funeral by half an hour, so clumsy that she has to bathe his grazed knees after a fall when he was rushing to meet the head verger.

Clearly Madré had a magic touch, in that he went on to be a prolific writer on theology and spirituality, appointed Librarian at Pusey House, a Residentiary Canon of Canterbury Cathedral, an adviser on Orthodoxy to Michael Ramsey and an honorary professor at Bangor University. His name was Donald Allchin.

At a party celebrating the opening of the new Westcott Common Room in November 1960, John met a certain Rosalie Boston, a distinguished teacher of music, violin and piano at King's College Choir School, and they talked for most of the evening. Rosalie fell instantly for this dishy cleric, but feared he was celibate, since he was dressed sombrely in black. She took advice from a good friend, Frank Bennett, Vicar of Maidstone, who enthusiastically encouraged her to pursue John. Just two months later, after their third meeting, they announced their engagement, ironically following Ken Carey's annual lecture advocating celibacy. Madré very much approved of Rosalie, and had counselled John throughout their courtship: 'The great moment will be reached when you find that being apart may be an ecstasy and you discover the real meaning of togetherness.'

They married in June 1961, with Frank Bennett officiating, and honeymooned in the South of France, near the Pyrenees. On the first night of their honeymoon, John knelt by the side of the bed to say his prayers while Rosalie shimmered beneath the sheets. After half an hour's praying she began to wonder whether she had married a saint, and deftly kicked her new husband. 'So sorry, Rosalie,' her beau apologized. 'I was so tired, I fell asleep!'

Initially they lived in a flat overlooking Parkers Piece, a grass expanse in the centre of Cambridge. Their next-door neighbour was Professor Donald MacKinnon, of whose lectures on doctrine and philosophy John was a devotee. Though utterly brilliant, MacKinnon proved as eccentric as Michael Ramsey: undergraduates visiting his rooms for a supervision occasionally found him perched sitting precariously on a high bookshelf, in a state of high anxiety, whimpering, 'There are lions in the room, ravenous lions!' Having had a lion in his own room in King's, John was very relaxed about such things, and got on with MacKinnon incredibly well.

With Carey's exodus to be Bishop of Edinburgh, Rosalie and John slept in the principal's rooms during term time, just to make sure 'Carey's boys' behaved themselves. But the House was in a very safe and indeed inspiring pair of hands during the interregnum, with John happily staying on to see in the new principal, Peter Walker.

Though John's fellowship at King's had concluded with his ordination in 1954, he still had high-table rights there, and regularly met with its Dean, Alec Vidler, a liberal Anglo-Catholic with an exquisite turn of phrase. He was editor of the monthly journal *Theology*, and appointed John to serve on its advisory committee and write the occasional article, such as on the 'Attractiveness of science' (December 1958). John was part of a favoured group, which included gurus like Hugh Montifiore and Harry Williams, who gathered around Vidler, basically very troubled about the mismatch between rigorous academic theology and the simplistic faith pedalled in parishes. In 1962, this symposium published *Soundings: Essays concerning Christian Understanding*, which highlighted their concerns. John's essay, 'The Uneasy Truce between Science and Theology', sketched the similarities and differences between effectively two faith communities, concluding that 'in the long run, those who care about science will make better theologians and those who care about theology better scientists'.

For the previous century Oxbridge dons had established considerable form with such publications, 'Young Turks' attempting to jump-start the Church to reckon with current thinking. *Essays and Reviews*, published only months after Darwin's *Origin of the Species* in 1860, encouraged the Church of England to adopt the radical biblical scholarship already prevalent in German universities. Two of the essayists faced charges of heresy in the Court of Arches; another, Frederick Temple, went on to be Archbishop of Canterbury. *Lux Mundi*, the Victorian equivalent of the Second Vatican Council, was a collection of 12 essays published in 1889, edited by Charles Gore, future bishop of Oxford. Though Anglo-Catholics, they championed a more radical and rational view of doctrine and biblical inspiration than traditional exponents.

At the same time, Cambridge scholars such as Westcott and Hort had produced a version of the Greek New Testament. During the nineteenth century a plethora of ancient biblical manuscripts had been discovered by Middle Eastern adventurers, and Westcott and Hort deployed logical textual critical criteria to establish a text that was as close as possible to the original Scripture. Not surprisingly, such a text differed from the much copied and redacted sources used by the translators of the King James Version, causing severe disquiet to the gullible majority who had hitherto believed the Authorized Version was infallible, having descended directly from heaven.

It was all heady stuff, and no doubt the contributors to *Soundings* braced themselves for considerable flak. John Robinson, Bishop of Woolwich, stole their thunder, by publishing *Honest to God* just months after *Soundings*, with its rallying call for a New Reformation. Robinson was an enfant terrible who had previously defended the publication of *Lady Chatterley's Lover* as a book that wives and servants could read to their great benefit. *Honest to God*, a racy read that condensed the theology of Bultmann, Tillich and Bonhoeffer, caught the public's imagination, especially when on the eve of its publication *The Observer* ran an interview with him with the headline 'Our image of God must go'. Ironically Robinson had not been included in Vidler's select group because he was thought too conservative. It seemed that the group thought he was too wedded to the biblical theology movement, which in the late 1950s had stressed the dichotomy between Hebrew and Greek thought, imagery and ethos. Biblical theology's premise was that the Hebrew viewpoint, in which the Scriptures were saturated, had been subordinated to, and indeed polluted by, all things Greek, from which it deserved liberating. Hebrew culture – good; Greek culture – bad. The *Soundings* group suspected that bracing though the dichotomy seemed, it was a false perception, in that the two viewpoints were inextricably interwoven over the centuries the two cultures had rubbed against each other, with both borrowing from and being enriched by each other. In short, it was as if the biblical theology movement was saying salt ($NaCl$) would be so much nicer if we removed all those nasty chlorine atoms; the *Soundings* group was saying if you did that, you would end up with no salt at all.

Soundings, and John's essay in particular, received some solid and even adulatory reviews, with martyrdom postponed. His literary and hermeneutic style shines through each sermon he preached during his time at Westcott. There were over a hundred, all written by hand, with occasional corrections by another hand, presumably Madré's, whom he clearly ran them past. His first sermon preached in November 1956 is typical. It is a very serious piece of work, seeing priests as merely touching and passing by most of those to whom they are called to minister. Nevertheless, they should touch their people with no less than the power of Christ, principally by what they are rather than what they say. They are called to be outposts of eternity, learning to be quiet and reflect the leisure of eternity, mindful of Evelyn Underhill's, 'He who hurries delays the work of God.'

He also encourages his hearers to strive to be impersonable, avoiding the cult of personality and popularity and the temptation to entertain. Priests should be wary of promulgating their winning ways as a second line of defence in case the Holy Spirit should let them down. Of course they should be approachable, sympathetic and human; but above all different, representatives of a Christ whose personality was extraordinarily elusive, instead inculcating a sense of mystery and something other.

His other sermons at Westcott warn against an image of the Church as a self-satisfied little clique of the sound, quoting William Temple that 'God is not nearly as interested in religion as the average curate'. John repeatedly stressed that every cleric's ambition should be channelled into preaching, a preaching that celebrates a Christ who is sensitive but selective, addressing full-on the need before him, without being distracted by all the needs he is failing to address. To some, Christ gave advice, others healing, others bread; to all he gave himself, a self that was true, child-like, believing in loveliness, believing in belief, hoping it might be so.

His style is typical of that I encountered during his York years. Essentially John comes across as a skilled pilot of an aeroplane circling the airport. Over several circuits he points out the topography and local landmarks, his meticulous detail giving them a three-dimensional air. He also wonders at the complex mechanism of the plane and the laws of physics that enable its incredible flight. He also sketches the dangers therein, and the deficiencies of the runway and weather conditions. And then, quite infuriatingly, he abdicates, leaving landing, or even choosing another airport, in your hands. Over to you . . .

John often quoted Emily Dickinson:

Tell all the truth but tell it slant —
Success in Circuit lies . . .
. . . The Truth must dazzle gradually
Or every man be blind.

His style is very simple, his vocabulary is very accessible, with no attempt at deliberate obfuscation to which other academic theologians tend to be prone. As a postgraduate I attended Cambridge Divinity School's D Society, a fortnightly seminar discussing the philosophy of religion. Over three years, I must have attended nearly 40 sessions, but hardly understood a word, with those around the table employing a specialist language to which I had no access. My daughter Hannah has observed similar sessions and has concluded that at some stage these theologians have had a secret tryst where they agreed only to talk bollocks to each other. There is none of that with John: his yes is yes, his no is no.

John's message is authentic, urgent and serious, with humour, and the concomitant risk of appearing flippant, used sparingly. When it is used, accompanied by a dazzling smile, it is like a glimpse of sunshine. The disappointments in ministry are manifold, like 'when your best confirmation candidate gets married and goes off to live in Tooting'. 'If we would understand St John's theology of the Resurrection, we must look mainly at the raising of Lazarus. That's the sort of comment one can make quite gaily when one doesn't have any responsibility for the teaching of the New Testament!' This is his wry take on a frequently visited subject, the mother of James and John and her ambition for her boys:

> The official hierarchy, the inner ring, consists of people in the know, the people with real power, the power that calls itself 'we'. It has no official membership and no rules, but a large number of people on the fringe either try to get into it, or think they are in it, much to the amusement of the people who really count. In times of emergency it may suddenly expand and call itself 'all the sensible people in this place.' Whereas from outside it is generally called 'So & So and his set' or simply 'that gang'.

Two views of former students. The first by former Bishop of Norwich, Peter Nott:

> 'What can you tell me about Amos?' John asked me on my first morning. 'Not very much, I'm afraid.' 'Jeremiah?' 'Very gloomy!' 'Ah,'

said John, 'I see we shall have to start from – ah – scratch.' Years later I came across a report John had written about my prowess: 'This young man gives the impression of great facility with this subject. His ability, however, is only moderate.'

There was always a freshness about his theological teaching, linked to the fact that he had not been trained as a theologian – the best teaching is often given by those who are continuing to learn. His seminars, talks and addresses were memorable, a fine teacher, although sometimes his mind operated at such a different level from most of us that he could lose us in complexities, which to him were perfectly straightforward.

Casual chatting with John over coffee would usually develop into an informal seminar. John sometimes gave the impression of being cool and aloof, and was reserved and uncomfortable with idle chatter – 'Reticence', he once said, 'is not a vice.' But he was underneath a warm person with a marvellous sense of humour, both admired and for whom we had a great affection.

There was an indefinable quality about the way he led worship that can only be described as communicating holiness. We wondered what the secret was, and asked him for tips on how to celebrate the Eucharist. 'There is no technique,' he replied, 'just pray the Eucharist. That's all.' At the beginning of Lent, John invited any who wished to come to his room to read T. S. Eliot's long poem, *Ash Wednesday*, together. I knew little of Eliot and found him obscure at first. But something was communicated and sparked a lifelong interest. Each year now I begin Lent by reading *Ash Wednesday*.

I spent an enjoyable evening with John, which as usual developed into regions of theology in which his mind strode on, leaving me stimulated but not completely understanding. The next morning his engagement to Rosalie was announced in *The Times*. 'Why on earth didn't you tell me, last night?' I asked. 'Oh Peter, didn't you realize that's precisely what I was saying to you.'

The second view by Ian Bennett, former Canon Residentiary and Director of Training at Newcastle Cathedral:

John had immaculate Old Etonian manners, but was intimidatingly tall and shy. Being shy myself, I found sitting next to him at formal meals something of an ordeal. Lectures and sermons were an entirely different matter. All three members of staff gave good, usually succinct, addresses at Eucharists and Compline, but John was outstanding, thought-provoking, imaginative in his use of imagery, and clear in language, very much a model, perhaps an unattainable ideal, for an aspiring preacher. In seminars and tutorials one discovered an erudite scholar who nevertheless corrected our crassness with gentleness and humour.

There was a time when it was whispered, 'John has a girlfriend!' This struck some as out of character or surprising for one so apparently remote and shy. Nevertheless at the beginning of a new term, Mrs Rosalie Habgood appeared. The rumour was that John had popped the question to Rosalie after taking her to see the film *Hiroshima Mon Amour*. Rosalie later entertained us with her piano playing at a House concert, where she encouraged John to revive a hitherto hidden talent for playing the viola.

After John left for Jedburgh, encounters were comparatively few and far between. Every so often he would be a keynote speaker at a conference I attended, always something to look forward to and always memorable. He also preached at the wedding of my colleague, his former student and gave the couple *The Joy of Sex* as a wedding present!

I recall a highly embarrassing Morning Prayer at Bishopthorpe, when I had to read the set Old Testament lesson from the Song of Songs. 'How beautiful you are, my love, how very beautiful,' I stammered 'Your two breasts are like two fawns, twins of a gazelle that feeds among the lilies . . .' John led the prayers, as always subordinate to the lectionary: 'We give God thanks for the sheer thrill of sexual love, and for the joy of family life,' he softly said, utterly unfazed. That joy is to unfold in all its fullness as he and Rosalie leave Cambridge for Jedburgh in the Scottish borders.

9

Jedburgh John

During John's latter years at Westcott, at least ten jobs were his for the taking. Both the Bishops of Worcester and Peterborough asked him to be their examining chaplains, an honorary role that puts candidates through their paces prior to ordination, an ecclesiastical equivalent of the Grand National's Beecher's Brook. There were three Cambridge jobs – he was approached about being Dean of Jesus College (1959), Dean of Corpus Christi (1961) and Dean of Trinity Hall (1961). Robert Runcie curiously offered him the latter post, which he himself was vacating to be Principal of Cuddesdon; presumably he was acting on the authority of his father-in-law, who was Trinity Hall's Master. There were two cathedral jobs: in 1961 the Bishop of Rochester offered him a residentiary canonry at Rochester Cathedral, also delivering post-ordination training and lecturing at the theological college; in 1962 the Bishop of Guildford offered him the post of canon theologian at his newly consecrated cathedral. Then quite a few parishes came his way: in 1960 King's College offered him the King's living of All Saints, Kingston on Thames; in 1961 the Bishop of Peterborough offered him St Matthew's, Northampton; in 1962 the indefatigable Robert Runcie (acting this time on behalf of the Dean and Chapter of Windsor) offered him St John the Divine, Kennington, along with some teaching at Cuddesdon; also in 1962 a desperate Bishop of Manchester offered him anything that he fancied; and finally the Bishop of Guildford offered him the Lord Chancellor's living of Bramley.

John wanted to see his time out at Westcott House, steering the ship as one principal left and another came, hence he declined jobs that crossed his horizon too soon. He was keen to get to grips with a significant parish job, to put into practice all the theory he had developed over his Westcott years, which is why he turned down prestigious jobs in Cambridge colleges and cathedrals, coupled with a view that being a cathedral canon induced death by cloister.

John and Rosalie seriously considered Bramley, but decided against because it was too major a post to give John time to study and write, but too minor a post to warrant additional staff to free John up to do other things. Ken Carey, conspiring as ever with Madré, came to the rescue, wanting to staff his new diocese with pastors, scholars and gentlemen and realizing that all three were combined in John. He initially suggested St John's Princes Street, Edinburgh – Madré reckoned that Carey had had that in mind for him even before he became Edinburgh's bishop. She wrote: 'I said to Ken, "When you and I are asked what we have got to say for ourselves, we'll say together, 'Please, we both did our bit in producing John H!'" and he agreed.'

However, the Vestry at St John's, who held power of appointment, did not agree to their bishop's albeit pre-existent suggestion, and rejected John: the first but by no means the last rejection he was to face over the coming decades. Instead, Carey suggested Jedburgh, which couldn't believe its good fortune in netting such a star. Describing itself as the prettiest market town in the Scottish borders, Jedburgh is some 50 miles equidistant from Edinburgh, Newcastle and Carlisle, boasting a magnificent ruined castle and Augustinian abbey. The church of St John's, built in the Tractarian style in the 1840s, is part of the Episcopalian Church in Scotland, a sister church to the Church of England. When John became its rector in 1962, there were three other churches in the town, one Roman Catholic and two Church of Scotland Presbyterian. Unlike in England, the Anglican Church was not established, so John spent his time in Jedburgh observing the effortless superiority of the Church of England through the eyes of the effortless superiority of the Church of Scotland.

He ministered to a gathered roll around 300 in number, a mix of local gentry and millworkers. Jedburgh's rayon mill had recently closed, so mill-workers commuted to mills in nearby towns. John hit the ground running, and was decades ahead of his time. His first magazine picks up on a comment, 'Rector, you tell us what to do and we'll do it!' Such Father-knows-best attitude was anathema to John, who rather saw a parish priest as a seeker, looking for buried treasure in the lives that surrounded him, a teacher who gently enabled his charges to discover their talents and be amazed by what they can do. John was no talk-and-chalk teacher, but a fellow traveller, in the spirit of Cardinal Basil Hume, who said a bishop was to come to where people were and take them to places they never dreamt of going. While John realized that faithful local Anglicans worship and socialize together, he wanted them to have the opportunity to think together. So he proposed a series of monthly meetings to do just that, which were complementary to the Vestry meetings, which focused on the nuts and bolts of church governance and protecting their congregations from English invaders. John's monthly magazine gives a lively and intelligent record of his ministry, termed by him as his 'productive period'. The first congregational meeting decided to sex up the weekly eucharistic celebration, banishing stuffy and outdated practices to free it up to be a meaningful meal for the gathered faithful. Former parishioner Jean Simpson writes of how John stood outside the church, warmly greeting each person on arrival, with a fine eye for the beauty of ceremonial, his hands a pleasure to watch as he performed the manual actions of the Eucharist. John himself issues practical advice: don't over-worry about fasting before communion – after all, the first ever communion followed a hearty Passover supper! Members of the congregation should sit at the front of the church, where the preacher is more audible, and should be poised to come up and receive their communion without delay. Although John always celebrated with grace and precision, there was an urgency about his conduct of worship, akin to performing a Shakespearean tragedy, with no room for dithering or people missing their cue.

He tells it straight, marvellously so. 'It is a mistake to try to be more religious than God,' he informed his readers in December 1962, setting his face against the oft-repeated criticism that Christmas is too commercial. 'God came into a very brash and vulgar world indeed, the rough and tumble of a pub. We cannot penetrate that mystery by pretending to be religiously superior to folk, when even God wasn't superior.'

Each month he snappily reviews the latest theology books that he has introduced into the church library – one month 15 in total! In May 1963 John Robinson's notorious *Honest to God* is heartily recommended, not least 'for grabbing hold of a few good ideas and working them to death in a very lively way'. In August he apologizes that his parishioners had not seen much of him because he was finishing his own tome, a textbook for sixth-formers on science and religion – the book was published by Mills and Boon, who had decided to broaden their repertoire beyond bodice-rippers. September marks the closure of St John's church primary school. The magazine gives no hint whether the closure was due to falling rolls or that building maintenance or rising staffing costs proved too expensive. Whatever, John would have to manage a major sense of bereavement at the loss of the school and the connections it enabled with the young. In the same month, John enthuses about Paul (accept-that-you-are-accepted) Tillich being introduced to the church library, which must have cheered school parents no end.

October marks John's disappointment that only four people attended a congregational meeting on funding the poorer parts of the Anglican Communion, with John scathingly speculating that everyone else was too busy watching ITV's *Double Your Money*, hosted by Hughie Green. Duly reproved, more turned out in November, although I fear John never drew crowds to these meetings. It seemed people were initially enthusiastic in the autumn of 1962, stopped coming because of the fierce winter blizzards and never came back. However, November's meeting jump-started the New Year's Vestry meeting to sponsor the training of an ordinand from Ghana, to the tune of £500 over two years.

The ordinand in question, Thomas Brient, trained at Coates Hall, Edinburgh, staying at the rectory during vacations. Sadly he proved an introvert who was not easy to get on with, adding little to John's ministry. He failed his ordination exams at Edinburgh, but was in denial about any difficulties with study, obdurately resisting advice and attempts to help improve. He returned to Ghana shortly before John left Jedburgh, and despite his academic shortcomings, eventually became Bishop of Sunyani. Rosalie had her typical take on the episode: 'I suppose we've been too kind and made him feel too much at home!'

John's Jedburgh sermons pull no punches. For the four Sundays running up to the 1964 General Election he preached on politics, international affairs, productivity and defence. In October 1966 he preached on sex, defending the doctrine of being chaste before marriage, but allowing for exceptions where even adultery can be an expression of the sacrificial love championed by 1 Corinthians 13. Sexual intercourse exposes our deepest vulnerability to each other, with sensitive legislation making sure no one is exploited – 'it is just when someone is under the influence of sexual passion, that they most need guidelines'. The next month the broad-minded congregation are treated to a sermon on abortion – Jedburgh was in the constituency of David Steel who was introducing a Private Member's Bill for an Abortion Act. John takes a classic Anglican via media approach, sensitive to those unmarried or married women who are daunted by an unwanted pregnancy, having become pregnant through fear, ignorance or irresponsibility. He emphasizes that sex is a gift of God that should be treated with reverence and compassion. He deems the Roman Catholic approach as too simple, bestowing a foetus at any term with full human rights, trumping the human rights of the mother – 'I simply don't know when it is sensible to talk about a new human being.' Faced by 50,000 illegal abortions performed each year in the UK, he feels that abortion should be permitted when pregnancy was a severe threat to the physical or mental health of the mother. He is less sure about David Steel's proposal that deformity or rape should be additional criteria, when the mother's mental and physical health is not under threat, but welcomes open debate on the issue.

Jedburgh got hot under the collar about teenagers dancing in the streets on a Sunday. Martha and the Vandellas' 1965 hit may have encouraged dancing in Chicago, New Orleans, New York, Philadelphia, Baltimore and LA, but unfortunately hadn't reckoned with Jedburgh's strict Sabbath-day observance. John, ever the diplomat, rather than telling the Sabbatarians to get a life, instead took pity on the teenagers and tried to get an ecumenical youth club going. The first planning meeting didn't draw any parents of teenagers at all. Things dragged on for over a year, arguing over a site, until in April 1966 John took matters in hand and launched a weekly club on Sunday evenings in the Drill Hall, which he ran until his departure.

John relieved the sheer hard slog of parish ministry by lecturing on ethics at Coates Hall each and every Wednesday, even managing the 100-mile round trip through the heavy snows of the winter of 1963. John's lectures may have wowed a Cambridge audience, but ordinands in Edinburgh found them over their heads. He also joined a high-powered group regularly meeting at Lambeth Palace discussing Christian ethics and natural law, which included professors galore, as well as John's former spiritual director, Harry Williams, by then Dean of Trinity, Cambridge, who broadened John's education by filtering theology and philosophy through a Freudian lens. Daringly for the 1960s, the group also included a Roman Catholic philosopher, Fr D. B. J. Hawkins, parish priest of Godalming, the first time a Roman Catholic had slept under Lambeth's roof since the Reformation – or slept there and walked out alive!

The group's chairman was Ian Ramsey, Professor of Philosophy of Religion at Oxford. In 1966 he was appointed Bishop of Durham, and horrified the group with terrible tales of life in Auckland Castle, where the huge, unmanageable rooms made his carpets look like postage stamps. Ramsey shared with them a photo of Auckland Castle from Hensley Henson's biography, with the bishop's residence looking more like a medieval citadel – John pitied him and his wife in having to cope with such a place. Probably because Ramsey was distracted by running such a pile at Bishop Auckland, the group never produced a report, but John published two papers in *Theology* in 1966 on censorship and moral discovery.

John also gave a series of talks for schools on the BBC Home Service to mark a century of the theory of evolution, which was followed up by his reading extracts from his book *Science and Religion* on the Home Service's *Ten to Eight* (later to morph into 'Thought for the Day'). People who mattered were noticing him, and in November 1965 he attended a dinner at 10 Downing Street, hosted by Harold Wilson. Ostensibly the dinner was in the Archbishop of York's honour, but, on the very night Ian Smith had declared UDI in Rhodesia, international politics inevitably loomed. Wilson, who didn't twig that one greater than him was there, held court and waxed lyrical, styling himself as JFK redivivus. John was not impressed.

Other outside engagements included addressing the five-day Sheffield Diocesan Conference on Science and Religion, leading Mirfield College's annual retreat, addressing a health education conference in Blackpool, and leading a retreat at his old college at Cuddesdon. His four addresses are masterly, using simple language to draw on salient examples of ministry in Jedburgh. He weaves the talks around episodes from King David's life, not so much episodes as the odd phrase. The Lord makes David king because he looked on his heart; at the end of the day, what is there in your heart? David keeps Goliath's heavy, cumbersome sword as a trophy, marking his role as a giant-killer; what cumbersome thing do you carry around, which could be the making of you? One of his examples is poignant, ahead of its time: 'The homosexual personality, if accepted and controlled, can bring its own gifts, greater gifts in terms of sensitivity and insight than those who are luckier in their sexual make-up.' David's wife Michal despises him for dancing enthusiastically before the Lord when the ark of the covenant reaches Jerusalem. While Anglican worship should be done decently and in order, shy John makes a case for the occasional bout of holy madness, shock tactics to break an impasse. Finally, John deeply reflects on David's grief at the death of his rebellious son, Absalom, and the whole dynamic of how the old and young relate, including elderly vicars and firebrand curates. Robert Runcie, Cuddesdon's principal, praised John's talks: 'No one has been more successful than you in carrying everyone.'

Angela Grant, a Roman Catholic from Jedburgh, also eulogizes about John, including 'his refreshing enthusiasm for ecumenism'. John was the force behind regular meetings of ministers from the town's four churches, resulting in a united evening service each Sunday and a united visiting plan, where each minister did door-to-door visiting in their designated sector of the town, and referred any lapsed they discovered to their respective colleague.

John also launched united services for Holy Week. Across Scotland a highly ambitious unity scheme for the Church of Scotland and Episcopalian Church to covenant was scuppered by vociferous opposition in the *Scottish Daily Express*. Mindful that their church was in a minority, Scotland's seven bishops were themselves cautious, and opposed John's proposal for a united Holy Communion in St John's, Jedburgh, on Maundy Thursday 1967. To do such a thing on such a day was a highly charged act. Despite the bishops' disapproval, which in many respects seemed petty, John bravely went ahead with the Eucharist. But as a mark that the Body of Christ was still very much divided, no one, not even the celebrant, received communion, which made the occasion far more poignant than had the bishops approved it.

In July 1963's parish magazine, John announces the birth of Laura Caroline, 'who doubtless will produce a change or two at the Rectory'. December 1964 records Francis' birth, reflecting 'that life will become even harder for the sub-organist!' January 1965's magazine leads on the installation of an automatic organ, installed by a local headmaster for £100, which includes a sophisticated tape and record deck for those times when Rosalie is otherwise engaged. But often she played with one child on each side of her:

I managed despite both of them swarming all over me. Then they sat on the pulpit steps and wouldn't let John down, then they followed him to the altar. During the blessing both of them were crawling around under John's cassock – he found it difficult to stand still with all the tugging! Everyone loved it – full of praise and admiration, and John said it didn't matter at all. He was quite proud of them. They did look very sweet – and they were quite quiet and solemn – and reverent in all their activities!

The parish clearly were very fond of John – 'bishop material' – and his family. When John was consecrated Bishop of Durham in 1973, Lord Stratheden had his head shepherd carve a sheep-horn crook to present to their former rector. Ten years later the parish were thrilled to receive tickets for John's enthronement as Archbishop of York, given pride of place behind Rosalie and the family in York Minster, happily chatting over old times, 'like Princess Diana and her flatmates all over again'.

Their third child, Ruth, arrived in January 1967, meaning John had to miss a diocesan clergy conference staged at a chilly Butlin's in Ayr. He clearly was a devoted father, supporting Rosalie, endlessly playing with them, using his carpentry skills to make them toys, which nearly resulted in tragedy when Laura was three. In a letter to her parents, Rosalie vividly recalled:

Laura had been on an orange box about to climb on the rocking horse and she overbalanced and fell backwards, hitting the back of her head on the runner of the horse. They were in the basement as John was making a new ear for the horse. John raced upstairs with her – she still was not breathing so he decided to do artificial respiration rather than the 'kiss of life' because she was bringing up a lot of saliva. Lying her face down meant that this could come up. She started breathing soon after he started the A.R. The ambulance drive to Galashiels Hospital was frightening, Laura was very semi-conscious but sang lah to 'Pop goes the weasel' very loudly.

I asked John about the way he revived Laura. He said he knew one can't not breathe for long without serious damage to the brain – but clever John, even in such a crisis, managed to keep his head. John obviously saved her life in the few minutes when he started artificial respiration. The doctors were amazed at John's presence of mind. They say knowledge is one thing but in a crisis like that, when one's own is involved, one can completely go to pieces and panic.

When Laura was in hospital (where the X-rays showed no permanent damage), John had a meeting in Edinburgh with the seven Scottish bishops discussing unity between Presbyterians and Episcopalians. Rosalie writes: 'When Ken Carey heard about Laura he was very distressed, but opened the meeting by asking all the bishops to stand in silence and pray for Laura. Wasn't that lovely? – we were so touched.'

In a later letter she concludes:

We have survived the week and we now have little Laura safely home with us. How different we all feel. It really has been the most ghastly strain and John and I are absolutely worn out. I think we suffered from shock, horrid reactions and quite honestly we've slept very little all week. We couldn't help going over it all again and again – and then one hates the separation. We are so relieved she's OK because John was so alarmed that she'd stopped breathing for so long. Laura remembers nothing at all of that morning. She loves her little horse still.

In conversation in 2006 John was very modest about the whole episode. 'Little Laura hit her head and I gave her heart massage. Thank God the doctor and the ambulance were in the right place at the right time and we brought her round.' Laura went on to be a highly skilled doctor; Francis joined the police, ultimately serving as Chief Constable of Thames Valley; Ruth became a speech therapist, practising in South Africa and New Zealand.

From the start at Jedburgh, John decided that at least five years was needed for his ministry to be effective. He therefore turned down posts that came his way during that period, including Principal of Salisbury Theological College; Harold Wilson's personal offer of a canonry at Worcester Cathedral; the Dean of Emmanuel, Cambridge; Principal of St Chad's College, Durham; Warden of Rochester Theological College (vacant after Stuart Blanch's appointment to be Bishop of Liverpool); and the post of Director of Post-Ordination Training and Vicar of Shincliffe in Durham. After Christmas 1965, John was approached by his alma mater, King's College, about being Dean in succession to Alec Vidler, and went down for interview. In March 1966 he heard from Ken Carey that church historian David Edwards had been appointed. Carey was very fond of Edwards, who had been a flamboyant student and briefly a tutor at Westcott in Carey's time, and had then gone on to be editor of SCM Press where he had published John Robinson's infamous *Honest to God*. Even so, he felt 'the Provost and Fellows must have taken leave of their senses if they had the chance of getting you'. Perhaps King's appointed Edwards because they wanted to project a more upbeat and less stuffy image, to down a dose of the 'swinging sixties' before the decade had expired. The Provost wrote to John, expressing the view that though the recommend-ation of the appointing committee had been unanimous, 'many of us regretted that the college would not be able to benefit from some of the particular qualities you display. I don't know how far this is a disappoint-ment, in that you have clearly so many possibilities ahead of you.' Carey similarly concludes 'that he had no doubt whatsoever that the Lord had some better thing in mind for you'. The letter contains an alarming PS about Madré's failing health; it seemed that the Lord would soon have the redoubtable Madré beside him to help make up his mind. Whatever, as a door to King's shut, a door to Queen's opened.

10

Queen's John

Yesterday I had a look around and had long talks with the outgoing Principal and all the members of staff. I do not know yet whether they will invite me to be Principal, so this letter may be redundant, and no one would be happier than I if this were so. The Principalship of Queen's in the present state of affairs is not a very enviable position.

So John writes to Canon Basil Moss, the Secretary of the Advisory Council for the Church's Ministry (ACCM) in May 1967, following an intriguing exchange of letters with the Bishop of Bradford (Chair of Queen's College Council) and the Bishop of Warrington (Chair of ACCM). It seems that Kenneth Woolcombe, Principal of Edinburgh Theological College, had warmly recommended John to the Bishop of Warrington for the post, but then John resolutely resists making any formal application. The best they can get out of him is that he puts in writing, 'Should I be asked to become Principal of Queen's College, I would give the matter most earnest consideration' – a form of words previously suggested by the Bishop of Bradford.

Certainly there was a culture within the Church that one should be sought out and never directly apply for things, since self-promotion was seen as counter-gospel. But from the veiled, secretive comments in the correspondence, I suspect that more was at play here and there was an episcopal job going. Yet no Scottish or Welsh bishoprics were up for election in 1967, and the post of diocesan bishop or dean in the Church of England did not brook any discussion, but would come out of the blue, with a letter of invitation from the Prime Minister. Which (setting aside election to an overseas bishopric) leaves three suffragan posts vacant that year, with their diocesan holding power of appointment. Probably forlorn Dunwich in the St Edmundsbury and Ipswich Diocese, whose bishop, Leslie Brown, was a fervent Evangelical, would be a non-starter. Penrith in Carlisle Diocese, close to Jedburgh, is a possibility, in that rumours of John's prowess would have spread over the border. Maidstone in Canterbury Diocese, vacated by Stanley Betts' appointment as Dean of Rochester, is a stronger possibility: Betts was John's former vicar at Holy Trinity, Cambridge, who thought very highly of John, and so could have recommended he succeed him; and Michael Ramsey would have had frequent communications from Madré extolling John's virtues.

At the end of the day, I can't quite see John, who had already taken on all seven Scottish bishops over his united Maundy Thursday Eucharist, as a biddable episcopal curate. John Robinson was just 40 when he became Suffragan Bishop of Woolwich, and many felt he came to episcopacy too soon, their fears realized by the Lady Chatterley trial and the aftermath of *Honest to God*. Probably it's wisest to appoint men to bishoprics when their libido is on the wane, in that otherwise the Church can't really cope with such highly charged ministry.

Whatever, nothing came of it. 'Sometimes the trail just goes cold,' John once shrugged, talking about promising posts that never materialized. Perhaps John just said no, as he had said no to other shining possibilities. Something did come of Queen's, with John accepting the post in May 1967, though with considerable reservations. The college, based at Edgbaston, was cash and building rich but student poor. In the 1930s Queen's had become a strictly Anglican foundation, beached in a strongly Nonconformist Birmingham, which had made quite a killing out of the sale of former premises in the centre of the city when it moved out to the leafy suburbs. Somehow it was also awarded a massive £150,000 grant by the Church of England in the early 1960s to develop its premises as a staff college to provide in-service training and courses for existing clergy. This avant garde proposal saw Birmingham as an excellent communication hub, which would free up the Church of England from its stuffy Oxbridge-based image. John's predecessor, while accepting the no-strings grant (which among other things financed a luxurious five-bedroomed principal's flat) fiercely resisted the very changes it was intended to facilitate, so by 1967 the complex was a white elephant, housing just 18 ordinands.

Not just Queen's but all theological colleges were struggling to attract ordinands in 1967's infamous 'summer of love', which is why John wrote to the Secretary of ACCM to check on the state of play. The Bishop of Bradford candidly replied that, though 'the building up of Queen's will take some years, I do not think there is the slightest doubt about the college remaining'. He felt its wealth and match-fit buildings would ensure its survival, as other theological colleges went to the wall, with Queen's set to absorb an influx from Cuddesdon (whose students already commuted to Birmingham University to complete a diploma in theology), Lincoln and Salisbury in the event of their closure. No less than Archbishop Michael Ramsey personally guaranteed Queen's future, 'if the best appointment possible could be made'. Joe Fison, the Bishop of Salisbury felt John's going to Queen's was a great and courageous new venture. Robert Runcie wrote, admiring John's courage in lowering himself into one of the hottest seats in the C of E. Both Kenneth Woolcombe and Sidney Evans, Dean of King's, London, thought John was one of 'the few men capable of doing the job that has to be done'. Woolcombe's only reservation was that John would no longer be available to be the keynote speaker at the diocesan clergy conference. He sweetly suggested that John should tape his lectures, which would then be replayed to the conference, with slides of John, in various poses sporting his infamous death stare, projected on to a large screen during the talks. Shades of Father Ted!

Displaying the same single-mindedness that had saved little Laura's life, John took decisive action. Attending his first College Council meeting as Principal-elect on 19 July, he informed them that he had been in touch with the Principal of the Methodist training college at Handsworth, who had made the first tentative approach about a possible merger. At his second coming on 24 October, he appointed a committee to establish an ecumenical college, the formation of which had been under discussion by the British Council of Churches since 1963. The committee included members of the United Reformed Church (URC) and Roman Catholics, as well as Methodists and Anglicans, and produced an interim report by February 1968, which was presented to and accepted by successive Methodist Conferences in May 1968 and 1969. The Church of England, braced by the conversations it was having with the Methodist Church about eventual unity, also enthusiastically proposed the merger, with the amalgamation being sealed on 14 October 1970, with a ceremony attended by the Archbishop of Canterbury, President of the Methodist Conference and representatives of all the other main churches. Any ecumenical venture is prone to be notoriously slow, a time span measured in centuries. John had achieved it in just three years. In that year the college staged a production of *A Man for All Seasons*: John was.

Along the way, John produced some crisp phrases in sermons, lectures and college magazine articles:

'Real unity could only be based on trust, with a shared and high sense of purpose.'

'Though undoubtedly an exciting time, excitement was not always easy to live with.'

'Despite our insecurities and sharp exchanges, God was asking us to do a new thing; all denominations must be prepared to put their traditions into the melting pot.'

'Differences should be respected rather than overridden, with many things deliberately left undecided; we desperately need to present a vibrant pattern of unity to shame the church and the world.'

With automatic access to key committee meetings in Methodist colleges, John found it extremely interesting getting inside Methodism, impressed that the Methodist formation and selection for ministry was much more searching than our own process. He was also struck by Methodism's great emphasis on preaching – it wasn't always good, with so-called impromptu sermons actually following a set form, but was taken very seriously. Surprisingly he found it a much more rule-bound church than the Church of England, with its committees treated with great reverence.

In 1968, Bishops' College, Cheshunt, closed with 20 older men migrating to Queen's, providing a welcome influx. The United Reformed Church sent the odd student to train without any formal unity scheme, and also the Roman Catholics had a peripheral presence enabled by a student and staff exchange with the Roman Catholic seminary at Oscott, where John lectured on the Reformation. The proceeds of the sale of Handsworth College enabled a block of 20 flats to be built; another block that had formerly been let to overseas students was being refurbished, with John and his students having to apply several coats of paint to walls seemingly impregnated with curry. The two libraries were amalgamated into a new library, built on the site of the former common room.

New ways of being college and relating to each other were being built at the same time. The combined staff had weekends away in cottages in Shropshire and Wales where they got to know each other, broke sacramental and secular bread together (it was only the second time in John's life he had received communion from a Methodist) and even climbed real mountains. During term time the staff met briefly every day, and for one full afternoon a week.

What was more astonishing than establishing an ecumenical college was that John firmly grasped the 1960s' zeitgeist and promoted a community, effectively a holy commune, that was non-authoritarian. The key phrases were 'self-discipline rather than imposed discipline' and 'personal freedom coupled with responsible commitment'. Each week staff and students (who were all on first-name terms) attended an informal debate led by a student, as well as a weekly no-holds-barred decision-making session, when there were some heated exchanges, with some of the staff disapproving of a forum where students could say anything and often did! John was in the habit of listening carefully (with the occasional raised eyebrow when a student was a tad too free with expletives), and then gave a masterly summary and proposed an utterly brilliant solution, which everyone else only wished they'd thought of in the first place. It was a trait I observed time after time in senior staff meetings in York and in interminable debates in Diocesan and General Synod; the rabble would let off considerable steam, but when the huffing and puffing was over, John would pronounce the verdict, as cool as a cucumber.

Each student joined a group that included a staff member, which focused on spirituality, ministerial formation and pastoral care in a relaxed forum where each group member exercised care over the others. The students wrote their own end-of-year report, which they discussed with their tutors, and could include actual criticism of them. One university lecturer took considerable exception to a portfolio John sent him, brim-full of anonymous criticism of his lectures on the niceties of accents in Hellenistic Greek failing to connect with his audience.

Each week one group was responsible for sensitive worship in chapel, a mix of traditional and creative. Attendance was voluntary, apart from the obligatory Sunday Eucharist and Tuesday preaching service. Attempts at syncretistic worship, containing a little bit of this tradition, a little bit of that, pleased no one, so each denomination played to its strong suits. About half a dozen Anglican students refused to receive communion from a Methodist, so on those occasions decamped to a nearby Anglo-Catholic church via a minibus paid for by the college. One Methodist would not receive from John, because he used alcoholic wine.

After much discussion, Queen's came up with its own rather beautiful eucharistic rite, drawn from the very accessible Roman Catholic Missal that emerged after the Second Vatican Council. Since it drew on the Canon of Hippolytus, the earliest Eucharistic Prayer known, few objections could be made. Hackles were raised about the phrase 'In memory of his death and resurrection, we offer you, Father, this life-giving bread, this saving cup,' with connotations of the sacrifice of the Mass, anathema to Protestants. *Regina*, the exceedingly critical college magazine, records how John came to the rescue:

In a way reminiscent of William Temple at the crisis of the world Missionary Conference in Jerusalem, the Principal produced a form of words which soon recommended itself to everyone: 'With this bread and this wine we represent his offering for our salvation; we share in his death and resurrection . . .' The use of the word 'represent' was a masterly stroke, with the studied ambiguity (re-present and represent) satisfying the whole churchmanship spectrum.

In another edition of *Regina*, John enthuses about a firework display of services, ranging from an early morning Methodist Communion service, celebrated as Wesley might have done it, to a carol service 'for the neighbours'. The college served its neighbours well, acting as an honest broker to end the student sit-in at Birmingham University in 1968, which had been spurred on by the Grosvenor Square and Paris riots. John became the voice of both the students to the university and the university to the students. Through pastoral and preaching placements, Queen's deliberately involved itself in the inner-city, such as the notorious Balsall Heath.

Reflecting on his time at Queen's 30 years later, John felt the generously resourced initiative had bought time for people from very different denominations to get to know and value each other and flourish accordingly. He brought the same spirit to the 1994 Act of Synod, whose aim was to enable two very different integrities to function in parallel and appreciate each other's strengths and vocation. Neither quite worked out like that, with the proposed Anglican–Methodist Unity Scheme rejected twice by the Church of England, with Graham Leonard, then Bishop of Willesden, leading a revolt that John described as 'utterly intolerable'. Shortly after that rejection in 1972, John preached to the college and certainly pulled no punches:

The Church of England has lost its authority as an ecumenical pace-setter and bridge-builder. The bishops have lost a good measure of their authority as leaders; they tried to lead, perhaps too half-heartedly and too late, and their lead was rejected. Methodist leaders may well find themselves under criticism for having led their rank-and-file members up the garden path. Both churches must have lost some of what little authority they have as agents of reconciliation in the world.

Jesus wept that night in Queen's.

There were lighter moments too. In 1968 John wryly reported to the College Council about a man who had ceased to be an ordinand, but still lived in college and attended an all-day psychological clinic. John got on well with his inter-denominational staff, most of whom he appointed, including Bill Grisbrook, an Orthodox layman leading on liturgy, and Rupert Hoare, a brilliant New Testament lecturer, who came to Queen's from a curacy where he had just translated Bultmann's commentary on John's Gospel from German into English. John also joined a 'fun' discussion group, which included Professor John Hick, Michael Goulder, Dan Hardy and Harry Stopes-Roe – son of Marie Stopes, affectionately known as 'the one that got away!' After John had departed and no longer stayed the ship, they emerged as the infamous 'Myth of God Incarnate' group.

In November 1971, ACCM and the Methodist Church jointly inspected the college, enthusing about 'a very exciting community with an adult and responsible tone, allowing a large degree of personal freedom within a setting of responsible commitment to the college'. They deemed the place very good, with just a few points for attention. At the time of the inspection, of the 79 actual students, there were 14 Methodist deaconesses, 34 Methodists, 24 Anglicans, 2 URCs, 1 Anglican woman worker, 2 overseas students and 2 research fellows, funded by a healthy budget surplus. Apart from the 14 Methodist deaconesses, who were housed off site, there was only 1 Anglican woman among the 79 students, so the inspectors encouraged greater female participation.

The inspectors, who presumably had never experienced the pressured life of a parish priest, felt that 30 hours a week timetabled activities was too stressful for students: 'To go to a lecture after an exhausting if rewarding day in a mental hospital is asking a lot of human endurance.' I have chaired a PCC after an exhausting and unrewarding day visiting a psychiatric ward, often wondering which of the two contexts was more insane. But certainly academic standards and expectations were high, for which John was a rallying point. He was once informed by a prospective student during an interview that one only had to trust in the Lord Jesus to be saved. 'Erm, what would Schleiermacher make of that?' John asked, with the clear expectation that the pretty impenetrable works of this German philosopher would grace every Midlands' ordinand's bookshelf.

While the inspectors approved the creation of a college crèche, they 'feared it could increase pressure on young wives to go out to work'. I suspect John had driven the creation of the crèche to allow Rosalie to go out to work! But they realized that Queen's was a victim of its own success, in that kitchens intended to cater for 80 had to cater for 120.

The 1970 edition of *Regina* had far more cutting edge than the inspectors, as evidenced by the following proposed college carol:

Doctor Habgood once looked out,
Over all Queen's College;
As he cast his gaze about,
He had to acknowledge –
Though the property was grand,

Hell as well as Heaven –
Yet the total student band
Was but thirty-seven.

Hither, Rupert stand by me,
Answer without dodging:
From my signal-box you'll see
Many an empty lodging;
Where do ordinands all go?
Why aren't they abundant?
If recruitment stays this low,
We shall be redundant.

Slave and master, with no fuss,
Forth they went together,
On the number 'leven bus,
Through the wintry weather.
Conned Doc Mitton with the theme:
Ec-u-men-ic-it-y;
Pulled off their pernicious scheme
Without shame or pity.

Took the Methodists with glee
Over to Edgbaston;
Thought they'd make them C of E
Thought they'd pull a fast 'un;
But the Methodists at best
Are all non-conformers;
Soon they'd got a viper's nest
Full of keen reformers!

Even three decades later, John always became so animated whenever
Queen's was mentioned, for instance, talking of the block of flats *he* built.
'It was such a nice place to live, with a lovely university campus and park
next door, complete with a children's centre and theatre and excellent
schools.' Their spacious flat was over the dining room, with a service lift

so the family could enjoy the same fare the 80 students and their families were devouring below, quaintly termed 'commons from the kitchen'. Rosalie did some teaching at Bluecoats School until Adrian's birth in 1971, Laura gained a place at Edgbaston High, and John bought a caravan, enabling them to reprise his boyhood camping holidays with breaks in Devon, South Wales and the Isle of Wight. All was very well with the world. And then on 26 January 1973, John received a letter from Prime Minister Edward Heath.

11

Nolo John

10 Downing Street

26 January 1973

Dear Dr Habgood,

The See of Durham is vacant by the death of the previous Bishop, the late Right Reverend Ian Ramsey. It is my duty to advise the Queen on the question of the succession to this See. After most careful consideration, I have decided, if you are willing that I should do so, to submit your name for appointment as the 68th Bishop of Durham.

I must, of course, ask you to treat this proposal as confidential. If, as I hope, you find it possible to accept my offer I shall have much pleasure in submitting your name to Her Majesty.

I am naturally anxious that the See of Durham should not be left too long without a Bishop. In your reply, therefore, I hope you will be able to give me some indication about the length of your present commitments.

Yours sincerely,
Edward Heath

Having received this bombshell on Saturday 27 January, John drove over to Hartlebury Castle, home of Robin Woods, Bishop of Worcester and Chair of Queen's College Council. Woods confirmed by letter dated Monday 29 January his enthusiasm for John's appointment: 'It is a wonderful next step for Christ and his Church in this country. You have both

81

the natural characteristic and the enormous asset of doing things efficiently and quietly.' I have always had a soft spot for Robin Woods, who chaired my father's selection conference in 1958. My shy dad hadn't got much to say, and certainly wasn't fluent in the religious psychobabble that held sway back then. He simply said he humbly felt the deepest calling to be a priest. 'That's simply wonderful,' Woods very warmly replied, 'what more assurance do we need?' As a very charismatic Dean of Windsor, Robin Woods stars in episode 7 of Series III of Netflix's *The Crown*, giving valued counsel to Her Majesty the Queen, the Duke of Edinburgh and the rest of the Royal Family.

In medieval times a candidate groomed for episcopacy traditionally declared 'Nolo episcopari' (I do not want to be a bishop) twice before reluctantly accepting on the third approach. There was no such feigned humility on John's part, in that he clearly had considerable, tangible misgivings. On Sunday 28 January, John wrote to the Archbishop of York, Donald Coggan, expressing his 'considerable turmoil' after receiving the Prime Minister's letter. He sensed he needed two to three years more at the helm of Queen's to steady things, not least to drive through the legislation to enable the appointment of a non-Anglican as Principal. While he fully allowed there might be a greater need for him elsewhere, he felt he was too young, his achievements too modest for such a responsible and senior post. 'This is not mock humility on my part, because the contrast is painfully obvious when I look at my own career and that of, say, Ian Ramsey.' John asked the Archbishop most urgently for his guidance, particularly to share with him any special factors in Durham or the wider Church that needed him rather than anyone else.

On Monday 29 January, John received a letter from Sir John Hewitt, the Prime Minister's Adviser for Appointments, assuring John that 'he was entirely at his disposal' over the matter. On the same day, John sent the Prime Minister a holding letter, informing him that he was consulting the Archbishop of York on the following Wednesday, after which he would be able to give a definite answer.

On Friday 2 February, John attended the consecration of Colin James, to be Suffragan Bishop of Basingstoke, and Aubrey Aitken, to be Suffragan Bishop of Lynn, in St Paul's Cathedral. The preacher was Basil Moss, Provost of Birmingham Cathedral, formerly the ACCM Secretary

John and sister Pam

Head Boy John at Hill Brow,
Eastbourne

At Eton

Bible Camp on the Norfolk Broads, with John as cook

John's Sunday Evening Youth Group at St Mary Abbots, Kensington

Graduating from Cambridge, June 1948

At Westcott House

John and Rosalie on their
engagement, with Rosalie's
poodle, January 1961

Wedding day, June 1961

With newborn Laura and Ken Woolcombe in the garden at Jedburgh, July 1963

With Laura and Francis at Loch Mary, summer 1965

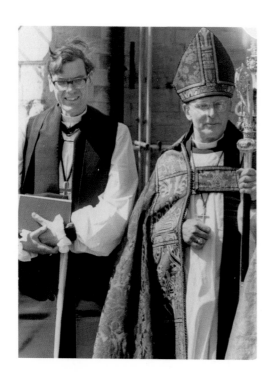

John at the West Door of York Minster following his consecration as Bishop of Durham by Donald Coggan on 1 May 1973

With the family in front of Durham Cathedral, May 1973

Going down a mine as Bishop of Durham

An armed Rosalie at Auckland Castle, hunting crows

The congregation at John's Enthronement as Archbishop of York, including Margaret Thatcher, Robin Catford (her Appointments Secretary) and the family in the front row, 18 November 1983

Loyal address at the opening of General Synod, November 1985

With Robert Runcie at the General Synod in York

With WCC General Secretary, Emilio Castro, in Zimbabwe in December 1985, discussing South Africa

John and the Queen admiring York Minster's restored Rose Window,
November 1988

'You like my Curia, eh?' With Pope John Paul II at Assisi, January 1993

John and Jasper, one of the family's many
Border terriers

Painting Bishopthorpe Palace by the Ouse . . .

. . . and the finished product

On holiday in Portugal, summer 1990

John and Adrian with indoor fireworks during Christmas at Bishopthorpe. The family thought they looked like dog dirt!

Summer Mission at Bridlington 1992, with David Wilbourne (left) and Malcolm Exley, Vicar of Emmanuel Church, Bridlington

Ennobled on his retirement as Baron
Habgood of Calverton, September 1995

The George Bruce portrait at Bishopthorpe,
1984

John and Rosalie in the garden at Malton

John feeding Anna, Laura's daughter, 2001

Grandad taking Joseph, Laura's first-born, for his first day at school

John and Rosalie in retirement

John in his pyjamas in the family's camper van

With the children and grandchildren at Malton

John holding Laura, July 1963

Laura holding John, Christmas Day 2018

to whom John had written prior to going to Queen's. The sermon was hard-hitting and very funny, which John was so impressed by that he procured a carbon copy. Warning that the Church of England still needed a rationale for suffragan bishops (at their consecrations they were only given a 5 amp plug for the mains compared to a diocesan's 13 amp), Moss came up with four new sets of symbols for episcopal office. He proposed a horse collar, halter and blinkers to equip them to be committee men, prone to chess-playing syndrome, obsessed with meeting after meeting, succumbing to 'Bishopitis administratalis', the grey fatigue and physical ill health symptomatic of a one-way ticket for Cardiac Alley.

Moss then talked of the bishop trying to be all things to all men, gracing sacred and secular occasions, going everywhere 'under a little purple cloud', too smooth by half, a master of platitudes, an underliner of conventional attitudes, a confirmer always of the received opinion. The fine robes donned at a consecration adequately symbolized this pomp, with the Bible presented to the new bishop recalling him to be the disciple of the man who rode on a donkey.

Moss was tempted to suggest a shepherd's crook and a tub of sheep dip to symbolize the bishop's role as counsellor and judge: 'Be so merciful that you be not too remiss, to minister discipline that you forget not mercy.' Rather, he suggested a crucifix, because 'we cannot bear burdens at the depth of which they need to be borne except in the power of the cross of Jesus, and with a grace not our own'.

His final symbol is a microphone, so that the Church and world can hear clearly what the Spirit gives him to say. Attached to his purple front, it is forever switched on, because 'everything the bishop says and does and is will be picked up, amplified and broadcast wholesale, in a most unnerving manner'.

Braced by Moss's vision and encouraged by the Bishops of Birmingham and Bradford that 'You *must* go to Durham!', on the following day, Saturday 3 February, John wrote to Archbishop Coggan. He confessed that though he still had forebodings about leaving Queen's, at the end of the day he had to trust the shared responsibility that he had implemented. He thanked the Archbishop for 'transforming the thought of going to Durham from being a nightmare into becoming a practical possibility'. When I travelled with John as his chaplain, we had a strict rule of silence in the car, rarely broken. Yet once, as we drove out west from York on the A59, John pointed out the very hotel where he had stayed at the end of January 1973, 'when I came up north to see Donald Coggan to make him see sense over the mad idea of me becoming Bishop of Durham!' Significantly, in 1955 Donald Coggan had similarly agonized over leaving the London College of Divinity (a place he had transformed as principal) to become Bishop of Bradford.

He also wrote to the Prime Minister, confirming that he had eventually decided to let his name go forward. Though aware of the risks of leaving Queen's, he was confident that the Prime Minister's advisors would themselves have been aware of what was at stake. Heath's curt reply reflected the pique that he had been kept waiting a week: 'I am confident that you will justify the choice that her Majesty has made.' Archbishop Michael Ramsey was far warmer:

> I rejoice in the news that you are going to Durham. I love Durham greatly and you will quickly come to love it. I am thankful for all you have done at Queen's, and they will grieve at your going – but it will be cared for somehow!

Ramsey concluded the letter by offering John help or service at any time in connection with Durham, 'except in March when I shall be touring the Anglican churches in South East Asia'.

John's appointment went public on Wednesday 14 February, just 20 days after he had received the initial approach. The next day, *The Guardian* gave its warm approval:

> The appointment will be seen as one of the most imaginative for years in the Church. It takes to one of the country's oldest and most influential bishoprics a comparatively young man, committed to the ecumenical movement, who has his own distinct views about a bishop's role. He said yesterday: 'I see it as a challenge to try to think through ways of making the episcopacy a possible job. It seems that at the moment bishops are fulfilling so many roles that they tend to fall between various stools. We are in a time of change in the Church. We have got to rethink the job of a bishop.'

The *Daily Telegraph* reported that Durham had wanted a 'pastoral' bishop, helpfully noting that with John's appointment there would be 17 former college principals on the Bench, with John the youngest, among them four Old Etonians: Bardsley at Coventry, Simon Phipps at Horsham, Bowlby at Newcastle (second youngest, aged 46) and John.

'The new bishop of Durham is a man of many parts – most of them rather impressive,' *The Journal* reported. 'He wears his learning lightly, has a gently courteous manner and not one iota of episcopal pomposity.' Misreporting a local paper's coverage of John restoring a rocking horse for Laura, the ever-accurate *Daily Express* described his hobby as 'making golliwogs'.

The evening after the official announcement, John and Rosalie attended a dinner for local dignitaries as guests of the Prime Minister at the Midland Hotel, Birmingham. Edward Heath asked John what he intended doing in his first days as Bishop of Durham. 'I plan to go down a mine,' John informed him. 'What on earth do you want to do that for?' the PM replied, totally astonished, 'Miners don't count any more.'

The many letters of congratulation were in the poor Queen's/rich Queen's genre. 'How we shall find a successor, I know not. But somewhere out there, there must be an Elisha . . . deeply and widely we shall miss you.' John Turner, Queen's Methodist Senior Tutor, wrote that John would grace Durham so well, having offered leadership in Queen's that was truly magnificent. 'I don't know what we shall do without you at the helm.'

The most moving letter is from John's 91-year-old father:

Your news is wonderful, and I am not surprised you have had a momentous decision to make. I have no doubt you have come to the right conclusion – you have the backing of the hierarchy and who are you to say to them nay? It is bound to be a very responsible job, and all you do and say will be hot news to the press – but probably your worst critic will be yourself. Much love to you all – and a father's blessing.

On 2 March, John received Durham Diocese's Statement of Needs from the Archbishops' Appointments Secretary, which the Archbishops sent to a new bishop, but only if they deemed it would be helpful. From 1972 onwards, Heath, who took his role in appointing bishops very seriously, insisted that the authorities of a vacant diocese filled in a pro-forma, setting out their particular needs. He found such pro-formas always showed a remarkable similarity. Every diocese wanted a man between 44 and 48, married with four children (preferably two at university and two still at school), and with a knowledge of both agriculture and industry.

Durham's statement covers just one side of A4, and is signed off by Alec Hamilton, Bishop of Jarrow. Durham's new bishop should have outstanding ability and wide vision, and initially should be allowed to concentrate on diocesan needs rather than distracted by wider church concerns. He should be an understanding pastor, sensitive to the whole ecclesiastical spectrum, a teacher of theological insight, able to communicate and interpret Christian faith for a contemporary context. He should win the respect of Durham's ancient university, in short be a man of sound learning, pastoral understanding, social concern, ecumenical outlook and administrative skill, keeping a cool head in the midst of massive change. He should have vigorous health, with the ability to relax and delegate, possibly lightening heavy burdens with additional episcopal help.

On 13 February, Bishop Alec had written to John, pulling no punches that succeeding Ian Ramsey would certainly be a formidable task, but reassuring him that he had many of the gifts that were needed. Prior to moving in before his consecration in York Minster on 1 May, John, Rosalie and the children went up to Durham for a flying visit at the end of February, meeting with each of the senior staff, checking out schools for the children, and having their first jaw-dropping visit to Auckland Castle, slightly reassured that the Church Commissioners had plans for its improvement.

Fortunately John's father provided more immediate help for an uncarpeted and uncurtained castle. 'Send me the bills for carpets, I will pay them direct, and the "refreshment" bill,' he wrote on 17 April, outlining his plans to come up to the consecration in his ancient Hillman, which had just managed to pass its MOT!

It was just as well that John's father had decided against a rail journey, since there was yet another rail strike on 1 May. Despite that, York's capacious Minster was as full as it had been for the service marking its

£6 million restoration, with 1,000 travelling down from Durham and 28 bishops assisting the Archbishop. A sign of the tremendous contribution John had already made to the ecumenical movement was that it was the first consecration ever where the preacher was a Methodist minister.

John Turner, Senior Tutor at Queen's, from whom John had received communion during those getting-to-know-the-staff weekends away in Wales, preached a trail-blazing sermon, complete with eight footnotes. Conceding Dr Samuel Johnson's point, that 'episcopacy is an apostolic institution it is dangerous to be without', he yearned for a bishop who was a friend of all, enemy to none, who, in the spirit of Cardinal Newman, 'was committed to people for ever'. Essentially, John should be a mark of unity, holding together conservative certainty and radical doubt, a successor of previous bishops of Durham like Lightfoot and Westcott, 'whose full-blooded Christianity was not frightened one wit by biblical scholarship'. John should 'get out the big maps to lift people out of parish-pump pre-occupation', equipping his clergy to be the exposed nerve of humanity, embracing an ideal church addressing the actual, a church of the ages appealing to the church of the hour, the church universal to the church on the spot.

Stressing that any bishop should have the moral integrity and fearlessness of a George Bell, Turner recounted how, on approaching Windsor, Bishop Latimer heard a voice within him, 'Latimer, Latimer, remember you preach before the great Harry this day', only to be drowned out by another voice, 'Latimer, Latimer, remember you preach before the King of Kings this day.' The church, à la Coleridge, should be 'the sustaining, correcting, befriending opposite of the world, the compensating counterforce to the inherent and inevitable evils and defects of the State'.

There was homely advice alongside these powerful quotes. Suspecting that the office of Methodist superintendent was more functional than 'the bleak sense of isolation' of a prince-bishop, Turner encouraged a bishop who lived in a castle to be seen in a supermarket. He stressed that John must learn to say no, must be given time to think, read and pray, lest he become little more than a dried-up orange. All bishops are just the servants of the strange man on the cross: at their consecration they are asked, 'Will you, will you, will you?' When they appear before their Chief Shepherd they will be asked, 'Have you, have you, have you?'

Nineteen days later, John, with his new mitre awkwardly perched on his head, yet to bed in, processed from Durham Castle, across the Palace Green, escorted by mounted horses, a trumpet fanfare and background pop music from a college open day. Having knocked thrice on the north door, he entered his cathedral and made the customary oaths on the Durham Gospels before the 2,000-strong congregation, with his toddler son, Adrian, soundly sleeping through the whole proceedings.

'What has all this to do with Jesus of Nazareth, or indeed the people of this area?' John asked in his sermon, clearly sensing that the pomp jarred with the One who humbly washed his disciples' feet. 'How dare the Church tolerate the status quo – the voice of radicalism is the authentic Christian voice, the voice of one who was crucified for being a nuisance.'

John draws back from the brink, assuaging the congregation's fears that they might have installed a firebrand as their new bishop: 'Though the Bishop of Durham has the highest throne in Christendom, in actual fact he sits over a tomb,' he asserts, mindful of the need to balance having his very public platform with the rich traditions of the past. He emphasizes the need 'to live with paradox, to live in the faith of the crucified one, painfully if need be, to make real for ourselves and for others the gospel that this same crucified one is risen, exalted and enthroned'.

At the sermon's beginning, John admitted he was overwhelmed by a sense of history, succeeding

saints and scholars and soldiers, powerful men, proud men, men of prayer who have made Durham to be conjured with all over the world. Then there is the more recent and the more poignant memory of the man who became known as 'the people's bishop', the man whom so many, including myself – perhaps too many of us – were privileged to call a friend. If it is hard to follow the saints and scholars of the past, how much harder to follow this loveable, brilliant man of God. The burden of history is hard to bear.

Aged just 57, Ian Ramsey had died of a heart attack after a meeting at Broadcasting House in London, casting Durham and the whole Church into massive grief. 'I shall be ready to speak only when I have something to say. Ian Ramsey tried to do too much,' John observed in an interview with the *Methodist Recorder* prior to his enthronement.

> Therefore, one of the main pieces of advice that I have been given is for heaven's sake learn to say 'no'. Primarily a bishop must be a man of God. If not that then he is nothing. The world is hungry for God, and unless the Church is on that level then it has nothing to offer.

Ian Ramsey's magnum opus had focused on the philosophy of language, particularly negotiating the interface between ordinary and religious language. Basically if you introduce God into a sentence, you massively alter that sentence, definitively beyond our experience. The Edwardian short story writer Saki wrote: 'When once you have taken the impossible into your calculations, its possibilities become practically limitless.' The Gospels are a series of word pictures, capturing what happens when God is introduced into the secular, combining the massively comedic (just think of the effect 180 extra gallons of wine would have on the wedding guests at Cana), the massively tragic and the massively miraculous.

Ramsey, worn out by styling himself as a man of the people, failed to apply his philosophical paradox to his own life, because essentially introducing a bishop into the mix also skews the sentence or the calculation or the context. The bishop's role is highly pressured, because everywhere he goes he has to be simply wonderful, from the moment he climbs out of the car until the moment he leaves. But what happens when, following the advice in the consecration sermon, he goes off piste and frequents the supermarket? Does he talk to everybody when he goes to buy a pint of milk, feigning interest in their life stories, which would make for a very long shopping trip and a lot of sour milk. Or does he blank them out? Leslie Hunter, Bishop of Sheffield, was once asked how with such a high profile he could ever have a day off unnoticed. 'I go to Goole!' he grinned. Chillingly, towards the end of his consecration sermon, Turner recalled Bishop Charles Gore looking at an early photo of himself: 'To think that I was once a man.'

12

Prince John

On 18 May, the day before his enthronement, John, by Divine Providence Prince-Bishop of Durham – the other diocesans had to make do with just Divine Permission – made the ceremonial walk across the Tees into his kingdom, via the Croft Bridge rather than actually walking on water. The ceremonial sword normally presented to the new bishop was under repair, too fragile to be handled, so gentle John was spared taking up Goliath's weapon.

It was a curious ceremony signifying a massive history, which John rightly admitted to being overwhelmed by in his enthronement sermon. After two unsuccessful attempts to send an earl to govern the troublesome Scottish borders, William the Conqueror had ceded secular powers to the Bishop of Durham, in return for his allegiance. So from 1075, the Bishop of Durham became a Prince-Bishop, with the right to raise an army, mint his own coins and levy taxes. He governed as a virtually autonomous ruler, reaping the revenue from his territory, but also ever mindful of his crucial role in protecting England's northern frontier from marauding Scots. In a phrase, he was Hadrian's Wall incarnate, immensely powerful and immensely wealthy, residing in Durham Castle, the foremost of his 13 castles.

In 1832, the Bishop of Durham made Auckland Castle in Bishop Auckland his chief residence, enabling Durham Castle to house the newly founded university. Auckland Castle has 78 rooms on 11 levels, a parkland of 800 acres and the largest private chapel in Europe, whose size would put most cathedrals to shame. The castle has a galaxy of features, including *Jacob and His Twelve Sons*, a set of large paintings by Francisco de Zurbarán, which hang in the Long Dining Room, having been purchased by the Bishop of Durham in 1756. Formal gardens surround the front of the castle, while a large medieval deer park features bridges, fish ponds, an ice house and a charming eighteenth-century Deer House. In 1994, prior to an engagement at Durham Cathedral, we once detoured via Auckland Castle so John could show his chauffeur and me, his chaplain, his former grandeur. Twenty minutes after we had left the castle, driving at speed towards Durham, John piped up, 'I think that's our back gate!'

In 1943, The Episcopal Endowments and Stipends Measure vested all endowments, investments and property, previously administered by the diocesan bishop, with the Church Commissioners. In return, the Commissioners guaranteed the bishop a stipend and pension, and funded the maintenance and day-to-day running costs of any episcopal residence. In theory this levelled the peaks and troughs of a former landscape, where some bishops had access to great wealth, others very little, ensuring all bishops were treated reasonably equally. It also removed from them the heavy responsibility of managing any real estate. While it undoubtedly benefited some bishops, in Durham it massively disadvantaged the bishop, who still had to inhabit the real estate, having ceded funding and decision-making to a faceless body nearly 300 miles down south.

There are some similarities with my father's situation in the mid-1960s, when he was vicar of a small rural parish in the Vale of York. Sixty-five per cent of his income was provided by glebe, church land that was rented to local farmers, with my dad employing an agent to collect the rents six months in arrears. Most of the farmers paid on the dot; a few were going through lean times and couldn't afford to pay, or paid in kind with produce; one or two refused to pay. It was a bit cumbersome, but as a system of local accountability and funding it sort of worked: my dad was a faithful parish priest and so the farmers were glad to finance his ministry rather than pay rents to some inscrutable landlord. By the end of the 1960s, the Church Commissioners took over the glebe, relieving my dad of the administrative hassle. But something precious was lost in terms of local ministry, locally resourced. For over 40 years now the parish has had no vicar, with its significant glebe diverted to fund other enterprises.

Initially, moving from a flat in Birmingham to a castle in County Durham brought great excitement. The family only had to occupy 36 (!) rooms, with the remaining 42 comprising State Rooms and a couple of private flats or used to house the Diocesan Office. In letters in 1973 and 1974, Rosalie writes of 'this beautiful castle in which we have settled in very quickly, unpacking 92 tea chests and John's 3,000 books, with the children much healthier than in Birmingham'. John's father came to the rescue – as well as funding the purchase of expensive carpets and curtains, he provided a veritable removal-van-load of antique furniture to transform 'sparsely furnished rooms into most adequately furnished'. Rosalie enthuses about it being grand and spacious, marvellous to have room for everything, including a room with a model railway laid out by John, play rooms up- and downstairs, and even a shoe-cleaning room. The castle easily accommodated 22 family members for John's enthronement, with 18 staying the following Christmas, when the State Rooms housed illicit games of badminton, golf, billiards and even cycle races. Michael and Joan Ramsey visited in the early days, played croquet with Adrian and told John to be ever obedient to the 'Ramsey rule' of having one Sunday in four off. The castle was a thrilling venue for diocesan events, ranging from the Durham Cathedral Choir singing Evensong for just the family in their 'cosy' chapel to hosting 500 visitors for 'treasures and tea' open days. John's domestic chaplain recalled:

> During the ordination retreat, the candidates were invited over to Auckland Castle for a day, to play a game of cricket on the lower lawn, and we all tried to have a go at seeing how far we could hit the ball out of the grounds. The then Bishop of Jarrow turned out to be quite a cricketer. As soon as he'd got the bat in his hand, we couldn't get it out of his hand, and I don't think we ever actually put him out!

The grounds, lovingly tended by Rosalie with some help from the gardeners, provided ample space for ten-year-old Laura to exercise her grey Welsh pony, bought for her just three months after moving in. One year, one single gardener grew 44 different kinds of vegetable and 365 leeks in the kitchen garden. In preparation for the botanist David Bellamy staging a TV programme in the grounds, one Holy Saturday the Habgood family dredged the massive fish pond, with Francis trawling the depths from a fibreglass boat, dragging tyres, rope, milk crates and parcels of newspapers to the shore.

But as the sheer slog of maintaining a castle took hold, Rosalie talked of the appalling nightmare wreaked by Ted Heath's letter of invitation. In conversation in 2006, John concluded the move 'had been hard on Rosalie', who often simply wished that the entire place would fall down. Even the saintly Ramseys had clearly found the place a struggle. Laura's bedroom was 100 yards from the chilly family sitting room/library, with heating used only sparingly as fuel costs soared; asthmatic Adrian, 'more ill than well', forced Rosalie to spend her evenings in an adjacent bedroom, while John worked in a distant study. With John away at conferences or meetings, Rosalie was often 'castle-alone', with letters to parents sounding increasingly desperate:

> It's almost a full-time job doing the shutters, locking up, renewing 180 light bulbs, making sure twelve lavatory cisterns don't freeze up, clearing gutters and downspouts, checking the many unused doors in the Castle and Park are kept locked, replacing wire cages on chimney pots, keeping an eye on the electric fuses serving the Diocesan Offices – on two occasions we nearly went up in flames – as well as keeping a vigilant watch that the gypsies don't invade the Park.

The much-maligned gypsies had let loose a wild black stallion, which kept trying to ravish Laura's pony.

The journalist Graham Turner interviewed the Habgoods in an exquisitely written article in the *Daily Telegraph* in 1982:

> The bishop's wife is envious of the statutory warmth in which the diocesan staff work, and tries to share in it by leaving open the door between the office and the house, but with only marginal benefit. It is enough to make Mrs Proudie rotate in her grave.

The Diocesan Office had moved into a wing of Auckland Castle shortly before the Habgoods' arrival, under the control of the Diocesan Secretary, Phyllis Carter, who ruled with a rod of iron. Her dynasty went back to the 1920s, in that she succeeded to the post on the death of her father, who had been appointed Diocesan Secretary by Hensley Henson. She was a tireless worker with detailed knowledge of the diocese, to which she was devoted. She was, however, a poor delegator and team player, resulting in her being over tired, tense and prone to fall out with her colleagues. John, his study just the other side of the door from the Diocesan Office, often had to step in to calm the latest crisis. He instituted a weekly meeting with Phyllis, to discuss the diocese and its boards and committees, which gave John the opportunity to gently nudge her into handling the office better and make it more efficient. The longer she worked with John, Phyllis noticeably became happier in her skin and more relaxed.

Improving the castle and park was a work in progress throughout their decade in Auckland, sometimes working with but more often working against the team of local contractors hired by the Church Commissioners, who wisely kept a safe distance. John had a furious row with them when, instead of simply changing a valve on the ancient oil-fired boiler, they decided to convert the whole system to gas, with laying new pipes and disposing of asbestos cladding promising months of upheaval. Auckland Castle went into siege, with John and Rosalie bolting the doors and refusing the workmen admittance. Another delicious quote from Graham Turner:

> At a party for 160 people, the Bishop noticed the floor moving up and down (he drinks only sparingly). An engineers' report concluded that the floor would safely bear the weight of 12 people, but only if they kept to the edges of the room. The culprit was beetle and the entire floor had to be removed.

It took a total of 14 months (the original estimate was six) to underpin the floor of the State Room with steel beams, forcing the family out of their sitting room below to take refuge elsewhere.

Ominously at a Church Commissioners' tenants' dinner, thousands of Pipistrelle bats, lured out of hibernation by the unaccustomed warmth in the chill dining room, flew from their haunt in the chapel, terrifying the august company as they dive-bombed the guests' heads. Protection of rare species notwithstanding, the Commissioners sent in a team of pest-control experts, who fumigated the place with sulphur candles, but to no avail. John ultimately dispatched them to new roosts by installing a stuffed owl in the rafters.

It all seemed a terrible muddle. The Commissioners had to prioritize a limited budget from afar, with advice from architects based in London jarring with that of local architects and contractors. They didn't always keep John and Rosalie in the loop about timings, undoubtedly trying to spare them being involved in some of the more menial works. But at the end of the day the Habgoods had to bear the brunt and, in the absence of an on-site manager, ultimately see through any project. In 1981 one friend, Canon Colin Brennan, described their time at Auckland Castle as 'seven years living in a builders' yard'.

Prior to the Episcopal Endowments and Stipends Measure, 14 full-time staff had been employed at the castle. Initially Rosalie was enthusiastic about their much reduced team:

> John's secretary is a mine of information, popular with the children; the gardener makes the park a show place, providing vegetables and fruit galore, his wife cleans for us and is an absolute treasure; Paul the chauffeur is thoroughly reliable and a very good driver; Barbara, the cook is marvellous, with Auckland Castle fare the talk of the county.

At first it seemed that the team shopped, washed, ironed, mended, cleaned, and managed to tend both hens and the children. But swans turned to geese as the impossible task of maintaining the castle meant relationships soured. 'We never had a good team,' Rosalie later complained. 'The new gardener was hopeless, the chauffeurs were desperately difficult – one took us to a tribunal, but the judge threw out the case. Nevertheless he went to the newspapers, who ran the headline, "Life with the bishop was hell!"'

How John was able to function at all given all this hassle, let alone run a diocese and take an increasingly major role in the national church, is an utter miracle. There would seem to be very few advantages and very many disadvantages to bearing all the trappings of a prince-bishop, who no longer had a kingdom to fund him. Yet there was one loyal sector who still regarded the bishop as their king: the Durham miners. Coal had been mined in Durham in substantial quantities in medieval times, when the Bishop of Durham had owned all mineral rights, culminating with 170,000 miners employed in the industry's heyday in the early twentieth century. Bishops of Durham and world-renowned scholars such as Moule (hailed by the miners as 'canny lad'), Lightfoot and Westcott (who had solved a miners' dispute) had found a surprising rapport with the miners. Miners trusted them to hear and resolve their grievances, welcoming them as the main speaker at the annual Durham Miners' Rally, bestowing on them the accolade 'The Miners' Bishop'. It wasn't an accolade easily won: in the troubled 1920s and 1930s, the ever controversial Bishop Hensley Henson had vehemently opposed their 1925 strike, and at the Durham Gala that year the miners attempted to throw him into the River Wear. Or they would have done had they not mistaken the unfortunate cathedral's dean for him and threatened him with a ducking instead; when you are a miner unaccustomed to the daylight, I guess one pair of ecclesiastical gaiters looks much like another.

John managed to win their hearts, visiting Easington Colliery in his first days as bishop, arguing against pit closures, praising them as a workforce whose distinct skills needed cherishing for the benefit of our nation. Though John was ahead of his time in being environmentally sensitive, he repeatedly championed the production of coal in articles in national newspapers, simply because in the 1970s there was no viable alternative to keeping the lights on, once North Sea gas ran out. In the industrial troubles at the end of 1973 and beginning of 1974, with a national miners' strike forcing a three-day week and a 10.30 p.m. curfew, the Durham Union of Miners asked for an urgent interview with their new bishop. On Monday 4 February 1974, one year and one day since John had agreed to be bishop, the miners shuffled en masse into Auckland Castle's State Room. John greeted each one, shaking hands criss-crossed with deep blue lines, looking into faces bearing the odd black scar where coal dust had contaminated a wound. Any winter chill was offset by a fire of Durham coal burning in the grate, which John himself had laid. As the flames crackled, John listened attentively to their concerns voiced in the gentlest of Geordie dialects; ever the doctor, John also noticed the persistent and racking coughs, symptoms of black lung and silicosis. With large portraits of previous prince-bishops scowling down at them, the miners admitted that they had been pushed further than they wished by the militant Yorkshire Miners' Union, and strongly felt, if championed by their bishop, that they could be a reconciling influence across the nation and bring an end to the strike. John was deeply impressed and promised to use all the powers he had at his disposal to help them. 'Is there anything else I can do for you?' he asked. 'Yes, Father,' the miners' leader requested, 'Pray give us your blessing.' To a man they all bowed their heads as John blessed them: 'Unto God's gracious mercy and protection, we commit you; the Lord bless you and keep you; the Lord make his face to shine upon you; the Lord lift his countenance upon you, and give you peace . . .'

Once they had departed, John immediately rang the Prime Minister, but since he was not around asked to speak to his Private Secretary, and briefed him about the Durham miners' offer, with the Private Secretary promising to brief the Prime Minister. Three days later, on 7 February, Ted Heath called a general election, claiming that since there had been no breakthrough in discussions with the National Union of Mineworkers, he had decided to go to the country to decide who governed the country. Since the Prime Minister never got back to him, John assumed he had set his face against his offer of mediation.

There is an odd twist to the story. Two years later, at a conference at Ditchley House in 1976, on 'Values and decision-making in modern democratic societies', John met up with Edward Heath and expressed deep regret that Heath had not pursued his offer of mediation. Heath claimed that the offer had never reached him. Talking with them was TV presenter and interviewer Robin Day, who doggedly pressed Heath – was he really admitting that an offer that could have saved the government, sparing the nation the Lib–Lab pact and Margaret Thatcher, among other things, was he admitting that such an offer had been kept from him? Heath firmly maintained that this was the case. On 2 November 2006, I wrote to the Prime Minister's Appointment Secretary, to check whether John's call had been logged. He kindly checked through all the files from the 1973/74 Miners' Strike, but no call was recorded.

Whatever, John proved worthy of the miners' trust in him. He made sure that there was a key lay person in the diocese to keep local communities together after pit closures. He gave considerable priority to funding ministerial posts in decaying pit villages, where the church was often the only thing they had left, persuading clergy faithfully to serve there rather than be lured by more glamorous ministry elsewhere.

He also prioritized ministry in the new towns at Washington, Peterlee and Newton Aycliffe, where many displaced miners and their families ended up after the collapse of their community. A true prince in the steps of the Prince of Peace, wielding no sword, but rather the weapons of gentleness, truth and trust, girded with the belt of truth and breast-plate of righteousness. Just John.

13

Shepherd John

'I didn't really know what bishops did,' John startlingly confessed in 2006 when we discussed his appointment to Durham.

> When I was a curate, the Bishop of Kensington used to drift in, in purple splendour, and celebrate on a Wednesday morning. Otherwise I never saw a bishop. I bumped into the Bishop of Birmingham now and then at Queen's, but he seemed fairly relaxed.

The closing prayers from the Book of Common Prayer service used at his consecration would have given John ample food for thought:

> Be to the flock of Christ a shepherd not a wolf; feed them, devour them not. Hold up the weak, heal the sick, bind up the broken, bring again the outcasts, seek the lost. Be so merciful that you be not remiss, so minister discipline, that you forget not mercy . . . be a wholesome example, in word, in conversation, in love, in faith, in chastity and in purity.

Fifty of those 67 key words are chiefly concerned with bringing lost sheep home. I have spent 20 years observing shepherds in the North York Moors and Yorkshire Dales, and have often wondered whether all the training bishops need is to take a leaf or two out of their very distinct book. When the shepherd comes, he comes, and traffic and the rest of life is forced to grind to a halt until he and his flock have passed by. His coming is not provisional, no 'if that's all right with you', no appointment, no permission. He actually seems to do very little, strolling at the back of the flock, watching them, knowing the terrain, knowing the usual suspects who are prone to make a run for it. He commands his collies, who have tremendous energy; clearly they know the flock and terrain too, but they are subordinate to his overview (episcope in Greek), and woe betide them if they display any hint of disobedience. The sheep know their shepherd, responding to the horn of his pick-up truck with feed piled in the back. I have seen shepherds really put themselves out, one in a wintry April, drenched to the skin by sleet, wearing the thinnest of gabardines, kneeling beside a ewe to ease her labour, almost in homage.

John as chief shepherd declared he wanted to watch and listen to appreciate both the flock and the terrain. 'But I had better come clean,' he confessed in his first Bishop's letter in June 1973. 'In saying I want to learn, I must not pretend that I start without ideas. All the ins and outs of life in Durham, I have still to discover. But I believe I know what direction we ought to be moving in.' One of John's collies, Michael Perry, the Archdeacon of Durham, had written to John prior to his arrival in March 1973, suggesting a possible restructuring of the diocese. John's reply was terse: 'I find myself very depressed by the complexity of the diocesan organization, and wonder if this multiplicity of sub-committees is necessary.' Amen.

It's worth pausing to see how John viewed the team of collies at his disposal, and how they viewed him and the diocese. The chief sheep dog was Alec Hamilton, who, having previously served as a vicar and rural dean in Newcastle, had been made Bishop of Jarrow in 1965, just before Maurice Harland had retired and Ian Ramsey had been appointed. So he had managed two episcopal interregna and knew the North East very well. Following his 'retirement' in 1980, Alec was acting principal of my theological college, and we had long conversations about Durham and its bishops. Alec felt that it took Durham Diocese a little time to appreciate John's true worth, since he appeared rather reserved and even cold and unfeeling in contrast to Ian Ramsey, his hyperactive predecessor. Clergy were hesitant to approach him at first, but John's expressed intention, to be available immediately to them in any time of crisis, made them appreciate his considerable pastoral gifts, driven by a warm and immensely caring heart. Ian Ramsey, ever the talker, had bubbled with ideas, and had launched several exciting projects, including establishing industrial Wearside and Sunderland as a mini-diocese with its own bishop. But Alec felt he was a chaotic administrator, with the diocese strewn with plans conceived but not born, the plethora of unofficial groups he had let loose reporting directly to him, with no strategy for how these initiatives related to each other, let alone the diocese.

In Alec's opinion, John played recently introduced synodical structures to his advantage, encouraging the diocesan and deanery synods to take power, led by deliberations at a bi-monthly Bishop's Council and Standing Committee. John also appointed a Board for Mission and Unity, which neatly brought under a single umbrella all of Ian Ramsey's projects, and was accountable to Diocesan Synod. Alec noted that John listened with care, kept control of any meeting, using his presidential address at Diocesan Synod not so much to dictate its direction, but rather to educate the synod so any decisions would be informed and well thought through. Though Alec found him courteous and friendly in senior staff meetings, his thinking well organized with an almost scientific rigour, he had a self-sufficient air that rarely lent to asking for advice. Alec never heard a bad sermon or talk from John, who came across as someone who knew, and knew he knew; he recalled one bishops' meeting at Salisbury where John led a tutorial on nuclear physics, with the rest of the bishops like the elders gathered in Jerusalem's Temple, wondering at this prodigy in their midst.

Alec of course saw himself as co-shepherd, not chief sheepdog, but John had firm views about suffragans being necessarily subordinate to the diocesan. He (unsuccessfully) opposed their full inclusion at bishops' meetings, feeling they had a predominantly pastoral role, with the diocesan legally obliged to make difficult decisions that could not be delegated. John did the majority of licensings and institutions, which Alec had previously shared with Ian Ramsey. John's view of Alec was that he was essentially a parish priest who happened to be a suffragan, who was oblivious to issues on a wider canvass. For this reason, and because he felt Alec was not impartial, with both a host of favourites and those he targeted for unfair criticism, he repeatedly refused to recommend his name go forward to be a diocesan bishop, despite having his arm twisted by Ken Carey and others who rallied behind Alec's cause.

The Dean of Durham Cathedral is neither a co-bishop nor a sheepdog, more a cattle-herder with a mutual respect for the chief shepherd. Until 1979 the Dean was Eric Heaton, who did much to establish the Cathedral as both a spiritual centre for the diocese and as a place of pilgrimage of national and international repute. In his diocesan letter of September 1979 John compliments the Heatons 'for their warm friendship and hospitality, which have won them a secure place in many people's affections'. He concludes, 'Our prayers go with them as they move to a tough assignment in Oxford.'

Eric Heaton was an Old Testament scholar, who was married to Rachel Dodd, daughter of C. H. Dodd, former Norris Hulse Professor of Divinity at Cambridge, also chair of the group of translators who had produced the New English Bible. The tough assignment in Oxford was Dean of Christ Church, in charge of both Oxford's cathedral and the House, the leading Oxford college, with several professors per square inch. I once led a clergy school at Christ Church where one of the canon professors led the intercessions, addressing the Almighty as if He had scraped a mere 2:2 in the theology schools.

Heaton was succeeded by Peter Baelz, who had been Professor of Moral and Pastoral Theology at Oxford, the brightest of sparks whose philosophical creativity energized John. In *Prayer and Providence* (1968), Baelz had deliciously speculated about whether our much prayed-for Queen and Royal Family actually showed any material benefits from such frequent intercession, over and above the rest of us un-prayed-for mortals. He then had explored the boundaries between the distinct spheres of the sacred and secular, paralleling John's impressive grasp of philosophy in *Religion and Science* (1964). In that book John had declared his admiration for Polanyi's *Personal Knowledge* (1958), particularly the distinction between 'articulate knowledge', championed by science, and 'inarticulate knowledge':

To admit that there can be inarticulate knowledge clears away one of the basic theoretical objections to religion. It allows us to believe that our gropings after the meaning of things and our sense of the mystery of existence are not simply mistakes and misunderstandings, to be removed by being a bit more scientific or applying the laws of logic more ruthlessly. It becomes possible to see how there can be a confused and partial knowledge of reality, which is genuine, even though it cannot be brought within the bounds of science. But the fact that knowledge is inarticulate does not put it beyond criticism. The history of any religion is in part the history of successive criticisms and refinements of its fundamental insights.

Ken Skelton was a shepherd who had wandered into the wrong fold. Like John Habgood, he had flown CICCU's nest at Cambridge and proved himself a bright cleric, whose intuitions were swift but rational, serving with John Robinson as tutor at Wells Theological College. In 1962 he had become Bishop of Matabeleland and quickly earned the nickname Red Ken for his opposition to Ian Smith's government. His phone was tapped by the Minister for Law and Order, hoping for evidence to prove Skelton's treachery, who thwarted him by conducting all important calls to the UK and the USA in Latin.

Despite resorting to the Classics, by 1970 things had got too hot to handle, with several death threats, so Skelton returned to the UK. Michael Ramsey, who was concerned about revolutionary bishops returning home and sowing discontent, made it clear no dioceses were available here. Another Ramsey made him Assistant Bishop of Durham and Rector of Bishopwearmouth, and champion of his proposal for a mini-diocese of Sunderland. After Ian Ramsey's death, Michael Ramsey resisted pressure to appoint Skelton as his successor and instead advised Edward Heath to appoint the curate of high promise he had visited in Madré's Kensington flat some 20 years before. Skelton felt that John tackled the administrative chaos with alacrity and efficiency, although was disappointed he didn't take the lead on wider ecclesiastical issues, or become a spokesman and advocate for the North East. He did, however, feel John listened with his mind as well as his ears, although noted he could appear aloof, remote and cold, which he suspected was due to acute shyness – the Head of Durham Chorister School (where Francis was a pupil) had told Skelton he had never met a shyer parent. Skelton, an honorary member of the senior staff, was surprised that John never asked after his health, even though for several months he attended sporting a surgical collar rather than a dog collar.

In 1975, there was a new Prime Minister and a new Archbishop of Canterbury, one who was less jumpy about deploying episcopal refugees from Rhodesia, so he appointed Skelton to be Bishop of Lichfield. John gives him a muted farewell:

He has done more than most to keep a vision of the world-wide Church before us, and those who have worked closely with him will know from personal experience the refreshing change of perspective which such a vision can bring. I am sure he and his wife can count on our prayers as they begin their new task.

The proposal for the mini-diocese of Sunderland, though pregnant with possibilities, effectively died with Ian Ramsey, with Skelton's exodus sealing the tomb. Having been charged with being Durham's bishop, John was resistant to any diminution of his kingdom, also kicking into touch proposals for a diocese of Teesside, which was set to combine the major industrial settlements, such as Billingham, Stockton, Middlesbrough, Redcar and Thornaby, on the north and south banks. The scheme had got as far as building high-rise flats adjacent to All Saints' Church in Middlesbrough to house proposed diocesan offices, but John kept co-operation with south of the Tees at a very informal level, such as blessing the boats at Whitby in September 1976. The Bishop of Whitby was welcome at John's senior staff meetings to discuss mutual concerns, provided he realized that the Teesside diocese boat had firmly sunk.

Michael Perry, Archdeacon of Durham, was clearly a sheepdog very unhappy with his new shepherd, snapping at his heels for his entire episcopacy at Durham. John had a poor view of him, sensing he had been appointed as archdeacon too young (aged 37) with nowhere else to go, and was particularly concerned about confidences restricted to the senior staff meeting being broken. Alec Hamilton felt that, though he had first-class academic qualifications and was hard-working, he was naive, talked too much, had poor judgement and was pastorally inept. Strangely, Perry felt any dissonance arose out of John's academic inferiority, in that he was a mere pharmacologist whereas he had gained a first in pure chemistry at Trinity, Cambridge. Slighted that his wife was never entertained at Auckland Castle during the Habgoods' time there, he found John cold and calculating, though surprisingly good at church bun-fights. He suspected that John's avowed intention to be a listener was just a front for a very determined man, who within two years had reordered and rationalized the whole of Durham Diocese to his master plan.

The archdeaconry of Auckland fell vacant in John's early days in Durham. Resisting Alec Hamilton's advice to appoint in-house, John instead appointed Bill Westwood, vicar of St Peter, Mancroft in Norwich. In the event, Westwood cried off, unhappy with combining the role of archdeacon with that of residentiary canon, and John then took Hamilton's advice and appointed George Marchant, who was vicar of St Nicholas in Durham city centre and chaired the house of clergy in the diocesan synod. He proved the most loyal of collies, enabling deanery synods to lead in plans for financial and pastoral reorganization, with the annual diocesan budget, and concomitant clergy and lay deployment, first circulated to them for approval. He was impressed by John, whom he felt built up, through regular meetings at Auckland Castle, a diocesan awareness of corporate involvement, with an increasingly informed and experienced participation in responsible self-government. However, Marchant feared that in giving him and others, including the chair of the new Board of Mission and Unity, a much greater autonomous administrative role, whose input was welcome at staff meetings, John distanced himself. Apart from the odd phone call in a dire emergency, matters were deliberately kept waiting until senior staff meetings, because John felt that these gave the opportunity for doing your homework, resulting in considered decision-making. John clearly resisted being bounced by a vociferous person bending his ear, which could only result in shoddy thinking, knee-jerk responses and superficial policies. Marchant observed that John's manner was always cool, seemingly aloof, yet when any personal need was involved he would break into great kindness or almost youthful fun.

Alec Hamilton retired in 1980, to be replaced by Michael Ball, a monk who was chaplain at Sussex University. I realize to make any comment on the Ball twins is to tread on extremely delicate ground, but as a chronicler my prime responsibility is to relate what happened at the time, and not attempt to rewrite history because of subsequent events. John admitted to 'falling for Michael' after debating alongside him at Durham University Union on the subject 'Religion is the opiate of the masses'. A few months later John wrote to him, 'I'm very taken with the idea of asking you to be the next Bishop of Jarrow.' Dinner at the Athenaeum followed, where they chatted a bit; John was impressed that Michael had learned the names of the deaneries off by heart and officially offered him the job.

I interviewed Bishop Michael in 2006 and reproduce his perceptive comments in full.

John was humble, shy, yet sure. In Durham people could be a bit hesitant, but came away reassured. He knew what was in men – his shyness led him into the nature of people, combining a wonderful efficiency which doesn't overwhelm and an amazing intellectual breadth of vision. Like a lot of shy men, John was brilliant with children, displaying a boyish excitement, knowing exactly the right language and words. John was a classic exponent of Anglicanism's threefold emphasis on Scripture, Reason and Tradition, producing brilliant music from the tension in which he holds those three strings. In a way he had the brilliance of Mozart yet the knowledge of Bach, a theological hybrid of the two, very quick at picking up other people's ideas and adapting them – though he never produced any good heresies, in that he was too careful an operator!

He was confident of his governance, and took to authority naturally. In meetings he neither dragged nor pressed on, ably letting everyone have their say, expert at guiding the boats into his harbour whilst making folk think they had piloted their own course.

Occasionally at staff meetings he could be acerbic, and even coldly angry, particularly if he felt Michael Perry had broken a confidentiality. I was naive about episcopacy, but he let me do my own thing, yet was always there if I wanted advice, allowing me to shadow him for confirmations and institutions etc. We had sessions together where he joked, 'You're the popular curate, I'm the vicar who has to take the flak!' But he sorted and straightened out my ideas, able to balance the actual need and wider need.

Apparently when he came to Durham, John found several months of unanswered correspondence. Ian Ramsey was inspired, but a chaotic administrator, with John having to close down things that Ian had bewilderingly started. Coinciding with the introduction of synodical government, he managed to clear up the mess without really offending anyone. When faced by a muddle at diocesan or national level, John would interject, 'Don't you think, perhaps, possibly . . .?' Alec Graham, then Bishop of Newcastle, claimed that

John was right 99 times out of 100, with the difficulty knowing the rare exception. But without doubt he is the greatest churchman I have ever worked with, the most competent, aware, intellectually exciting bishop of the last three decades. Despite his height, he never dwarfed anyone, but would raise them up, with an incredible gift of opening people's eyes. Did I see angels and chariots of fire around John? Very probably!

John's domestic chaplain for most of his Durham years was Canon Alex Whitehead:

He always impressed us Queen's students as being one of the best brains in the Church of England, but he was a profoundly quiet person, and very, very thoughtful. With him being an Old Etonian and me being the grandson of a miner and the son of a railway worker, I sometimes thought that he was out of touch with where a lot of people were. He thought that I was just being awkward for the sake of it, and we had some quite vigorous discussions.

But before I left Queen's, he and I understood each other and respected each other. My father was dying in County Durham, so I wrote to John and said he knew me well enough, was there anything going in the Durham Diocese that would enable me to be much closer to my family. And within just a few days, he'd invited me to be his personal chaplain. It was one of the best experiences of my ministry. He and I already had an understanding, we already had a mutual respect, and my respect for him only deepened during six years as his chaplain. One of the delightful things about, of course, being his chaplain at Auckland Castle, was Rosalie was an amazing pianist, and you'd sometimes walk into Auckland Castle on your way to work and there would be Debussy echoing all around the corridors and so on, and so that was always a very joyful experience.

I was also vicar of Escomb and Witton Park, which were two small village communities that had seen some rough times. John wanted a chaplain, who was both a young man, so would have a contrasting experience from himself, but also someone who was in the frontline of ministry, working in some typical parishes in County Durham. So

I brought into his office something of the life, vitality and problems of those sorts of communities. He said what he wanted was someone who would speak the truth to him, in a way that no one else would. I've never had a senior colleague who's been quite like that, who was ready to listen, and if you said something that was worth saying, he would take notice of it and respond to it.

In John we had a bishop with real stature, presence, spiritual and intellectual integrity, real discipline and a natural seniority, a real desire to serve pastorally; added to the life of a strong family.

14

Bishop John

Jesus' commission to Peter, 'Feed my sheep', was a text John was often recalled by.

Alex Whitehead tells how

John spent his first years as Bishop of Durham just going round the parishes, meeting people, thinking, reading, writing, putting the people of Durham first, and that was something that I profoundly respected. And this came out very powerfully in his preaching, which was always relevant, always good, and always focused on the lives of the people to whom he was speaking. One of the things he told us at Queen's was as far as possible to reply to any correspondence the same day we received it, if it needed a bit more research, give it another day or two more, but get back to people, if people have asked you something serious, and something that was important to them, it was your duty to do it.

Over his ten years in Durham he wrote 68 letters to his flock, bimonthly from 1975. The letters were professionally printed, with the typesetting and proofreading inevitably time-consuming and labour-intensive. They would have to be written some six weeks before publication, usually inserted into parish magazines, with the danger that John's subject matter could by then be very old news. Remarkably, they come across as contemporary and upbeat, wisely focusing on the big picture, which tends to be immune from vicissitudes. He doesn't comment on the Falklands War until July 1982, and clearly didn't see it coming; but, then again, who did?

Initially the letters also contained diocesan news of clergy comings and goings, but within a few months John's musings are their sole subject matter, effectively a 1,500-word essay with John's signature squeezed in at the end. John's target audience strikes me as being the congregation of St Oswald's in Durham city centre, a highly articulate bunch with a lively, engaging faith, a heady mix of academics and others who were committed to a common familial life, rather than being lured by the more exotic fare put on at the cathedral and elsewhere. Apart from Durham itself, the rest of the diocese would form a very mixed-ability class, a heady mix of scattered failing mining communities, new towns, old towns, England's highest and most remote dales, and industries gathering around the mouth of the Tyne, Wear and Tees. What would the miner in Pity Me or the ship-builder in Sunderland or Hannah Hauxwell in the high Baldersdale make of John's latest offering? They certainly wouldn't feel patronized, but rather definitely stretched by a map far bigger than that proffered by the tabloids or TV. I recall Bishop Michael Ball's comment about John raising people up and opening their eyes. I also recall in York even quite bright clergy asking me to explain his diocesan letter, which otherwise baffled them: 'You think like him – what's he trying to say?'

Many of the letters are in-house: 'Without Christ the Church might as well die,' he boldly declares in his first letter, despising introspective, parochial religion, which 'went out with Jeremiah'. Administration should not be an end in itself, but there to enable Christ to come through loud and clear. John repeatedly hoped that he would never be too busy with administration to be available to help in a crisis. Just over a year in, he carefully sets out the workings of the new Board for Mission and Unity, which clearly got the diocese working like clockwork.

A lot of the letters deal with the machinations in General Synod and Parliament. He clearly was disappointed that General Synod rejected approving the marriage of divorcees in November 1973, and generously invites any remarried divorcees, who understandably felt excluded from or rejected by the Church, to touch base with him so he can make amends. In 1974 he regales the Diocese with the slow progress of the Worship and Doctrine Measure through Parliament, intended to enable the Church to fashion its own liturgy freed from parliamentary interference. Since the Measure had been approved by 344 to 10 by Synod, John rightly assumes that the government, especially a minority one, wouldn't dare to oppose it. 'Ee, Bonnie Lad, ah just hoop that that lot doon sooth don't wreck the Worship and Doctrine Measure this time roond,' must have been a sentence on every Durham miners' lips. In the same letter, John argues that God's grace comes first, and proves ahead of his time, hoping that full sacramental participation can precede any mature profession of faith and that unconfirmed children can receive communion and not feel excluded at the altar rail.

Other letters outline John's role in the production of the Alternative Service Book (covered in the next chapter) and successive reports on doctrine, *Christian Believing* (April 1976), *Believing in the Church* (March 1982) and *Varieties of Unbelief* (January 1983). John commends them for their subtlety and balance, wisely steering clear of the trumpet rally mentality that infected Call to the Nation and the Festival of Light, national initiatives in John's scathing sights. Unfortunately the reports were slammed by MPs and in the press precisely for their lack of a clarion call, 'even by *The Times*, which ought to know better'. John concludes his letter in November 1981 with this broadside, obviously rattled by the aforementioned politicians: 'I am more firmly convinced than ever that the most dangerous people in the world are politicians who believe they have exclusive access to God (Dr Paisley please note).'

Not surprisingly, given his role at Queen's, and his increasing role in the British and World Council of Churches, in August 1976, July 1980 and September 1982, John repeatedly leads on unity, and the choppy seas surrounding proposals for covenanting, despairing at the eventual defeat in Synod in July 1982, deemed by him 'a death blow for unity'. He covers in detail the Pope's UK visit in 1982, followed by a BCC delegation to the Vatican and the Middle East, and his chairing of a WCC symposium on nuclear disarmament, but concludes, 'All this activity is useless, though, unless Christians at a local level are making the effort to know one another better, and to work with one another more effectively.'

John was a very shy man, who had episcopacy thrust upon him in what is essentially a shy church. In one sense his whole life and outlook were a rationale for being shy. In January 1981 he writes a lengthy essay on evangelism, concluding:

Evangelism is not an obligation because somebody says we ought to evangelise. It is what happens when we look at the tragic-comedy of the world, and yet dare to believe that God has entered into the mess and muddle in order to transform it.

In his next letter he majors on mission, with the strength of the Church visually present in its parishes, 'through wise and generous use of occasional offices and basic pastoral care.' Ever the biologist, he senses the Church is an organism, which it is, none other than the body of Christ. But organisms affect how we use language, both limiting and enhancing it. You can run a bus, but you can't run a person; you can improve a machine, but you can't improve a child. You can observe a child, cherish a child, desire its flourishing, but you can never control that child, unless he or she becomes an automaton rather than a person. In short, John sees the Church as a 'you' to be encountered and adored and wept over, rather than an 'it', to be dragooned and controlled and organized.

John clearly was not a fan of unfocused national religious movements, however well intended, precisely because they tend to treat swathes of people as commodities rather than cherished children of God. In June 1974 he rails against the excesses of the Charismatic movement, especially when it champions spirit-filled Christians, with their hands held high and gibbering in tongues, as superior to more rational souls. 'It is a safe rule of thumb always to think of ourselves as related to the Father, through the Son, in the Spirit,' he assures his readers, proving that even rational souls are capable of gibberish. 'Reet, Bonnie Lad, make shoor thou gets the reeght preposition before the correct person of the Trinity, otherwise thou'll be proon to Corinthian anarchy!'

In April 1975 John targets the Festival of Light, for obsessing with sex and violence and failing to address any other ills, such as homelessness and inequality. Several letters form a thinly veiled attack on Archbishop Donald Coggan's call to re-moralize the nation. John outlines how the use of language and its perception is relative, and re-casts the naive discussion topics that the Archbishop has put to the nation, such as 'What is the right attitude to work?'

He follows this up in February 1976, brilliantly juxtaposing Coggan's further question, 'Where does the power lie?', with the powerlessness of Christ:

In the swirl of intrigue and power politics surrounding the trial of Jesus, men destroyed each other's credibility, and so lost their power by the way they exercised it. Whereas Jesus, who chose the way of silence and restraint, made this the supremely powerful expression of the love of God.

John majored on such silence. Following George Marchant's appointment as archdeacon, the Church Pastoral Aid Society (CPAS), the patron of St Nicholas, Durham, his former parish, wanted to appoint one George Carey as his successor, which needed John's approval. John saw George and Eileen Carey in his office at Auckland Castle, but George admits to being unprepared for the silence that followed his opening remarks:

> I started again and said that I was looking forward to working at St Nicholas and hoped that I had his blessing. Again there was total silence. I then did the unforgiveable, turning to Eileen I said, 'Is there anything you want to add?' She said there was nothing at that moment, although later she was livid at my putting her on the spot! But that was a trait that I recognized often in John's relationship with people. It gave the impression that he was aloof from others and insensitive to their needs, leading some clergy, perhaps feeling inadequate intellectually to cope with such an able bishop, to withdraw in terror from him.
>
> But one winter's morning I was on my way to Low Newton Remand Centre, where I was a prison chaplain, and because of icy conditions collided with a Land Rover. I ended up in hospital and had to have a week's convalescence. He paid for that and showed another side to his personality – that of his concern for his clergy. And he took confirmations brilliantly, speaking with great intelligence and insight to the candidates and their families. It left a great impression on me and influenced me later, when I became a bishop, to never speak down to people but to endeavour to make every confirmation very special to those offering themselves to God.

John certainly didn't talk down to people, with sundry letters that firmly grasp nettles. In May 1974, he judges abortion as the lesser evil, in promoting the health and life of the mother over the foetus; he is less sure when abortion promotes the happiness, convenience and good name of the mother over the foetus. In November 1979 he tackles the subject of homosexuality, pondering whether 'it may not be right for some of those whose homosexuality seems irremediable (!) to enter into the best and most faithful relationship they can, and give it sexual expression'. In June 1976, February 1978 and Sept 1980 he fiercely argues against discrimination, quoting a personal example where he defended a West Indian ticket inspector, suffering a barrage of verbal abuse from a member of the National Front.

John was equally unafraid to comment on national and international events, ranging from inflation, the Queen's Jubilee, elections, strikes and NATO, reaching typically gnomic conclusions. Such as on Watergate, September 1973: 'Democracy only works when there is enough in common between different power groups to make the loss of power by the ruling party a tolerable prospect.' Similarly he encourages church members to say yes in the EEC Referendum in June 1975, 'gladly committing themselves to the reconciliation of European enmities, the responsible stewardship of European resources and the enrichment of Europe's contribution to the rest of mankind'. In May 1979 he urges his flock to participate in the forthcoming European elections: 'Anything which strengthens our sense of belonging to one world, and helps us to act effectively within it, is to be welcomed. The European Community is a significant step along this road.' His belated take on the Falklands War (July 1982) is masterful:

> Bearing pain and suffering wrong, putting into practice the message of the cross, are not concepts which translate easily into political programmes. The kind of pain which has to be borne in the Falklands issue . . . is the upheaval involved in both countries reassessing their past, and then deliberately putting that past behind them. It is the pain of letting go part of one's image of oneself, the pain of acknowledging that 'honouring the dead' does not entail endless political intransigence. This is the level, I believe, at which true reconciliation takes place.

Inevitably, John occasionally majors on a scientific theme, such as in October 1976 when he boldly ponders extraterrestrial life and their faith systems; ten years later, considering whether animals have a primitive sort of soul earned him the immortal tabloid headline, 'Apes have souls too, says Primate!' There are letters about nuclear disarmament and the nuclear deterrent, with his 1976 Christmas letter defending nuclear power. However, he concludes that the enforced slowdown of society if it resorts to non-nuclear options is not all bad, taking its cue from none other than God, who scaled down big time at Christmas, abandoning the luxuries of heaven for the deprivations of a stable.

There are some surprising omissions in the 90,000 words John sowed during his time in Durham Diocese. Over ten years he would visit many varied parishes, celebrating new ministry, confirmations, centenaries, the liturgical round, but he never mentions one in his letters, no personal moments of elation or depression, consolation or desolation. I once asked him how he felt as he drove away from a parish occasion: 'Chiefly that I have managed to get away with it, and pull the wool over their eyes yet again!' Not once does he dwell on the striking landscape running from the high Pennines to the North Sea, carved by the Tees, the Wear, the Tyne, nor the myriad saints who inhabited them and still inhabit them in the modern day. Little mention is made of the towering cathedral, and the towering events and services it contained, including ordinations, with John serving breakfast, cereal and freshly boiled eggs, to each ordinand prior to their ordination.

No mention is made of his family: Laura thriving at school with a natural aptitude for the sciences; Francis equally brilliant, playing the cello and horn at concert level; Ruth as angelic at 11 as she was as a baby, her mother enthusing she had the same qualities as John; Adrian, described by Rosalie as 'a thoroughly active, exceedingly bright and mischievous boy, whom I lose several times a day in the vast castle, having heart attacks running around and calling him'. No mention is made of the heartfelt letters the children sent to their very busy daddy, missing him:

Bishop of Durham,
Will you come to the Library for tea.
We miss you.
Adie.

To the Bishop of Durham:
Are you going out tonight?
Can Laura and I watch *Top of the Pops*, please?
I hope you are well!
See you soon!
All best wishes,
Francis

Nor is mention made of the encounter John had with a fellow parent, queuing at a school parents' evening, who confessed that her son was one of the naughty ones. 'You should be supporting him, not briefing against him!' the Bishop declared.

No mention is made of the family's happy caravan holidays motoring through Scotland, or driving a 2,500-mile round trip in a motor-home through North America, passing through LA, Palm Springs, the Grand Canyon, San Francisco, and driving down the western coast. Nor of the trip to Vancouver, driving through the Rockies down into Yellowstone and back through Oregon and cowboy country. Nor of the trip to Denver, through dinosaur country, with its incredible rock formations, to Salt Lake City.

Undoubtedly John's family humanized him, enabling him to relax. Alex Whitehead tells how

Rosalie, if she felt that he was overworking and getting too drawn and tired, would put a model kit on his desk in his study, and that was a hint that it was time he just took an hour or two off and make a model, rather than flogging away at the job all the time.

It would have made for a brilliantly funny and very personable bishop's letter had John delegated it to Rosalie from time to time:

It is quite fun accompanying John to some civic events in the evening – he in his gorgeous purple cassock, me in my best (getting ready in five minutes) and usually forgetting my gloves and hat and having to swop my handbags in the car. There is much handshaking, formal introductions, speeches, bouquets, nice eats and then we get away as soon as possible. At one such do I spied my former headmistress who was sitting goggle-eyed with quite a look of awe on her face. She was obviously proud to know me as Rosalie and was delighted to introduce me to her friends. We get a lot of laughs in the car after these dos.

For reasons of discretion, no mention is made of their encounters with the Queen, feasting with her on the Royal Yacht *Britannia* for her Jubilee in 1977, led by police escort to its moorings in Teesport. Again, if John had let Rosalie write the Bishop's Easter letter in 1976 it would have been a bestseller, pure *The Crown*:

I nearly fell down in a faint when John came in one tea-time and said, 'We are going to the Queen!' Out of the blue the Secretary to the Queen's household had rung and asked us to dinner and to stay the night at Windsor Castle in four weeks' time. Well, that is an invitation that no matter what one is doing previously, one has to accept!

Luckily I discovered I wouldn't need to buy any clothes. I would wear a dress I had made for a wedding to be presented in – a fashionable short dress in rust-coloured nylon jersey – and for the evening a shocking pink terylene dinner gown I bought when we first came here.

We left the children happily settled here and were driven down in record time – four hours. The chauffeur remarked that he must have exceeded the speed limit in some places. 'Only in some?!' John replied. We were checked in by the police at the Castle gate and from then on we drove unchallenged to the front door. By this time I was feeling quite ill with nervousness. The Lady-in-Waiting, Lady Abel Smith (a relation of John's) and the Queen's Secretary were on the steps to greet us. Our chauffeur, in his excitement, leapt out, accidentally leaving the car in gear, and as we turned to go into the Castle, we left a scene of consternation – our car slowly advancing on to the bumper of the Peruvian Ambassador's Rolls in front. There were enough footmen and chauffeurs around to extricate the cars!

We were shown to our suite in the Lancaster Tower. I couldn't believe my eyes, the three rooms and two bathrooms were so exquisite. John's valet was unpacking his case and my chamber-maid offered to unpack mine. I had very little, and my dresses were in John's case, but I accepted and they didn't seem bothered by the muddle. When she had gone, I ventured into my room. Things were laid out most methodically, and I had fun trying all the many drawers and cupboards to find out where my few belongings were put. The maid reappeared and muttered something about a bath before dinner, but I wasn't sure if she intended bathing me, so I declined.

We were ushered along vast corridors, past footmen, into the beautiful white drawing room to meet other guests, the Queen's personal staff and trays of huge cocktails. There was so much to see, I couldn't take it all in. Suddenly there was a hush and, turning around, there was the Queen, smiling beside me. I was presented to her and then the Duke, and the other 11 guests were presented. The Fijian greeting was extraordinary – the Ambassador and his wife shook hands, stepped back, knelt low on one knee and clapped their hands three times very slowly. The Queen came over to us and remarked what a charming custom it was, and she then chatted with us for the rest of the time until we all had to change for dinner. She went on rather longer than was intended, and I noticed anxious glances between her staff, but no one can move until she does. However, 20 minutes was plenty of time for me to change, when usually I only have five disrupted minutes, and then I only decide what to wear at the last minute.

Dinner was announced, and I expected the Queen and the Duke to lead the guests in, but the Queen just made a vague movement towards the door, and no one knew what to do. No one moved, but by the time the Queen had reached the door I decided to follow. This was obviously correct, because as we took our places at the table she remarked to me how slow everyone else was.

The Queen wore a rich peach-coloured lace dress, embroidered with sequins and jewels – with enormous diamonds for jewellery. Her dress was magnificent for a Queen, but she obviously found it tiresome as she kept catching her diamond bracelet in it! The table was laid with silver and gold, candles everywhere, beautiful flowers, enormous oil paintings around the room all lit up, and although there were only 25 guests, the table could have seated many more. One tended not to notice the many waiters standing around, they were so discreet. I sat next but one to the Queen, beside her Private Secretary. The meal was sumptuous and of respectable portions, smoked salmon, veal, crème brûlée and fresh fruit so polished it looked unreal. Coffee was served, and the waiters all went out, taking with them the three dogs from around the Queen's feet. The Queen took the ladies to retire, and another awkward moment followed when the Queen asked us to bring up chairs and sit. No one moved, so in desperation I did and sat next to her. John's eyebrows shot up when he came through and saw me.

Later on, the Queen showed us all round the state apartments. This was fantastic. We spent a lot of time in the library where the librarian had laid out relevant documents for each of the guests. Rather footsore and weary we arrived back in the drawing rooms at 12.30 a.m. for a nightcap and a final farewell to the Queen and Duke. We were escorted back along miles of passages by relays of footmen!

Our bedrooms were immaculately laid out and all three beds turned down – we weren't sure which beds we were expected to use! After a scorching bath in the marble bath, I slid into the finest linen sheets I have ever felt. It had been a long and exciting day, and I imagined I'd never get to sleep in such magnificent surroundings, but it was all so quiet (where do the jets go at night at Heathrow?) that we slept soundly.

The chambermaid called us with tea in Royal china and later breakfast was served to us alone in our sitting room. What a sight – five morning papers for us, bacon and egg and coffee on a hot plate, fruit juice, fresh fruit, toast and rolls. Our car was brought around at 9.30 a.m. and we were waved off by Lady Abel Smith and the Queen's Secretary. It was a warm and friendly farewell, and I was glad in a way it was all over and none of the awful things had happened that I feared might! I only wanted time to dream it all over again. It had been like being wafted into a fairy-tale land, and it was strange to come back to reality.

As the Queen says, in Alan Bennett's play, *An Englishman Abroad* (1983), 'I suppose for someone like me, heaven will be a bit of a come down.' For me, the best of a brilliant bunch of letters comes in March 1980. John begins by jesting about C of E being a modern acronym for Centres of Excellence, but then concludes that the Church of England is precisely that, holding to its traditional threefold combination of Scripture, Tradition and Reason. He quotes from *Lord, I was Afraid* (1947) by Nigel Balchin, who was clearly disaffected by causes, creeds and the tub-thumping certainties of those who knew exactly where they were going in life:

> We stood at a cross road of time, with all the signposts down. We saw error and ignorance and prejudice and stupidity go marching boldly down the roads away from somewhere and towards anywhere. The bands were playing and the flags flying. It would have been easy to follow. But we stood there, fumbling for our lost compass and our missing map – waiting for the stars to come out and give us a bearing; waiting until it was light.

John comments:

> Sometimes the Church of England seems to fumble, or speak with too many voices, or act too late and too feebly. There are penalties in a competitive age for those who cannot climb quickly onto bandwagons. But even when all has been said about the dangers of patient reasonableness in times when others refuse to be reasonable, it is still a kind of excellence.

15

Alternative John

At only his second General Synod, John, along with his old chum Robert Runcie, had attacked a report by the Church of England Commission on Broadcasting, which criticized the BBC for taking a neutral or critical stance on the Church of England, rather than reflecting the deep respect fostered by John Reith. The report, presented by the Commission's chair, Stuart Blanch, the Bishop of Liverpool, boldly proposed setting up a Church of England centre for radio and TV, forming a national committee monitoring the mass media and appointing a broadcasting officer in each diocese. Basically, they wanted to recall the BBC to heed the motto on its 1934 crest, *Quaecunque* (whatsoever), flagging up St Paul's Epistle to the Philippians: 'Whatsoever things are true, whatsoever things are honest, whatsoever things are just, whatsoever things are pure, whatsoever things are of good report: if there be any virtue and if there be any praise, think on these things.'

John went for the jugular, claiming the report had misquoted the BBC's Director General and had mistaken the above motto for a manifesto:

> May I make it absolutely clear: I believe that this report is inaccurate, biased, and likely to lose the Church the confidence of the broadcasting authorities, whose avowed aim is to promote and defend things that are good. There is an element of deliberate distortion in order to make a case. I therefore shall vote against it and I hope the synod will too.

Synod did, rejecting all the Commission's proposals. 'Never has a document been more savagely mauled by Synod or the Church Assembly,' concluded Sir John Lawrence, a leading churchman, diplomat and travel writer. As British Embassy press attaché in Moscow during the Second

World War, he had set up and edited *Britansky Soyuznik* (British Ally), the only uncensored official publication ever produced 'back in the USSR'. Having survived Nazi and Stalinist suppression, he would not use the words 'savagely mauled' lightly. The *Church Times* reported: 'In a long debate in which praise for the report was mixed with an increasing amount of criticism as time went on, Dr. Habgood caused something of a sensation by the strength of his language.' John later withdrew the word 'deliberate' in the phrase 'deliberate distortion' because he didn't want to impugn the honour of the Commission's members; not that they had much honour left after his blistering critique!

Not having shown much interest in broadcasting before, John had certainly mastered his brief, and was strikingly sure of his facts. I do wonder if John was a bit of a stooge, fed bullets to fire by the Machiavellian Runcie, who was chair of the Central Religious Advisory Committee. Runcie himself had argued – though deploying a rapier compared to John's blunderbuss – that the report was uneven, regretting that there was no recognition of the high quality of the programmes put out by the BBC. Fourteen years later, following the publication of the infamous *Crockford's* Preface, John again fired Runcie's bullets, with fatal consequences, as I will make clear.

My instinct is that, for the last six decades, the BBC has benefited from treating the Church of England as a soft target, ruthlessly taking advantage of the very generosity of spirit that it so pillories. It woefully fails to reflect that the Church is implicitly or explicitly supported by a majority of the population. Its oft-repeated mantra of church decline is little more than a smokescreen for the BBC's own decline as an institution, and it is nothing short of miraculous that the Church is still standing despite such splenetic criticism. As for promoting and defending the good, more often than not its programmes promote as a norm a murky lifestyle which denigrates conventional family values and their concomitant stability.

Twenty years later (in January 1993) John lived to regret his championing of the BBC. Joan Bakewell filmed a *Heart of the Matter* interview with him in the drawing room at Bishopthorpe, asking his view on a range of issues, including disestablishment and the role of the Church of England in the future coronations. One slightly odd question was connected with Alan Bennett's *The Madness of King George*, and whether the

British public would ever tolerate an imbecile as king these days. 'The nation has been extraordinarily tolerant of all sorts of behaviour among its monarchs. But all tolerance has its limits, and I would not want myself now to say where those limits might lie,' John loftily replied. After the interview, Joan and her team remained in the drawing room to do a few head shots. When the programme was eventually broadcast, Joan's question had subtly changed to reflect the state of the present monarchy following its 1992 'annus horribis', with John giving the identical reply. Following the broadcast, John wrote in *The Guardian* about the perils of edited interviews, where the answer to one question can be presented as the answer to quite a different one. 'Who would have guessed, for instance, that what I said about the limits of tolerable royal behaviour was in answer to a hypothetical question about a fictitious monarchy which had become totally corrupt and debauched?'

Back to John's attack on the 1973 Broadcasting report, it was an amazing outburst by a newly consecrated and very shy bishop, especially given his avowed intent to spend his first year listening. It could be that John had gone over the top in compensating for his newness and shyness: or that he and Runcie were trying to get themselves noticed, with vacancies at Canterbury and York pending. Rising Young Turks have to have their sacrificial victims, but make enemies for life when those victims live to fight another day.

John had definitely got himself noticed, because Archbishop Ramsey immediately appointed him chair of the General Synod working party aiming to produce a new prayer book. J. F. Kennedy had concentrated the USA's mind, promising to land a man on the moon by the end of the 1960s; Ramsey, even more ambitious than JFK, promised there would be a new prayer book by the end of the 1970s, with John the Church of England's equivalent to Neil Armstrong.

Though a royal commission way back in 1906 had deemed 'the Book of Common Prayer too narrow for the religious life of the present generation', the trajectory of the Starship Liturgical Revision had been repeatedly scuppered by hostile missiles. The most notable was the 1928 Prayer Book crisis, when a modest revision of the BCP was rejected by Parliament for its allegedly Catholic sympathies, resulting in the Archbishop of Canterbury resigning. After that, the Church trod carefully, waiting until

1965 to promulgate the Prayer Book (Alternative and Other Services) Measure, which enabled modest experimentation with worship no longer to be a criminal offence. John used his maiden speech in the House of Lords in November 1974 to reassure a twitchy House that the proposed Worship and Doctrine Measure (finally passed in 1975) would bring an end to such experimentation and a period of consolidation. Basically, from then on, the responsibility for firing missiles at any liturgical revision switched from an aggressive Parliament to an equally aggressive General Synod.

In conversation with John in 2007, he recounted how he had foolishly read through the liturgical papers before his first bishops' meeting, so, much to his surprise, found himself appointed chair of the working party to produce a new prayer book. On the eve of that book's publication in November 1980, in a *Church Times* interview with Brian Rice, John described his task as no less than seven years' hard labour, and had he known what lay ahead, would not have said yes so readily! Though John had devoured the works of Shakespeare during his student days, and was capable of producing many a poetic and numinous turn of phrase, he was aware he had no formal liturgical qualifications, unlike the experts who made up the working party, such as Ronald Jasper, Dean of York. John played this to his advantage, unprejudiced, with no particular party axe to grind other than common sense, he felt able to look openly at the various options.

Undoubtedly there were warring liturgical factions within Synod and the working party, yet there was an unequivocal desire to contain everything in one book. John's genius harnessed this, seeing his task as 'helping the Church to make up its mind about what it really wanted and then stick to it as the publication date approached'. John argued that the book should be cheap enough to be affordable by any church member, and involved several publishers in its production, with market forces thereby driving down its eventual price. John wanted worship to have an authenticity that reflected the present-day understanding of the gospel, keying in to contemporary issues, while holding this in tension with people's understandable desire for stability, which comes through familiarity with traditional resonances. He realized that sensitivity to the present and loyalty to the past was impossible to reconcile, unless the tension was a creative one, respecting different approaches, following the classic Anglican line of taking a mean between the two extremes.

Inevitably the task was one of compromise, but John was bold in asserting that the gospel of the living Christ is too rich in content, and spiritual needs too diverse, to be contained in just a single book. John insisted on the title *Alternative Service Book 1980* (ASB), both to indicate that the work was complementary to, rather than a replacement for, the Book of Common Prayer, and also it was not the final word, flagging up that liturgy was necessarily a work in process.

Even so, following the ASB's publication, John hoped for a period of liturgical stabilization, to encourage familiarity with the new work, which could be used in the home to browse and memorize, cutting deep grooves in the mind and soaking into the soul. The ASB contained every liturgical permutation possible, along with a two-year cycle of Sunday and festival readings printed in full. These skilfully drew on different translations to provide a wide range of attractive scriptural material to revive society's appetite to immerse itself in the Bible.

John and others clearly felt considerable relief when the straightjacket imposed by the BCP was relaxed in 1965. But he stressed that the Liturgical Commission had encouraged considerable feedback to the experimental services introduced since then (including Series One, Two and Three), which a wide number of parishes completed, with responses in questionnaires broadly positive and seldom radically critical. At the age of 11, I recall responding to one such lengthy questionnaire on Series Two Communion. Oblivious to liturgical fashions and fads, I praised it simply for omitting the BCP requirement that people make their confession 'meekly kneeling upon their knees', a rubric that was proving increasingly tricky for ageing congregations with arthritic limbs.

Congregations with arthritic minds, while clearly having trouble taking in words whose meaning had changed since Tudor times, were also uneasy that twentieth-century language lacked resonances, with little sense of exaltation and mystery. The scriptural echoes, deliberately and carefully introduced into modern liturgy, failed to connect with a generation that no longer read the Bible.

People in the pews and hacks in the media didn't seem to get the point that liturgical revision was not so much a novelty but rather a recovery of several early Church practices overlaid by centuries of well-intended and not-so-well-intended improvements, and then mauled by the Reformation. John felt that the process of assimilation would have been helped by including some BCP gems and Sunday readings in the ASB, but the Privileged Presses (who had exclusive control over publishing the BCP) refused permission for including parts of it in the ASB. It seemed they feared this would reduce the demand for the BCP and cause its price to spiral. John just couldn't win, accused of turning his back on the BCP's treasures, while bowing to the Privileged Presses' view that the BCP was best protected by leaving it distinct, as well as having to honour the 1975 Worship and Doctrine Measure, which safeguarded the BCP as the doctrinal standard.

John preferred including a modest revision of the BCP Psalter, but was overridden by Michael Baughen, the Bishop of Chester, who mustered General Synod to include a psalmody which he himself had penned. John felt this was so jejune that he persuaded the publishers to produce an alternative Alternative Service Book that contained no Psalter whatsoever. With a distinct sense of disconnect with a nation crippled by the Winter of Discontent and all creation groaning, Synod scrutinized each page of John's new book, waging battles over the perils of parallel printing, such as placing different versions of the Lord's Prayer side by side, the Filioque clause in the Creed, and whether the production should be monochrome or technicoloured. Little wonder that John hoped he would not be personally involved in any further revision, as he makes all too clear in his diocesan letter, August 1978: 'If some future Archbishop of Canterbury asks me to chair a working party on the ASB 2000, my answer will be "No!"'

John's hope for a period of liturgical stabilization was a forlorn one, for several reasons. The Revised Common Lectionary (originating in the Roman Catholic Church as the *Ordo Lectionem Missae*), with a three- rather than a two-year cycle of readings, was authorized for use in the Church of England in 1996. It became, after revisions, the Common Worship Lectionary in 1999, replacing the ASB scheme; but, unlike the ASB, it failed to draw from different translations and, annoyingly, its explanatory glosses paraphrased or even rewrote Scripture.

John felt an undoubted strength of the ASB was that it was rich in seasonal resources, compared to the BCP. Unfortunately the ASB was the victim of its own success here, in that it whetted the appetite for even more seasonal resources, culminating in the publication of two additional books (*Lent, Holy Week, Easter* (1986) and *The Promise of His Glory* (1990)), expanding into the whole Common Worship canon, the books of which would fill a medium-sized bookcase. So much for John's vision of one book 'which encompasseth us'!

Similarly John's vision of the ASB being used as a resource for the home caught the imagination, spawning such books as the Franciscan *Celebrating Common Prayer* (1992), which provided a host of offices for use during the day. Probably the ASB's weakness was that it failed to offer Night Prayer (the monastic office of Compline) or a midday office. Full and abbreviated forms of Morning Prayer and Evening Prayer (for home use) span some 60 pages, whereas the widest spectrum of occasional offices (irrelevant for use in the home) span a disproportionate 185 pages. The book therefore seemed more a *Vade Mecum* than an *Omnibus*. Another weakness was that it failed to anticipate the revolution in inclusive language, which dominated the run-up to the millennium, with the ASB's Benedictus committing the heinous sin of 'promising to show mercy to our fathers' rather than 'promising to show mercy to our ancestors', one of the many clunky inclusive phrases that sound more Taoist than Christian.

I was ordained in 1981, so the leather-bound ASB, an ordination present from my wife, inevitably became the book that fashioned my ministry. It contained the dates of Easter up until 2025, so I expected it to see me out. I became immersed in its cadences, anticipated what Gospel was coming up when, could have chosen its Sunday themes (who can forget 'The Remnant'?) to get full marks as my special subject on *Mastermind*, and found the tour de force through biblical history in the nine Sundays running up to Christmas bracing. In short, I felt a strong sense of connection with my Archbishop, who had been its bold architect, a truly shared cure. And then at the turn of the millennium, authorization for its use was withdrawn and I was bereft, not least because my tower of Sunday sermons built up over two ASB decades was virtually redundant. But the wisest of words John wrote for the ASB Foreword transcend its demise:

Christians are formed by the way they pray, and the way they choose to pray expresses what they are. Few books can have had their origin in so much, and such detailed, public debate. With the exception of the Psalter and the readings at the Holy Communion, the wording of every part of the book has been subject to repeated scrutiny by the General Synod. But words, even agreed words, are only the beginning of worship. Those who use them do well to recognise their transience and imperfection; to treat them as a ladder, not a goal; to acknowledge their power in shaping faith and kindling devotion, without claiming that they are fully adequate to the task. Only the grace of God can make up what is lacking in the faltering words of men. It is in reliance on such grace that this book is offered to the Church, in the hope that God's people will find in it a means in our day to worship Him with honest minds and thankful hearts.

By the end of the 1960s we did land a man on the moon, and by the end of the 1970s we did have one prayer book, which was a remarkable achievement, a masterpiece of political compromise due to John. The process, which required intensely focused thinking and the frequent acerbic put-down, won John enemies as well as friends, which, combined with the way he had handled one or two refractory members of his senior staff in Durham, earned him an undeserved reputation for being cold and ruthless. That undoubtedly contributed to the reason why he was not nominated for Canterbury in 1979 – the *Church Times* (3 April 1981) reported on its front page that Runcie was the second choice on the Crown Appointments Commission list.

The same issue of the *Church Times* claimed that Margaret Thatcher had chosen Graham Leonard, the Bishop of Truro, to be the new Bishop of London, even though he had fewer votes than the other nominee from the Crown Appointments Commission (CAC). The *Church Times* revealed the other nominee as John, and that he was passed over for the appointment after intensive eleventh-hour political lobbying by Leonard's Anglo-Catholic supporters. The *Church Times* reported that while John

received more votes than Leonard, he did not have the two-thirds majority required for any resolution of the Commission to be officially accepted as passed. So the names may not have been given in order of preference, though Mrs. Thatcher would have known that

John had a simple majority of votes. Even if the names had been placed in order of preference she would have been within her rights to select the second one – as, under the agreement which set up the Commission, it was provided that the Prime Minister would have the right to do this. During the 1976 General Synod debate on the new system, it was stressed that a Prime Minister would not lightly disregard the Church's first choice, and that in most cases this would be the one appointed. Leaders of the main political parties (including Mrs. Thatcher) agreed to the proposals for the new system, which came into effect in 1977. But there has also been dogged opposition to the Bishop of Truro, although these people have been much less organised and much less politically active than the Anglo Catholic lobby. It is understood that many of the diocese's senior staff (including the area bishops) were opposed to Dr. Leonard being nominated. It is also understood that the Archbishop of Canterbury, who is chairman of the Commission, favoured Dr. Habgood rather than Dr. Leonard. After a long period of discussions and deadlock Dr. Leonard's opponents managed to carry the day, in the sense that marginally more votes were cast for Dr. Habgood in the final Commission meeting. But then somehow the Anglo-Catholics got wind of the fact that the names of Dr. Habgood and Dr. Leonard were going to the Prime Minister – and that their man did not have the majority vote. Immediately they swung into a burst of last-minute lobbying among Members of Parliament – including, it is understood, direct approaches to Mrs. Thatcher herself and to the Leader of the Opposition, Mr. Foot. Shortly afterwards, Mrs. Thatcher decided to recommend Dr. Leonard rather than Dr. Habgood.

It is being said that the Queen was dismayed at the choice, and contacted the Archbishop of Canterbury to see if the nomination could be reconsidered, but was told no. Bob Edwards, the Vice Chairman of the Vacancy-in-See Committee for London, and leader of the Anglo-Catholic lobby, claimed their action had been justified because Leonard was wanted by a very large majority of the committee, while the representations to MPs had been actually to make it plain that Dr Habgood was quite unacceptable to the diocese, which is not the same as asking for the Bishop of Truro.

A lot of clergy wrote to John, expressing their dismay at such a slur, along with their relief that he was to remain in Durham. Stephen Sykes, Van Mildert Professor of Divinity at Durham, later to be appointed Bishop of Ely, wrote a supportive letter, claiming that 'this is the work of that part of the Church of England which will stop at nothing to prevent the ordination of women; what they conceive to be "defence of the apostolic ministry" takes precedence over the mere conventions of moral integrity'. David Carey (Bishop Ken Carey's brother), the Legal Registrar to the Archbishop of Canterbury, wrote, 'The way your name has been dragged through the media is quite terrible, and Ken would weep for you.' John received similar powerful letters of personal support from the Bishops Cyril Bowles of Derby, Simon Phipps of Lincoln, Alec Graham of Newcastle, David Say of Rochester and George Reindorp of Salisbury. David Lunn, the Bishop of Sheffield, wrote, 'I mind about the diocese of Durham and the Province of York and feel we need your wisdom and learning in our midst. It is not fair that the South of England should have all the best brains!' The retiring Bishop of London wrote:

> What really worries me is the distress which this must have caused you, with all the cruel and unwarranted things that are being said. It is all highly distasteful and I want you to know how much I feel for you in having been brought into the controversy so undeservedly. There are some evil and ambitious people around who want their voices to be heard.

The most significant letter is from the Archbishops' Secretary for Appointments:

> I write to say how deeply sorry I am for you and Rosalie, and how exceedingly I regret the publicity which has been so outrageously spread about, concerning London. The Crown Appointments Commission has large reason to know of the immense importance of doing all it can to retain confidentiality. And yet, and yet. I am furious without being able to disclose it on a wider canvass. But I would weep if I was to think you and Rosalie were hurt because you were nursing an apprehension that the Commission had insensitively

ignored deeply human implications. That you have been hurt, no one can doubt, and I bitterly regret it.

Rosalie was certainly hurt for John, also hurt that a possibility of escaping Auckland Castle was denied her. Speaking in 2007, John seemed his usual sanguine self about the whole episode: 'I can't think of anything worse than having to go to London. It would have been impossible for the family. Thank heaven!'

16

Ecumenical John

John was frighteningly clever, one of the cleverest people I have known and worked with. And yet, for all this brilliance he was humble and modest, truly wise as a serpent and gentle as a dove. He was humble and even when an Archbishop never pulled rank. He was patient with those much less able than himself. He was imposing physically, graceful, kind and he had a sense of fun. John was a good, patient listener around ecumenical tables and the House of Bishops' tables and never dismissed anyone's thoughts out of hand. John was open to the thoughts and practices of others. In this one could call him a receptive ecumenist before receptive ecumenism became the fashionable way of ecumenism today. He could sum up a discussion in an inclusive way. He could see the other person's point of view and work with it without dismissing it out of hand and he could change his mind. He understood, as few did, what living with those who held different views with integrity meant. While people spoke of 'the two integrities', John knew the difference between that and two different opinions held with integrity. John knew that deeply held differences between those who shared the faith in Jesus Christ could be and was painful.

I realised that John's qualities and dispositions were the very ones needed in an ecumenist. No wonder John in his ministry was a leader in the ecumenical movement nationally and internationally.

The warmest words from Dame Mary Tanner, European President of the World Council of Churches (WCC) from 2006 to 2013, member of the WCC Faith and Order Commission since 1974, Moderator from 1991 to 1998. An Old Testament and Hebrew scholar, from 1982 to 1998 she was General Secretary of the Church of England's Council for Christian Unity, involved in Anglican–Roman Catholic and other conversations.

> I have one special memory of being at a Conference in Africa and walking home from a meeting in the dark with a small group. Suddenly one of the group said look at the stars. The night was very dark – no light blight. John had us all lying on the ground looking at the stars and explaining the heavens to us. I remember thinking that he must love the Psalms – 'I will consider the heavens, even the works of thy fingers: the moon and the stars which thou hast ordained.'

Obviously John came to Durham with a considerable head of ecumenical steam. Bishop David Hawtin was a young priest back then, somewhat fazed by John's 'awesome presence' but impressed by his willingness

> to bring home his widening ecumenical experience through the World Council of Churches and the British Council of Churches, to the benefit of the North East. As a member of the North East Ecumenical Group, he supported the visit of an international ecumenical team to the North East to explore 'Christian Mission in an Industrial Society' there and to make recommendations. There had been similar visits in Sweden, Canada and Holland. The team's report, entitled *As Others See Us*, was published in 1979. John was committed to working across the whole range of ecumenical encounter, international, British, regional, diocesan and local. This gave him a rare overview, and much scope for networking, communicating, interpreting, and at times calming.
>
> John's ecumenical credibility was established by attending routine meetings, sharing in the ecumenical 'slog', listening, contributing, knowing and being known by leaders and representatives of many denominations. The result was that when he spoke and gave leadership, he did so from within, not as a prelate from outside.

John went ecumenical from day one at Durham when his first ever preachment as bishop was at the Elvet Methodist Church in Durham City on the Sunday after Ascension Day, followed by addressing an open meeting of

MethSoc. It was actually a diary mix-up by his PA, who thought she had committed her new bishop for an engagement a year hence. But John made light of it, describing it as 'a fortunate accident and he was absolutely delighted to be among his Methodist friends'. One rather suspects he was happier there than at some formidable Anglican occasion staffed by elderly acerbic clergy with sharpened knives. Whatever, his sermon was brilliant, focusing on how at the Ascension Jesus took our humanity into God, flagging up that, with God as its destination, every human life was glorious and deserved to be cherished as such. The corollary was that every human had a duty to live each and every day as if heaven was their destination. At the MethSoc meeting afterwards John championed steam train enthusiasts, seeing them not as cranks but rather as those who have set their face against a throw-away society and want to restore and cherish and integrate everything as purposive. For steam train enthusiasts read ecumenists.

John took up the reins of Donald Coggan's 'Call to the North' after his exodus to Canterbury, organizing the annual meeting at Scargill for all northern church leaders, as well as a monthly meeting of regional church leaders at Auckland Castle – 'We got to know each other pretty well,' is John's modest take. As at Jedburgh, John was prepared to be bold with intercommunion, consistently supporting flagship projects such as the Washington town-wide Local Ecumenical Partnership (LEP). Hawtin notes:

> Knowing that the local Church Councils were in favour, he went beyond what was permitted by the current House of Bishops Code of Practice for LEPs, by authorising Methodist and United Reformed clergy to celebrate the Eucharist in all Anglican churches involved in the town-wide LEP. He gave this authorisation in 1977. It was not until 1989 that this was made possible nationally for ministry in LEPs through the new Canon B44 – twelve whole years later.

Hawtin realizes that John was increasingly involved in national and international ecumenical bodies, but strongly feels he was able to steer, enable and liaise so effectively, only because he was already a committed participant in the local hard slog of ecumenical working.

From his early days in Durham, John represented the House of Bishops on the British Council of Churches (BCC) and earned the deep respect of the World Council of Churches following his keynote address at their conference on faith, science and the future, at the Massachusetts Institute of Technology in July 1979, when he also contributed to plenary sessions dealing with nuclear power and molecular genetics. In a quintessentially Habgoodian sermon, John took a conference, which seemed over-pleased with itself, back to the Garden of Eden, focusing on the serpent's seductive plea, 'Eat the fruit and you will be like God.' John hammers home gem after gem:

God enters into our human point of view, bearing the pain of our distortions, and offering the promise of transcending them. The reality we are most conscious of is ignorance and confusion – the bigger the conference, the more conscious we are of our ultimate inadequacy. It is just then, in the failure of our godlikeness, that we can dare to go to the man on the cross.

The veteran broadcaster Gerald Priestland was covering the conference for the BBC, in utter despair at some of the extreme views expressed. John recalled consoling him over 'some very powerful concoctions on roof-top restaurants, almost weeping, "Boston, O Boston, if only you had known the way that leads to peace . . ."'

At the Vancouver Assembly, shortly after the Massachusetts conference, John was elected a member of the WCC Central (or governing body) Committee. Tanner writes:

John made a significant contribution as the Vice Moderator of the section on Confronting Threats to Peace and Survival. In the final presentation John stressed that whilst our Technological society tended to fragment and deal with each major topic in isolation, the Church, rather than denouncing secular *mores*, should promote creation's inter-relatedness and attempt to see the picture whole. The Section report is an elegantly written, clear report and one can be sure that John had much to contribute to the eloquent prose and succinctness of what only too often are verbose and confused reports written under the strain of Assembly timetables. The first part of the report dealt with Justice, Peace and Militarism. The second with Science, Technology and the Human Future. There were many statements placed before the Assembly for adoption, one on peace and justice. Bishop John spoke from the floor arguing for a more pragmatic and less 'utopian' emphasis, arguing for greater specificity about conditions of injustice and what the churches could do about it.

The Revd Dr David Gosling, who served with John on the WCC, catches this bracing period well:

In 1983, after my own appointment as director of the sub-unit on Church and Society, John became our Moderator. During those eight years, John earned the respect of the various WCC constituencies for his meticulous commitment to complex scientific and ethical issues. His realism during Central Committee discussions was not always welcome, but he could stop an impassioned debate by asking the most simple question, such was 'What happens when the poor become rich?' Major church leaders such as Archbishop (now Patriarch) Kirill and US Presiding Bishop Edmund Browning treated his views with the utmost seriousness. The funding for my own programme came from the state-subsidised German churches, which made no bones about the fact that their confidence in our work was largely based on John's active participation. We held conferences in Brazil, Argentina, East Germany (as it then was), Russia (at Tambov, south of Moscow), and many other places. Often travelling with John I came to know him as a shy but warm and deeply caring man with a quixotic sense of humour. I will not forget the look of rapture on his face when a waiter in a restaurant in Buenos Aires served him a huge 'knickerbocker glory'. In addition to holding ecumenical conferences, our sub-unit was expected to respond to topical science-related issues such as the Chernobyl and Bhopal disasters. Sometimes we referred these to members of our advisory committee, and then to John, who helped to make a statement for the General Secretary (Emilio Castro for most of my time at the WCC).

These sessions could be very contentious, as when a representative of Union Carbide stormed out of a meeting after the Bhopal disaster.

At the beginning of the AIDS pandemic, the World Health Organization and the US Episcopal Church approached the WCC with a request to help understand why some conservative churches were blocking funds for AIDS-related research on the grounds that AIDS is God's judgement on homosexuals. After a consultation – the first ecumenical and international of its kind – we raised the issue at the WCC Executive, after which John presented a series of recommendations for the Central Committee's approval. They were:

1 that AIDS is a virus;
2 that the churches must rediscover their ministry to the sick and dying;
3 that the rights of people with AIDS must be protected;
4 that there must be education for prevention.

The recommendations were passed unanimously, but some of the General Secretariat were so unhappy that they blocked their dissemination. We therefore leaked them in French through sources in Paris.

One of John's regular visits to Geneva was almost cancelled because York Minster was hit by lightning the previous day, shortly after the controversial David Jenkins had been consecrated as Bishop of Durham. John had been up half the night helping to put out the fire only to find, on arriving in Geneva, that his luggage had disappeared en route. But the press were relentless. 'Was the lightning an Act of God?' 'Look,' replied an exhausted John, 'in addition to the lightning, my luggage has disappeared', and, glowering at a rapidly retreating reporter, 'that's neither more nor less an Act of God than the lightning!'

In the 1970s, Sydney Bailey, a Quaker and expert on international law, had persuaded John to become President of the Council on Christian Approaches to Defence and Disarmament (CCADD), whose aim was to bring together Christians involved in defence matters. With regular meetings in London and an annual conference, it included generals, chiefs of staff, politicians and clergy, and became an open forum, entirely off the record, for sharing concerns, particularly acute ones such as the Cold War, Northern Ireland and the situation in the Gulf and Middle East. In short, committed to the interface between Christian conviction and political realism, it picked its way through many enormously complex areas. In the 1980s, CCADD organized a series of secret meetings, mostly in Dublin, on the situation in Northern Ireland. They involved leading lights such as Garrett Fitzgerald, Mary Robinson and David Trimble, as well as other more shady characters. I recall John shocking my congregation no end when, during a confirmation sermon in January 1988, he recounted his previous day's conversation with an IRA terrorist, matter-of-fact, as if such conversations were routine parts of everyone's day. The Dublin meetings came up with a cunning plan to encourage both sides of the border to implement the European Convention on Human Rights into their respective legal systems. The thinking was that fearful minorities would be reassured that both the British and the Irish had committed themselves to recognizing the basic worth and dignity of every human. In 1990, CCADD was granted a surprise audience with Saddam Hussein, so, with the Foreign Secretary's reluctant approval, John was set to go to Baghdad, along with Sydney Bailey and an expert on Islam, to play the religious card by appealing to the best in Islam to persuade Hussein to step back from the brink of war. No doubt terror-struck at the prospect of enduring one of John's searing silences, Hussein had second thoughts and immediately attacked Kuwait, forcing CCADD's mission to be aborted.

Back in 1981, undoubtedly drawing on the major connections afforded by CCADD, John chaired a WCC conference in Amsterdam on nuclear weapons. The conference, broadcast live on Dutch TV, involved leading civil servants, politicians, clergy and military, enabling top US and Russian experts and those directly responsible for nuclear policies to discuss, in a safe Christian context, very different options. While the conference aimed at expanding people's horizons, the sheer complexities of the international dimension alarmed John, who felt out of his depth compared to the known and safe waters he chartered in Durham. In the same year, John led a BCC delegation to the Middle East, detailed in the next chapter.

In 1984, at a WCC gathering in Geneva, the then General Secretary of the British Council of Churches, Philip Morgan, asked John to invite representatives of all the churches in Britain to a meeting to discuss ways forward that would be acceptable to the Roman Catholic Church. John modestly claimed Morgan had approached him just because he was a senior cleric who had dipped his toe into the ecumenical movement. But Mary Tanner thinks that

> there was far more in the choice, not least of all his towering intellect and the respect in which he was held by the different churches and his commitment to the unity of the Church and the world. He was able to hold the diverse agendas of faith and order, life and works and mission together and relate local to global.

The year previously, John had accompanied the BCC on a visit to Rome, at the Vatican's expense, following up the Pope's visit to the UK in 1982. They toured the different departments, including the Holy Office (with conversations with Cardinal Ratzinger) and International Office – John observed he had seen something in the Roman Catholic mentality with which as an Anglican he did not feel at home. John was more at home in a relaxed audience with Pope John Paul II, whose opening greeting was, 'You like my Curia, eh?' He had then conducted them on a tour under St Peter's Basilica, praying at Peter's tomb. The cardinal in charge of ecumenical affairs massively encouraged John to include Roman Catholics in any new ecumenical ventures, which, combined with the high-profile visit, gave John major clout in his dealings with the Roman Catholic hierarchy in the UK.

In 1987 a conference in Swanwick rebranded the British Council of Churches as Churches Together in England (which evolved into Churches Together in Britain and Ireland). Mary Tanner reports:

> Not all were happy with the proposal. Dr Pauline Webb, for example, an inspirational and international ecumenist, feared it might lead to the loss of a prophetic voice of the churches. This was because the intention was to see that the new ecumenical instruments were more located in the structures of their own churches, and actions

taken had to have the approval of the churches. The authority for statements and actions must lie with the churches and not with an ecumenical group not located in the churches. The declaration coming from the Swanwick Conference resolved to move the churches from co-operation to clear commitment to each other in the search for unity and for the union for which Christ prayed. The 'Called to be One' process which followed led to intensive discussion within and between churches: the Inter Church Process culminating in *Not Strangers but Pilgrims*. A prayer was published to accompany the process, one which continues to be used more than 25 years later – at the end of the Swanwick meeting someone suggested the need for a prayer just as delegates were leaving. Legend goes that John is said to have written the prayer on the bonnet of his car:

> Lord God, we thank you
> For calling us into the company
> Of those who trust in Christ
> And seek to obey his will.
> May your Spirit guide and strengthen us
> In mission and service to your world:
> For we are strangers no longer
> But pilgrims together on the way to your kingdom.

When the new instruments came into being in 1991, John played an active role in both Churches Together in England (CTE) and Churches Together in Britain and Ireland (CTBI). He was a member of the forum of CTE and was on the enabling group that met four or five times a year. At the first forum he moderated section three on social and political issues. In CTBI he was a member of the assembly and one of the presidents. The inauguration ceremony of CTE was staged in both of Liverpool's cathedrals, venues particularly appropriate, given the close relationship between the Archbishop of Liverpool, Derek Warlock, and the Bishop of Liverpool, David Sheppard. Fearful of the ecumenical repercussions should the Roman Catholics not play ball, John had conspired with Archbishop Warlock and Vincent Nicholls (at that time General Secretary of the Catholic Bishops' Conference of England and Wales) to persuade

Cardinal Basil Hume to commit to Churches Together. John was acutely aware of the danger of gesture politics in large ecumenical events involving Roman Catholics, which actually had zero local impact or expression. He felt that the World Day of Prayer for Peace when Pope John Paul II had gathered faith leaders at Assisi in October 1986 was one such occasion. At that event John, and other WCC luminaries who had a privileged audience with the Pope, had tried to convince him that greater co-operation between denominations would be both fruitful and an exemplar of the way that leads to peace. While an obvious subject to raise, John was surprised the Pope was 'not terribly interested' and wouldn't admit that Catholics could be perceived as stand-offish where unity was concerned.

John was much more encouraged by his participation in the Malines Conversation Group, with open and fruitful discussions with Cardinal Danneels of Belgium. Danneels (who died in the same month as John in March 2019) readily admitted that the Roman Catholic Church had got to a point where it was becoming ungovernable, desperately needing a regionalism with self-autonomous local popes answerable to the one Pope.

Prior to preaching at the inauguration of the BCC's own regionalism process in Liverpool, John was interviewed live by a BBC reporter in the cathedral's confessional, simply because it was reasonably soundproof. Unfortunately they were interrupted by someone wanting to actually confess, which must have made for an arresting broadcast. In his sermon, John declared:

> We shall know that we are making progress ecumenically when our own churches begin to be changed by the demands of working together; we shall know that we are making progress when it becomes automatic to ask ourselves in all our planning processes, ought we to be doing this together? We shall know if we are making progress when at every level in church life we are conscious of being in partnership in the Gospel and feel a sense of deprivation if we try to go it alone.

The move from BCC to Churches Together was intended to widen the ownership for ecumenism, empowering the local. John yearned that the all-powerful WCC would make a similar evolution, as he details in the Epilogue of *Making Sense* (1993):

As Moderator of the Church and Society Sub-Unit in the WCC from 1983-1991, I was involved at world level in planning a variety of projects, all aimed in some way to help local Christian communities to tackle issues raised by scientific and technological development. In Central America and South East Asia, for example, groups of scientists were encouraged to work with local church people on the subject of deforestation. In the Marshall Islands we were able to focus public attention on the long-term social effects of nuclear testing. For a time we worked with the World Health Organisation on AIDS, and in 1988 I had to face an audience of African church leaders to try to persuade them, in the face of considerable resistance, that AIDS was not just a special problem for Western homosexuals, but was of vital concern in their own countries. In the Soviet Union we discussed with Russian Orthodox theologians their understanding of the uniqueness of human life, as made in the image of God, and the significance of this understanding in the way we should treat animals.

John tried to abort plans for a World Convocation in Seoul in 1990, majoring on the Justice, Peace and Integrity of Creation programme, re-placing it with a much smaller working group, in the hope that it might produce some ideas of real and intellectual practical worth. He was un-successful, and the convocation took place on the basis of ill-prepared and tendentious documentation. The result, in John's eyes, 'was a rhet-orical report full of high-sounding but impractical aspirations, which had scarcely been discussed by the participants'.

After retiring from the WCC, John chaired a small group of seasoned ecumenists (convened by Paul Abrecht, Director of the WCC Department of Church and Society, and entitled 'The Berlin Group'), who tried to ana-lyse why the WCC had suffered such a disastrous loss of credibility among opinion-formers in the Western world. The tabloids often ran reports that the WCC was funding freedom fighters, or that the Russian Orthodox presence were KGB stooges, censoring the WCC from criticizing the

Soviet regime. John's critique rises above scare-mongering and is more level and informed:

> Partly it is that the problems of the Third World are so huge and so pressing that the temptation to go for grandiose but inadequately researched prophetic denunciation is irresistible. It is also partly due to the failure to produce a convincing social ethic for the pluralist world. I am convinced that the only way to learn about ecumenism is not just talk about it but actually to do it.

Ecumenical John certainly did.

17

Beyond John

On his move to Durham in 1973, John co-founded the Council of Science and Society with former professor of physics and fellow King's man John Ziman. The Council was a heady mix of lawyers and scientists, with John describing himself as 'the token cleric' – some cleric! Styling themselves as a postgraduate version of the BBC TV series *Tomorrow's World*, they aimed to foresee precisely what was coming up in science, particularly its social implications, writing key reports identifying salient issues. Those reports included *Harmless Weapons* (1978), *Nuclear Energy Policy* (1979) and *Expensive Medical Techniques* (1982). John reflected that 'the Group had uncanny foresight, kept me up to scratch with Science and gave me insight into difficult problems'. John gained similar inspiration from the Society of Ordained Scientists, where by definition the clerical presence was more than token.

John also chaired regular meetings of medical consultants at Victoria Hospital, Newcastle. They discussed issues in medical ethics and produced regular papers, such as 'Resuscitation or Repair', focusing on children with acute spina bifida. John published these, along with his Council of Science and Society reports and his contribution to the 1979 MIT WCC conference in *A Working Faith* (1980).

As Bishop of Durham he had been invited by the Medical Council to join an ethics committee, which explored further funding Robert Edwards' and Patrick Steptoe's pioneering IVF research. The legislation on IVF was debated in the Lords prior to going before the Commons, with John one of the few Lords who knew the technique in lurid detail. He gave a talk at the Royal Society to interested peers, took prominent part in debates and was instrumental in getting legislation passed, stressing the need for future major research on the use of embryos. In regard to his presence in the Lords, John was sensitive but selective, only speaking when he felt he had sufficient weight as an expert witness. When in 1988 he spoke against Clause 28 (banning local authorities from 'promoting homosexuality'), Roy Jenkins wrote:

> I had never previously heard you speak, although I had greatly respected your intellectual rigour and positions. I had perhaps expected a certain austerity of expression, and was therefore more struck by what I found an exceptionally persuasive and sympathetic statement of the case. It was to my mind the best speech that I have yet heard in the House of Lords.

The Chief Rabbi, Immanuel Jakobovits, who was the first Chief Rabbi to enter the Lords that year, also expressed his gratitude, looking forward 'with intense and happy anticipation in joining you in promoting precious causes uniting us'.

Speaking of unity, John felt that the 1978 Lambeth Conference of Anglican bishops from across the globe was not well planned. Archbishop Donald Coggan had decided to leave it all to the Holy Spirit, who apparently is averse to detailed forward planning. For John the highpoints were the devotional addresses by Archbishop Anthony Bloom, and the 'extremely perceptive and extremely funny' plenary addresses by a very relaxed Stuart Blanch, Archbishop of York, whom John felt saved Coggan's ill-prepared day. Archbishop Desmond Tutu chaired section one, 'What is the Church For?', but proved a poor chairman at focusing on issues or gathering conclusions. John, as secretary to one of the section committees discussing twentieth-century technology and its effect on human life, rescued things by collaborating with consultant David Jenkins (at that stage Director of Manchester's William Temple Foundation). Excusing themselves from a planned trip and then working into the night with wet towels wrapped around their heads, they wrote up a substantial report from scratch. Fellow committee member, W. B. Spofford, Bishop of East Oregon, described John as non-excitable, a reality-tester, a cogent thinker, a sharer of information and, in group-dynamics terms, an enabler, never forceful, but always on top of everything. The hyper-controversial John Spong, Bishop of Newark, was also in the same group as John. Initially he deemed him:

England's number one stuffed shirt. But as the days of the Lambeth Conference went by, I came to respect his brilliance and academic background, and I had the feeling that he began to respect the fact that I had contributions and comments to make that he had not yet even thought of. He proved to be a cool customer rather than a cold fish, and I considered my association with him to be among the most pleasant that the Lambeth Conference afforded me.

The anarchy of Lambeth 1978 was as nothing to what John witnessed as part of a three-week BCC delegation, which visited seven countries clustered around Israel in a very troubled Middle East in September 1981. The fourfold aim of the delegation was to express goodwill; to incarnate itself in the political predicaments at the deepest and most prayerful possible level; to learn from those putting their lives on the line for understanding and reconciliation; and finally to feed back to their sending churches, enabling them to target their giving and support, and make sure any future resolutions on the Middle Eastern situation were informed rather than ill-judged. As the only bishop among the seven delegates, John was hailed as the supreme authority and spokesperson for the group, especially by Middle Eastern bishops from sundry denominations, and theocratic leaders, who clearly deemed conversing with anyone below episcopal rank as beneath them.

It was truly a tour de force, meeting a breathtaking succession of key figures. I will season my account with extracts from a bracing diary John kept of a dystopian world where they were daily pounded with propaganda and over-rich, unfamiliar, fatty food. In Lebanon the line-up included the General Secretary of the Middle East Council of Churches, the Chairman of the PLO (Yassir Arafat), the leaders of the Armenian, Assyrian, Maronite and Greek (Arab) Orthodox churches, as well as Camille Chamoun, the ex-President of Lebanon, the Prime Minister, the ex-Prime Minister, and many more.

Tuesday 8 September – Beirut
Terrifying taxi drives through the devastated zone between east and west Beirut. The old city centre was a pile of rubble, streets filthy, crumbling ruins with constant checkpoints in passing to and from

areas controlled by different militias. Traffic moves at breakneck speed – with overtaking on either side. At times the road virtually disappeared in potholes and dust. We saw three accidents – one actually taking place as a large saloon skidded into the back of an army lorry.

First stop the heavily protected British Embassy. The Ambassador described how a Kurdish gang controlled that part of the city – embassy servants have to be paid £10 more than the going rate for the gangs. Saw President Chamoun, Chairman of the Lebanese Front, in his office in an apartment block, half of which had been gutted. He stressed the Syrians are 'responsible for everything', and all that is needed is Western help to remove them. Arab league is powerless.

Our visit to the Armenian Catholics was a different world: enclosed, undamaged, prosperous. Much property destroyed in Battle of the Bridges (2,000 houses and 19 churches, but all rebuilt in 6 months). Clearly this is a prosperous, internationally orientated community tasked to preserve Armenian identity.

Lunch in a splendid restaurant near a mountain spring began with a table groaning with 'appetizers' – various kinds of oily dip, cheese, salad, and spinal cords (discovered too late!) and whole sheep's brains, followed by chicken and meat kebab and watermelon. The waiter dropped all the empties after clearing them.

A hair-raising ride up to the coast to Jounieh, with hair-pin bends to Bkerki, brought us to the headquarters of the Maronites, who were suffering severe losses – almost 150,000 have emigrated since the war. The Vicar General said Israel had been born out of Western persecution of the Jews: 'You are here: you have been persecuted: don't persecute others.'

Back to Beirut to the Syrian National Social Party's HQ, a large conference room dominated by huge ashtrays. An armed guard kept coming in and out. Dr Fares 'responsible' for external relationships launched into a long diatribe in French. Describing himself as 'Catholic' at times, the real hatred in his voice and face was startling.

At 12.30 a.m., just as sleep was coming on, the call came: Yasser Arafat would see us. It was a cloak and glasses affair. Two cars were waiting downstairs with some confident-looking PLO officials.

147

We were raced through the night at breakneck speed to the PLO headquarters, armed guards everywhere. Arafat, who had just returned from Damascus, received us in a very luxurious conference room, and was obviously concerned to be warm and friendly. A strange-looking man with enormous blue lips, three days' growth of beard and his trademark headdress. His hands by contrast were curiously delicate, and his eyes desperately tired. So were ours!

He is not interested in compromises – only in solutions. He heads a stateless people and is aware of their daily suffering, with no land and no passports. Despite many casualties they don't teach their children hatred. But why then do they have Military schools for 10–14-year-olds?

Arafat felt Israel's concern about secure boundaries is a 'big lie', but he is willing to accept UN forces on boundary of Palestinian state. Britain especially has moral and historical responsibility and knows more about the situation than any other EEC country. Britain and the USA are spoiling 'the naughty baby Israel'.

And so back to the cars in which we screeched through the deserted streets at 3 a.m. I tried to avoid sitting in the front seat, but was motioned to do so – and found myself sitting on a machine gun.

Wednesday 9 September – Beirut

Our driver drives with one hand, so he can shake his fist with the other. Am beginning to feel safe with him, despite a minor bump from a lorry. We picked up a young French-speaking PLO girl, near Palestinian university, who took us to a check point. Our armed guard had served in the Monty's Eighth Army, a humorous, vigorous 75-year-old, in startling contrast to the other PLA soldiers who were little more than boys.

The Refugee Camp itself holds 64,000 refugees. It looks higgledy-piggledy, the streets and passages wind around as if houses had just been planted anywhere, and the water pipes are laid along the ground. Although dirt and rubbish are everywhere, the insides of the houses were clean and looked quite prosperous. We were turned away from a school where they are trained militarily, its children clutching English text books.

There are minor industries in the camps – including car repairs. Expensive bicycles are on sale, and even chromium-plated hat stands! Two Israeli planes flew high overhead, and we heard some gunfire. Visited a training centre for girls, run by the Middle East Council of Churches (MECC), which taught typing, dressmaking, traditional embroidery etc.

A tour of the Red Crescent Hospital – still being built. Blood on the floor of the operating theatres, and every single ward. On-going building and the general dirt and squalor of the area, must have created enormous problems of cleanliness. The hospital administrator was proud of the way the hospital was able to deal with hundreds of casualties during bombing raids.

In Syria, John consulted with the Greek Orthodox Patriarch of Antioch, the Deputy Minister of Foreign Affairs, the Minister of State for External Affairs, the Director of the Presidential Office and the Deputy Minister for Religious Affairs, the Grand Mufti of Syria, the Vicar General of the Syrian Orthodox Church, and finally had dinner with the Syrian Government.

Friday 11 September
By this time I was feeling distinctly sick, and dreaded the journey over winding mountain roads through yellow-baked countryside. There were several evidences of fighting, and army checkpoints every few miles. At Zahle, Syrian tanks surrounded the town, and Lebanese soldiers confronted them with armoured cars. There was quite a lot of destruction, but no difficulty in getting through the check points.

We drove to Baalbek, looking round magnificent Roman ruins. It was very hot and I was sick behind a large Roman pillar. On the road to Baalbek were enormous fields of marihuana, and occasional Bedouin encampments. It was strange to find them there as the valley was fertile and cultivated. As we approached Damascus there was a very different feel about the country, evidenced immediately by the greater discipline in driving; there were actually road signs, the roads were better, and there was evidence of huge road construction programmes.

The Government has provided a fleet of three cars for our use – long black sleek ones, complete with motorcycle escort. We sped through the streets with sirens blaring, pushing our way through the traffic, ignoring the lights and sending cars and pedestrians scurrying to the side. Government cars don't stop in crowded streets for fear of assassins. It was a vivid illustration of the meaning of power in a one-party state, but we were assured that it was good for the local Christians to see Christian leaders being ferried about in this fashion. I hope so. We sped down Straight Street disrupting all its business.

Saturday 12 September – Damascus

After a light lunch at the hotel at about 2.30 p.m., and a short rest, we were taken on a whirlwind tour of the city – down Straight Street at 60 mph, a quick look at the well where St Paul was let down in a basket, and a slightly more leisurely one at the house of Ananias – little more than a stone-lined cavern. The houses and streets around looked incredibly old, and were covered with about a century's worth of dust.

In Jordan, John and his team were received by the Crown Prince, the Minister of Religious Affairs, the Minister for Information and his Under-Secretary. They also met with Dr Hanna Nassir, exiled President of Bir Zeit University of the West Bank. As in Syria and Lebanon and elsewhere, they were briefed at length by the British Ambassador. Emerging themes included the problem of moderation for Middle East states; Jordan's concern for Jerusalem and the West Bank; the relationship between Palestinians and the PLO; and differing perceptions between the West and the State of Israel.

Sunday 13 September – Damascus and Amman

Had a learned conversation with the two Bishops about the precise meaning of the word 'of' in the phrase 'born of the Virgin Mary'. They insisted that we visit their cathedral, which proved uninteresting. I suspect they wanted a lift back and the kudos of arriving with a police escort.

We set off in two taxis for Amman at 4.30 p.m., an hour late. The drivers were either mad, or up to some game, or under the influence of hashish. They drove alternatively very slowly and then at breakneck speed. We could see Mount Lebanon in the distance, and then the Golan Heights.

The road became mountainous, and we found ourselves hurtling round mountain bends on the wrong side of the road using full headlights to push other cars out of the way. By shouting at him we eventually got him to behave more reasonably, but it was a horrid experience. We arrived exhausted at 10 p.m., and had a hilarious supper – largely sheer relief at being alive. I had to mend the plumbing before going to bed.

Monday 14 September – Amman
Amman is a white city, mostly new and built of local stone, obviously very prosperous and orderly with lots of luxurious houses and flats. We saw little poverty, even in the old centre. The palace was up a steep hill in the old part of the town, and after going through the guards at the gate we wound up a long drive which curled between high walled banks. It was a good defensive position, but the outward signs of security were very few.

The Crown Prince arrived at about 5.15 p.m. and we questioned him until 6.45 p.m. He was very impressive – articulate, knowledgeable, balanced and realistic and he seemed to be speaking very frankly. He spoke about the attempt to find 'middle ground'. The new buildings around Jerusalem were built by Arabs on Arab land. Why should they not be inhabited by Arabs? Advice to Britain – stop the neurosis about security; stand up to the US; don't relinquish policy making in the Middle East to Israel.

Tuesday 15 September – Amman
Off to tea with the Mayor of Jerusalem, an old man exiled in 1968, who sat surrounded by a chorus of serious-faced business men, clutching their worry beads. Various photograph albums were passed round which were said to show the visit of an Archbishop of Canterbury to Jerusalem. But the smiling ecclesiastic in the pictures was unknown

to me. The mayor's story was a sad one – deportation, expropriation of property etc. He also talked about Israeli interference with ancient buildings etc., but it was difficult to be certain that we were getting the whole truth.

In Israel, the West Bank and Gaza, John and the team visited historic sites in the Jordan valley, and met with Jerusalem's Consul General, its Mayor and Israel's President, along with his Assistant Director for Information and his Minister for Jewish arrangements, David Ephrati, an expert on the interface between secular and religious Jews. They consulted with Archbishop Ajamian of the Armenian Patriarchate, along with 40 heads of the sundry churches gathered in Israel. The team visited the West Bank and Gaza and met local mayors, including the Mayor of Bethlehem and the Military Governor of the West Bank. In Beersheba they observed Sabbath preparation and in Gaza they consulted with local relief workers, visited a UN refugee camp and toured settlements around East and North Jerusalem. On the Sunday they attended a dawn service in the Church of the Holy Sepulchre and then lunched with the Israeli government, with a long interview with the Prime Minister's Adviser on Arab Affairs. They also met with representatives of the United Christian Council of Israel, visited the Yad Vashem Memorial to Victims of the Holocaust, before meeting with Likud and Labour MPs and a member of the peace movement. The group noted the grave view Israel took of its security problems, the impossibility for the Israeli government of permitting a sovereign Palestinian state to emerge on the West Bank and the dual loyalty of Israeli Arabs, many of whom had emigrated into Israeli territory because of its superior lifestyle. John was particularly struck by Israel's mystical and historical attachment to the land and the strong survival instinct of Israeli Jews, expressed in T. S. Eliotesque terms: 'Those who ask us what our end will be do not understand our beginning.' On their final day in Israel, John and the group met with a rabbi of the Moshav settlement movement and Yoram Dinsteen, Rector of Tel Aviv University.

Wednesday 16 September – Jerusalem
Allenby Bridge was a bleak spot in the Jordan valley, where we sat on stone benches under a corrugated iron roof from about 10.15 a.m.

till 12 waiting for the minibus to take us across the bridge. It was sweltering and the flies were swarming everywhere. Occasional busloads of Arabs went to and fro, presumably workers commuting. When our own turn came to be searched, my hand luggage wasn't even opened, which is just as well as it contained an empty cartridge case I had picked up in Balluk.

We drove up the road from Jericho to Jerusalem as the sun was setting. At a buffet supper at the British Consulate, I had long talks with the CMJ [The Church's Mission to the Jews] representative about the corrupting effect on the churches in the Middle East in having no outlet for mission. Social work is a help, but on the whole they have been too dependent on handouts from the West. The structure of Christian cooperation is very fragile and would collapse if pushed too hard. He also talked about Israel's bad conscience at having displaced the Palestinians, and located much Israeli vehemence in this fact.

Thursday 17 September – Jerusalem

Our day started at the British Consulate at 8 a.m. who described the settlers as commuters and weekenders with a smattering of farmers in the Jordan valley. Arab villages have been obliterated. The future looks depressing, made worse by Israel's 'Massada mentality'.

Next stop, the Jerusalem Municipality where we had more than an hour with Mayor Kollek, a vigorous 70-year-old in white open-necked shirt bursting with self-confidence. He gave the impression of being a liberal, intelligent man, proud of his achievements, yet not really conscious of the way his forcefulness might appear to underdogs. The settlements prove that the Jews will never give up Jerusalem. But there are no restrictions on Arab building. Now there is absolute freedom of access to sites, freedom of religion and education . . . but has anyone said thank you?

After a quick change into a cassock we went to the Armenian Convent in the Old City. We were met at the door by about 30 cowled figures who led us in procession into the church, chanting as they went. We stopped by the burial place of the head of St James the Less. The church was almost in darkness, but thickly hung with unlit lamps, and looked very mysterious. From there we were led up stairs to a huge reception room with about 40 leading Jerusalem clerics of every shape, size and dress sitting round the outside, including a splendid Ethiopian Bishop as well as a delightful black Franciscan. They stressed their friendliness with one another, and clearly most of them knew each other. But I did not detect much cooperation. We were offered huge glasses of gin. I realized what it was just in time, and took lemon instead. Walked back to the YMCA through the Old City.

Friday 18 September – Jerusalem and Gaza

We set off at 8 a.m. in a small taxi, and drove through well-cultivated, blossoming land on the way to Ashkelon. Near Qiryat Gat we turned off down a dirt track to see the site of a former Arab village, Faluja, which had been totally destroyed and replanted with trees. The only remains were a ruined shrine and the hedges of prickly pear. This is one of 350 Arab villages destroyed to make way for agricultural developments.

Suddenly just outside Gaza, there were camels, Bedouin and tumble-down Arab houses. There was quite a formidable barbed-wire fence separating off the Strip, but no road block. The city was obviously once a fine one, but is now very ramshackle, with a central area near the beach occupied by a huge refugee camp. The head man sat surrounded by younger henchmen, one of whom dropped an entire tray of coffee cups outside, and told us about his great days in Ashkelon – a city so hospitable that it didn't need any hotels. They refuted extreme statements about destruction of Israel: 'We will not be Nazis.'

The Mayor of Gaza lived in a magnificent house with enclosed garden. Though against terrorism, he stressed the world knew nothing about the PLO until the hijackings of the early 1970s. 'All we want is human recognition.'

We had a puncture on the way back. David Bleakly and I changed the wheel in record time. Our host, Mary Khass's parting remark: 'Are you really a bishop?' And then a final wave and shout from her car: 'I meant it as a compliment!'

To Beersheva, arriving at about 5.30 p.m., where Phil Reiss took us straight to the Sabbath Preparation services at his conservative synagogue – in a school room. It was all in Hebrew, much of it excruciatingly out of tune, and went on till nearly 7.30. It seemed interminable – mostly chanting psalms and prayers, with different people taking the lead, and a very informal atmosphere. At supper the young liberal rabbi accepted that the Jews were now treating the Palestinians as others had treated the Jews. 'By day the Israelis fight the Arabs, but at night they fight the Germans.'

We drove back to Jerusalem through rather eerie mountains with not a car in sight for 30 miles. Back at 11 p.m.

Saturday 19 September – Jerusalem

We had moved to the Moriah Hotel in West Jerusalem – a rather jazzy new building. My room is blue, orange, pink and purple: but comfortable and with a good view over the hills. We decided to stay in East Jerusalem for supper and a meeting, and took a quick walk into the Old City beforehand. I also visited 'Abraham's Bazaar' and bought some jewellery – our first opportunity to go to a shop! I tried twice to ring home, but without success.

Sunday 20 September – Jerusalem

An early start to walk to the Holy Sepulchre for the Greek Orthodox service. About 50 people attended the service, mostly old women in black and young men and boys who did all the singing and may have come from the monastery. The bishop presided, resplendent in a long train and sitting motionless on his throne while priests conducted the service behind the screen. It was strangely moving and we walked back to the hotel across the valley of Gehenna. It was a lovely peaceful walk, with the city glowing behind us and very few people about. But it was getting hot.

Then off to the King David Hotel for an official lunch – turkey (smoked to taste like ham!), then rather tough steak, and a sort of ice cream. We finished at 3 p.m. and spent a marvellous afternoon going round the Old City. Back, footsore, at about 6 in time to have a shower, and ring home. None of my postcards have arrived!

Monday 21 September – Jerusalem

Our bus took us to the Knesset, a fine modern building on the other side of Jerusalem, to meet the speaker, Mr Savidor, a brisk self-confident Likud MP, who wants to extend as much sovereignty as possible to West Bank. We dashed across Jerusalem to see Rabbi Zolti, the Rabbi of Jerusalem in his rather squalid office. He turned out not to be able to speak English. He sat there in a dirty frock coat with a black Homburg hat on, and refused to shake hands with the women for fear of polluting himself. He didn't really answer my question about the moral and theological basis of the state. The Rabbi was disappointing, reflecting the inability of that ultra orthodox tradition to give any help in the political scene.

To Yad Vashem – the Holocaust Memorial. It was deeply moving, but also hot and tiring. When shown the symbolic embers from which Judaism will arise I couldn't help remembering the charred cross in Coventry Cathedral with the words 'Father forgive'. Remembering is not enough.

Finally in Egypt they spent lengthy and fruitful sessions with the Coptic Orthodox Church's Bishop Samuel, and met with the Secretary of the Coptic Evangelical Church and other Christians, touring a church-run technical training project in Shubra's suburbs. They met with an Egyptian member of the Camp David negotiating team, and explored how President Saddat's negotiations with Israel, though deeply courageous, had alienated and angered other member states of the Arab League.

Tuesday 22 September – Tel Aviv to Cairo

We drove down the mountains to Tel Aviv, where it became hotter and hotter, then down to the coast for about an hour where we made the Hilton Hotel our base. The sea was blue and the sun grilling and it would have been lovely to have bathed, but like the Holy Family, we had a flight to Egypt to keep.

First impressions of Cairo were of endless crowds of people, many wearing ankle-length robes, cars hooting, old faded imperial streets, totally inadequate for the traffic they are now carrying, and above all heat, smell and noise. The Windsor Hotel (where two letters were waiting!) was faded like the rest of Cairo, and become slightly eccentric. It took about half an hour of furious argument in Arabic to work out which rooms we were occupying. The lift just manages to carry two people and an Arab driver in a kind of open cage, but I generally prefer to walk though my room is on the 6th floor.

Supper at 10 p.m, where we were served by a marvellous old man in a red fez who had been a waiter there for 55 years. The bed is like a board, and the pillow, I think, must have come out of one of the pyramids, but I slept soundly.

Wednesday 23 September – Cairo

Visited the offices of the Evangelical Church, founded by Scottish missionaries 125 years ago, and soon indigenous. It now has 250,000 members in 400 congregations, active in education, social work, youth movements etc., defining its mission as 'to present the love of Christianity to the total community, Christian and Muslim'. We lunched with them at a large restaurant where a line of black-skinned waiters in turbans and nightdresses served us four heavy courses. I sat next to one of the pastors who was heavy going, and did not derive much from the conversation.

We escaped at 3.30 p.m. and had a few minutes to change before setting off for the pyramids at Giza. They are right on the edge of Cairo, and the landscape changes dramatically from suburb to desert. The pyramids are surrounded by camel drivers, necklace sellers and numerous others clamouring for attention, and pressing goods into one's hand. The sphinx was difficult to see properly, as the light was wrong, but it looked magnificent later in the evening when it was floodlit. After leaving the pyramids we called at one of the innumerable workshops where papyri are made, and bought some. The process of making papyrus was demonstrated to us – marvellously simple and ingenious.

We were taken back to the pyramids for son et lumière – huge crowds, mostly American, but our bus driver managed to park very cunningly so that we could beat them on the way out. The lighting was spectacular – surely the best way to see the pyramids, and especially the sphinx. The night was cool and clear, and the whole setting unbelievably romantic – a night to remember.

Thursday 24 September – Cairo

To the Cairo Museum for a quick tour – concentrating mainly on the Tutankhamen collection. This was overwhelming – so much artistry, skill, wealth concentrated on death.

Met again with Bishop Samuel who talked about the spiritual revival in the Coptic Church, starting with the Sunday school movement in the 1930s. It has now spread through the whole life of the church, and there is a large adult education programme with seven evening seminaries with 200 students each, including women. Nine monasteries are full. 'These are the blessings of the pressures under which we live.'

There is a high church attendance, and the church fulfils its mission by the 'silent spontaneous witness of daily life'. This has led Christians to be trusted for their honesty and skill – trusted in the professions.

We were taken on a quick tour of the cathedral, a huge modern bare concrete building, holding up to 7,000. It was filthy and looked unused but was impressive none the less. We were then taken to the northern outskirts of Cairo to see an evening college for men sponsored by the church. It taught simple electrical and mechanical skills in a barrack-like building, guarded by the inevitable soldier.

Friday 25 September – Cairo

Our last day was practically all sightseeing. Discovered traces of original Roman walls with a few people even doing their washing in the Nile.

We went to the ancient 'hanging church' built over the main Roman gateway to the old city. Was struck by the transition from Roman paganism to Christianity with a cross replacing Venus in her shell, which then itself transforms into rays of light.

There was a service in progress (Copts tend to worship on Fridays so as to keep in line with Muslims), and the church was about half full with all ages represented. The service was entirely chanted, and we were told that communicants had to fast completely and go to confession.

After lunch we went into the Al Azhan mosque, having left our shoes at the door. It is said to be about 1,000 years old, and consists essentially of two huge spaces, one open and one covered. The closed space was a huge room, dotted with columns and arches, and with carpets on the floor. Men were sleeping, sitting, praying, talking where they chose.

From the mosque we plunged into the Cairo bazaar. The bazaar itself is an enormous maze of tiny streets, even more claustrophobic than the old city of Jerusalem. I bought a leather bag and managed to get £1 knocked off the price. Some of the others had a very long session with a voluble scent seller.

Then off to the British Ambassador's house for drinks. This was British Imperial splendour at its zenith – a beautiful house filled with servants in long white robes who produced a continuous stream of drinks and snacks. The former Ambassador has known the Middle East since 1947 and spoke about the frustrations of US indecision and Israeli intransigence, and said that Israel would be storing up trouble for itself if it tried to annex the West Bank. The Ambassador's wife spoke about charitable work among the 7,000 Arabs who live on the Cairo rubbish dump, and earn their living by collecting it in donkey carts, and then picking it over. Had supper back at the hotel, including a bottle of 'Ptolemy' wine which tasted as if it had come straight out of the Nile. Spent another night warding off mosquitoes.

September 26th. Saturday.
The drive to Cairo airport showed how close the desert is to the city. The outer parts of the town are built on pure sand, and the airport itself is just an oasis in the desert. Good views of the Nile delta, Southern Turkey and the Danube. It was raining in London.

On their return, at a press conference at Heathrow, John stressed the urgent issue of the unresolved and all-pervading conflict between the State of Israel and the Palestine people, with its legacy of fear, insecurity and frustration. In his view, failure to resolve this would threaten any fragile peace in the region and could threaten the peace of the world. The disintegration of, and near anarchy in, Lebanon was already a tragic consequence of muddled diplomacy, aggravated by the presence of half a million stateless Palestinian refugees terrorised by over 40 rival militias. On behalf of the group, John urged that the highest priority should be given to resolving the legitimate rights of Palestinians alongside Israel's requirements for absolute secure boundaries, and that Palestinians should be fully involved in any negotiations. John stressed that all Palestinians they had consulted with were convinced that the PLO represented their aspirations and could deliver the obligations made by any future agreement. Finally, John prayed for the peace of Jerusalem, starkly emphasizing that another war in this geographically small, but politically and religiously so significant, area could destroy a land and city whose gift to the world should be peace.

Just ten days after the group departed, President Sadat and Bishop Samuel were assassinated.

John felt the gist of this firework display of encounters was that no one can understand the Arab–Israeli conflict or do anything about it. The Israeli Adviser on Arab Affairs told John the story of the frog who gave a lift to a scorpion across a river, 'We sink or swim together.' Halfway across, the scorpion stung the frog. 'Why did you do that?' said the frog. 'Now we shall both sink together.' The scorpion replied 'This is the Middle East!'

18

Ebor John

In 1983 John's colleagues, all too aware of his heavy workload, persuaded him to take a sabbatical after ten years hard labour in Durham. In January 1983, John received a letter from Canon John Sweet, New Testament Scholar and Fellow of Selwyn College, Cambridge, sounding him out about being the College's next Master, in succession to Professor Owen Chadwick. Sweet wrote:

> It would be lovely to have you and Rosalie back in Cambridge, but I do see that for all sorts of reasons it may be just not on. If so, I hope you'll take it as a sign of the esteem in which you are held! One or two people have read *A Working Faith*.

During his sabbatical John wrote his third book, *Church and Nation in a Secular Age* (1983), and returned to Durham for the tenth anniversary of his consecration, at which Archbishop Stuart Blanch preached.

> I didn't recall thinking about succeeding Stuart at all. Towards the end of his archiepiscopacy he developed a fear of large services, so as senior bishop I often deputised for him at consecrations. But after my sabbatical I was looking forward to another longish spell in Durham, so I was shattered to have to return and say good-bye.

The fateful letter from Margaret Thatcher came in mid-June, asking to let John's name go forward to be approved by the Queen for York. It was the very middle of the children's O- and A-level exams. The restored chapel at Auckland, which had been a work in progress throughout John's ten years in Durham, was rededicated with great pomp, attended by ten Church Commissioners, with gnomic looks shared by members of the congregation, who knew but didn't know. Then all the family travelled by train to London early on 4 July, 'tiring, very hot but so exciting' in Rosalie's description.

After a look around the Lords and Commons, the news of John's appointment to York was announced at a press conference at Church House, followed by a reception at 10 Downing Street, where John recalled Margaret Thatcher was charming and motherly with the children, and couldn't have been more friendly. There were whispers that she had preferred Graham Leonard rather than John for London in 1981 in order to keep him free for York. Rosalie was annoyed by a *Church Times'* reporter, who wanted to know 'why she was called Rosalie and Robert Runcie's wife Rosalind, and wasn't it a strange coincidence they were both pianists?' 'I hope they realize the likeness ends there,' Rosalie secretly thought, while smiling sweetly and saying nothing.

Rosalie describes how she and Laura wept buckets on leaving Auckland Castle, although were pleased to downsize to a 'more compact and easier' palace at Bishopthorpe, with a mere nine acres of grounds. The original palace, consisting of a hall and chapel, was built by the Ouse in 1215 by Archbishop Walter de Gray, with various additions through the centuries, including a Strawberry Hill Gothic front, the latest fashion in the eighteenth century. The cellar and terraces frequently flooded, necessitating keeping a dinghy in the cellar for John to service the boiler. Rosalie thought:

the rooms are beautiful and the situation by the river, surrounded by private secluded lawns and arboretum is superb. I just hope the Church Commissioners will be co-operative and considerate after all we have put up with at Auckland. I'm insisting on a thorough survey.

General Synod at York followed hot on the heels of the official announcement, with John's appointment 'warmly welcomed and congratulated by all'. During Synod the Habgoods stayed with David Blunt, lay chaplain, which Rosalie declared great fun. According to Rosalie, the only cloud on the horizon was a young couple who served as houseman and cook, and lived in the Palace with their three children, all under four.

Knowing their family commitments and having seen them on our brief visit to Bishopthorpe, my worst fears have foundation. I am insisting we are under no obligation to employ them. They have taken over, so to speak, and I know the family and I would find them intolerable. John wants them to see us in, but I would find this very awkward.

Margaret Thatcher's attendance at John's enthronement at York Minster on 18 November (which involved anti-government protestors throwing themselves in front of the archiepiscopal car, in the mistaken impression it was hers) was unprecedented, with her awarding John 11 out of 10 for his sermon. Following his enthronement, she wrote to John, warmly thanking him for a copy of his latest book, hoping 'that he would still find time for writing despite the additional demands upon him'. In his early days at York, John had met with his fellow northern bishops, canvassing what they expected from him. 'We want an archbishop who thinks,' was their unequivocal reply.

John's enthronement sermon was a studied piece, exploring how an archbishop could represent the public face of the Church. Grateful that the occasion was more modest than in previous centuries, when guests at the feast following had been described as 'eating their way through a miniature zoo', he took his text from Psalm 11: 'If the foundations are destroyed, what can the just man do?' Public faith should mark the very foundations, the shared values and goals that bind us together. Amazed at what people believe, John set his face firmly against what he termed a jackdaw kind of religion, merely gathering random dazzling trinkets, a hotchpotch faith providing no defence against mere self-indulgence. Faith had to be coherent in order to make it powerful and effective, with religion containing an essential conservative element so we could believe in a gospel as something given, not merely chosen or made up. Any faith could only touch the robe of the infinite and everlasting God, who is not static but forever pulling down and rebuilding. The necessary balance to coherence was radical criticism, with a critical mind collaborating with a believing heart and making faith grow strong. The enthronement service, rather than being 'a mere puffing up of Christian self-importance, was actually a reminder of how fragile and vulnerable our life is together, and yet how securely we can be held in the loving hands of God'.

John spent his first few months touring York Diocese, spending a day with clergy in each of the 26 deaneries, from the Humber through the Yorkshire Wolds and North York Moors to the Tees, and from the North Sea to the A1. York, Middlesbrough and Hull were the major urban centres, with lots of bustling market towns with bustling vicars, pretty seaside resorts, stunning countryside (championed by *Heartbeat*, Herriot and *The Yorkshire Vet*), completed by ancient abbeys at Kirkham, Rievaulx and Whitby.

Measured John asked Robert Runcie to chair the CAC to appoint his successor at Durham instead of him, with John not even sitting on the committee, in order not to influence the appointment. The CAC process had only been running for six years, so there was no precedent for this situation, certainly not in the Northern Province. Reflecting on the appointment over 20 years later, John concluded that his deep knowledge of Durham Diocese would not have impaired his impartiality as chair, but would have made the chair's role far more informed.

Certainly Runcie bowled John a googly with David Jenkins, whom John viewed as someone who was interesting, said some profound things, read books and was capable of inspiring faith. Durham wanted to continue to have an academic as its bishop, and Jenkins had done some good work with the William Temple Foundation in Manchester, with a good track record with social policies. But his failure to take his audience through the stages, instead using an ecclesiastical form of shorthand, meant he was easily misunderstood, combined with a naivety that was either careless or staged. John felt the professorial sure touch Jenkins had about his subject material bordered on self-satisfaction, and tended to antagonize his opponents, such as those opposed to the ordination of women, with whom he was not good at dealing or keeping on board.

The first of a series of doctrinal storms, which wracked the rest of the 1980s, blew up when a highly enthused Jenkins appeared on ITV's *Credo* on 29 April 1984, discussing the Virgin Birth, the Resurrection and the Incarnation. 'I wouldn't put it past God to arrange a virgin birth if he wanted, but I very much doubt if he would, because it seems to be contrary to the way in which he deals with persons . . .' His take on the

Resurrection was actually quite orthodox, but he ended the interview asserting that someone who affirmed that Jesus was a great moral teacher, a divine agent who led people Godwards, but denied he was God-made-flesh, was still Christian. In a follow-up interview on the BBC's *Sunday* on 27 May, he impishly stressed 'that no single historical fact could be certain, nor could prove anything, and that there was absolutely no certainty in the New Testament about anything that is of importance'.

Initially, TV crews were ecstatic about Jenkins' marvellous soundbites and his ability to communicate with the media, which had been chiefly friendly and compliant during John's days in Durham. But the outrage that quickly surged in some parts of the Church alerted the media, which thrived on controversy, to deep-seated differences, not helped, in John's view, either by the Minster fire or Jenkins' description (in his Durham enthronement address) of Coal Board Chair Ian Macgregor as 'an elderly imported American'. The heady scene was set for the C of E to play the role of Opposition during the rest of Margaret Thatcher's tenure.

Whatever John's private views, in public he supported Jenkins' consecration, fearing that had that appointment, approved by the Queen, been overturned by General Synod or a critical crowd, it would have resulted in a trial-by-television episcopacy which played to please the gallery, rather than one which was prophetic, bold and independent. Jenkins himself had declared that his faith in God was too great and too strong to resist dodging real questions. I suppose ever since the Passover crowd preferred Barabbas to Jesus, the Church has had understandable reservations about public opinion.

On 1 July, six days before the planned consecration, John received a petition of 12,565 signatures, gathered by Fr William Ledwich, Chaplain of Hereford Cathedral School, asking that David Jenkins' consecration should only proceed after a formal, public affirmation of faith. John replied immediately, stressing that Jenkins 'had already declared to the Durham clergy that he would unhesitatingly respond affirmatively before God, in complete good faith and total dependence on his grace, to the questions put to him at his consecration'. From what he knew of him personally and of his writings, he felt this was sufficient assurance. Admitting that Jenkins would grow to appreciate the way a bishop is heard is different from the way a university professor is heard, John nevertheless felt that his works and writings spoke for themselves, carrying far greater weight than a soundbite or misreport on the media, which tended to be more interested in image than reality.

Noting that his critics had shown no evidence of having acquainted themselves with his thought as a whole, John saw no valid grounds for Jenkins making more declarations than the Church had seen fit to prescribe. He cited 1938 and 1981 Doctrine Reports, which recognized that the creeds contained many types of statement in which the borderline between the symbolic and the historical dimensions cannot be precisely defined.

The Doctrine Reports' point strikes me as salient. If only the Gospel-writers had used different-coloured pens, say red for history and blue for myth (profound story expressing eternal spiritual truths), then our work would be so much easier. But the two are inextricably bound up in a shade of purple, impossible to separate, especially by a very different culture two millennia on. After a lifetime's reflection, my take is that the jury is out as to what is history and myth, which is the best place for a jury to be; when the jury returns, that is when we have burnings and pogroms and crucifixions. John often used to talk about a 'healthy uncertainty'.

Yet sometimes Jenkins gave the brash impression that the jury had returned, and was in his favour. Those who had read theology in the 1950s and 1960s, John included, often reverted to a sort of Bultmannian fundamentalism that demythologized most of the gospel, claiming the intellectual high ground over those benighted souls, for whom the penny hadn't dropped for 2,000 years until Bultmann enlightened us all.

As a student majoring on New Testament studies, I have to admit, I have been there. My first Christmas Eve, following my ordination, I spent fiddling around with an anglepoise lamp that was arched over the crib figures in our so cold church in Middlesbrough – my boss had given me fierce instructions that the Christ-child should cast no shadow, since he is the Light of the world. As I heard the world outside partying, my vote went with those radical New Testament scholars who avoided taking the Christmas story too literally!

Yet very quickly scepticism about the Christmas story was replaced by a scepticism about the sceptics themselves, for several reasons. For 2,000 years, those touched by the truth of the Christmas story had been inspired to produce the most marvellous pieces of music, Handel's *Messiah* and Berlioz's *L'enfance du Christ* among them, which invariably move me to tears. And then there are thousand upon thousand works of art, tender scenes, the holy family, shepherds, wise men, all bearing the marks of the artists' own culture, casting the nativity afresh for their time. Not to mention the myriad poems and plays that point to new depths and insights in this timeless story. What treasures have those who deny the veracity of this story produced?

But what finally tipped me in favour of the story's truth was the year-by-year experience of ministry. Anglican congregations in England and Wales tend to be talented, articulate and urbane. I have worked hard with the laity to enable ministry, trying to produce and enhance striking acts of worship and teaching material, but more often than not the mountain labours and produces nothing more than a mouse! Certainly no Christian congregation that I have encountered would ever be capable of concocting a story with a thousandth as much depth as the Nativity. As I realized that inventing the story was a far, far greater miracle than the story actually happening, I opted for the lesser miracle, as it were, that the events really took place. And why shouldn't God-in-Christ, the Word made flesh, speak to us through event as well as word?

Whatever, the petition correspondence was unfailingly courteous, with Fr Ledwich stressing that though for him it was a matter of deep distress of conscience, there was no question of animosity or breach of Christian love and respect to our fathers in God. John added a kindly personal note to his formal reply, expressing he was conscious of Fr Ledwich's deep concern and the trouble he had taken in organizing the petition, but that at the end of the day he was swayed by quality of arguments rather than numbers. In a personal comment to me in 2006, John expressed profound regret that he hadn't shown greater tenderness to Fr Ledwich, who later was to resign from ordained ministry.

John made a similar reply to the Revd David Holloway, Vicar of Jesmond, who on behalf of some proctors in the Northern Convocation, asked him to postpone the consecration, and a small group of Durham clergy, who met with him to share their concerns.

In a press conference John defended Jenkins' *Credo* pronouncements as 'standard text book stuff', claiming that people had misunderstood him and that he actually believed in the Incarnation and Resurrection. As for the 12,500 signatures, he noted that most of them were from a limited number of parishes (where the possibility of arms being twisted to sign could not be ruled out) and included no bishops, archdeacons, deans and few clergy. Significantly, only 475 signatories were from Durham, where the majority were in favour of the consecration proceeding.

The consecration took place on Friday 6 July with two objections being made (which were heard but overruled) during the service. In the early hours of Monday 9 July, York Minster was struck by lightning and the south transept roof was destroyed, with massive concomitant damage. John visited the scene at 5 a.m. that Monday morning, checked the fire was out, then flew to a WCC meeting in Geneva. Mrs Thatcher rang the Dean to express her deep sympathy, then rang Bishopthorpe but had to make do with sharing her regrets with Rosalie as John was in Switzerland.

There were already towers of correspondence and press comment about the consecration; these escalated with speculation that the lightning was an instrument of divine displeasure, including a letter from a scary woman, among many others, suggesting that the lightning was an expression of divine discipline, the brave firefighters extinguishing the fire an expression of divine mercy. In a letter to *The Times* (12 July 1984), John wondered what sort of God the complainants believed in: 'To interpret the effect of a thunderstorm as a direct divine punishment pushes us straight back into the kind of world from which the Christian Gospel rescued us.'

Jenkins' continued political and theological soundbites guaranteed continuous media attention, with ITV's *Credo* given a new lease of life with successive programmes on the controversies Jenkins stirred up, including *God in the World* on 23 February 1985. At that programme's conclusion, John himself was interviewed and confessed he found it

extremely difficult to believe in the kind of universe in which there was some enormous heavenly computer which was logging in a million requests a minute and then ordering the universe in some inconceivably complicated way in order to see that the maximum number of requests was fulfilled without messing up everyone's life.

I suppose these days we'd call that the Internet! He went on to declare 'the absurdity of a universe in which my prayer about my Auntie Annie who is going on a railway journey is going to affect all the workings of the railway and everything else and everybody else's lives'. Almost as absurd as believing that hands that threw stars into space to cruel nails surrendered.

The controversy raged in General Synod as well, with various debates and reports, including one on the nature of belief at Synod's York session on 6 July 1986, caught by Chris Armstrong, my predecessor as archbishop's chaplain, in his diary:

> The Bishop of Durham spoke from a prepared script. The atmosphere was electric, especially as the Bishop faltered with emotion, referring to his stupidity in delivering a meditation on mystical theology to the Synod. He denounced the fundamentalists as believing in a God who produces miracles with 'laser beam' accuracy. The speech was long, moving and finished to prolonged applause and a standing ovation. He sat down close to the Archbishop, who wrote him a compassionate note which I was asked to deliver. It was not the only note he received in the space of about ten minutes. The Bishop was followed by David Holloway who was clearly unnerved by his adversary's performance.

It seemed that, with John's support, David Jenkins had won folk round. But another controversy was waiting in the wings.

19

Titanic John

Well: while was fashioning
This creature of cleaving wing,
The Immanent will that stirs and urges everything

Prepared a sinister mate
For he – so gaily great –
For the time far and dissociate.

Alien they seemed to be:
No mortal eye could see
The intimate welding of their later history,

Or sign that they were bent
By paths coincident
On being anon twin halves of one august event.

Thomas Hardy's *The Convergence of the Twain*, written on the loss of the *Titanic* in 1912, had eerie echoes on the seventy-fifth anniversary of the tragedy as ecclesiastical *Titanic* and iceberg converged in the affair of the anonymous *Crockford's* Preface.

The bare detail of the event itself has become as well known as gospel narrative. *Crockford's*, the Church of England's clerical directory, was traditionally introduced by a preface, whose author was anonymous. Behind the Preface lurked an unwritten gentleman's agreement that the author's anonymity would be closely guarded, provided the piece, which could be critical in its scope, shied away from personal abuse. With responsibility for publication of *Crockford's* passing from the independent Oxford University Press to Church House Publishing in 1984, the Preface took on the nature of an in-house publication, criticizing its own house. The Preface tradition thereby suffered a grinding change of gear, tantamount to the Secretary to the Cabinet commissioning Edward Heath to write an anonymous piece on Mrs Thatcher's Government for the preface of Hansard. The *SS Church of England* seemed to be steaming towards icy waters.

Memos between the Church of England's media and publishing department immediately prior to the Preface's publication express clear concern that 'the writer seems to have dipped his pen in vitriol', and suggest giving prior warning about the writer's 'spiteful views' to those cruelly pilloried in the Preface. However, the media department resisted giving the Preface any kind of publicity prior to publication, fearing that such action would inflict gratuitous damage: 'If anyone wants to read it, let them buy *Crockford's.*' I hear the captain bleating, 'Iceberg, what iceberg?'

As it happens, I bought my first ever *Crockford's* in 1987, and dutifully ploughed through the Preface. It struck me then as it strikes me now, as a thorough document, struggling to analyse the problems inherent in the Anglican Communion, but offering little if any solution. The tone purports to be objective, but, by using a combination of studied understatement and waspishness, seeks to undermine and ridicule the perceived foes of the 1980s' faithful Anglo-Catholic.

Graham Leonard, then Bishop of London, who had recently extended his episcopal care to troubled traditionalist parishes in the Episcopal Church in the USA (ECUSA), receives muted praise, as does Derek Pattinson, the General Synod's Machiavellian Secretary General, who had solely commissioned the piece and allowed its publication without any editorial alteration whatsoever. Initially the same muted praise is rained upon Robert Runcie, described as someone who listens well, whose speeches are warm, persuasive and witty, a notable holder of the primacy who has intelligence, personal warmth and a formidable capacity for hard work. But then the accusations positively rain down: Runcie doesn't know what he is doing, takes the line of least resistance, puts off questions until someone else makes the decision, thereby nailing his colours to the fence (a phrase borrowed from MP Frank Field). His own lack of rigorous theological study gives him a preference for men of liberal disposition with a moderately Catholic style that is not taken to the point of having firm principles. Good looks and an articulate media style excuse their certain theological deficiency. The whole splenetic piece accuses Robert Runcie of repeated cronyism, preferring Oxbridge contemporaries with a Westcott/Cuddesdon hue.

The press, who were able to afford to buy their *Crockford's*, or certainly the curiously produced offprint that contained the Preface alone, had a field day. Following an indecisive General Synod in November, where the Church of England had faced heavy media criticism for seemingly failing to condemn the sexual mores then prevailing, the *Crockford's* Preface was leapt upon as evidence of Runcie's woeful lack of leadership qualities.

Into the fray leapt John, Archbishop of York, who himself was lampooned in the Preface as the prime enforcer of the liberal trends and tendencies it so decries. In a brief press release, John himself decried the Preface as an outburst from a disappointed cleric, abusing the cloak of anonymity to raise charges that anyone with actual experience of the machinations of central church committees and appointments would realize were scurrilous. Clearly John felt the Preface's observations were either at best misinformed or at worst mischievous, and either way deserved to be treated with contempt.

There then followed days of fevered speculation in the press and within the Church as to the author's identity. Names included Dr Margaret Hewitt, General Synod member and lecturer at Exeter University, Roger Beckwith of the Oxford Evangelical Association, Peter More, then Dean of St Albans, David Edwards, then Provost of Southwark, Professor Henry Chadwick, Edward Norman, then Dean of Peterhouse, and Professor Roy Porter of London University. On the Saturday after the Preface's publication John was accosted at the opening of the new SPCK bookshop in York by a vicar from Withernsea, one of the most forlorn and faraway parishes in his diocese. 'I'd just like to assure your Grace that I didn't write it,' the cleric informed the Archbishop, in all seriousness. John responded with a withering look, as if that cleric in particular had never even crossed his mind as the remotest possibility.

The increasing favourite was Dr Gareth Bennett, who, in the face of media pressure to go public, took his own life. His body was discovered on Monday 7 December 1987, his having committed suicide at some stage over the weekend. The energies that days before had been devoted to finding the anonymous author were now diverted to finding the reason that pushed him over the brink. Prime suspect was the media, with rumours of the *Daily Mail* promising undisclosed sums should Bennett go public; this was closely followed by the demands of anonymity itself, which compromised Bennett's high integrity and forced him to lie to his trusted colleagues in denying he was the author; suspect number three was John's stinging rebuke to stinging criticisms.

Most pertinent of all was Bennett's state of mind during that first fatal week in December. A formidable scholar of ecclesiastical history, a committed Anglo-Catholic whose unease with women at times verged on the misogynistic, he is nevertheless remembered by many students and colleagues as someone whose sarcasm and cynicism was mediated by a certain gentleness and tenderness. At the time of his death, John was contacted by an ordained psychotherapist, a former student. After reading the Preface he had commented to his wife that he thought the author was unwell. Having first wondered whether the piece had been composed by two writers, he then concluded that its author had a divided personality and suffered from endogenous depression. Such depression is cyclic in nature, with excitement occurring during a low, producing rapid alternating shifts between a serious and responsible vein to one that is flippant, irresponsible and self-destructive. John V. Taylor, the former Bishop of Winchester, not a natural Runcie crony, came to this conclusion in an article in *The Times* only three days after Bennett's body had been discovered:

> he was temperamentally unable to fulfil conditions for the Preface authorship. He was too emotionally involved in the current political and ecclesiastical controversies, and his anxieties preyed upon a naturally depressive disposition. He was a tragic victim, at the very least, of a thoroughly misguided selection.

Bennett undoubtedly had been a long-term close friend, trusted speech-writer and confidante of Robert Runcie, from whom he received what turned out to be his final communion when the Archbishop celebrated at New College on Advent Sunday 1987. Bishop Michael

Ball recalls listening to a speech by Robert Runcie and sitting next to Bennett, who had the text of the speech before him. Bennett occasionally winced, 'Ah, the Archbishop is so much better when he keeps to my script!' Probably the disappointment both behind his Preface and suicide was that Robert Runcie, who had originated from a similar Anglo-Catholic stable, had failed to keep to that script and there was a feeling of a deep friendship betrayed. Certainly the Preface has the air about it of a lover spurned.

John was from a similar stable too, or rather counted the Anglo-Catholicism of 1950s Cuddesdon as one of his stables. He could reasonably count the post-war CICCU as another stable, coupled with an Erastian and even atheist stable of previous years. Those with only one stable to their origins are often suspicious of those who multiply theirs beyond necessity, and maybe this soured Bennett's view of him. If I had to plump for one Habgoodian stable, I would go for the Cambridge natural sciences that John had thoroughly immersed himself in in the 1940s and early 1950s: all heady stuff, where you ran with your results, no massaging, no turning a blind eye. You measured what you saw, and dispassionately constructed your theories accordingly, and fearlessly truckled to no person or opinions that were slipshod or not experimentally proven. This is probably overdrawing what was in the main a tedious time of data-gathering, but there is a feel that those who excelled in that time were like the child in Anderson's fairy tale who dared to proclaim the emperor had no clothes, and thereby were able to move on to a new level of perception.

This dispassionate observer, on moving from the natural sciences to the more personal sphere of priesthood, obviously tempered his wind to the shorn lamb, realizing à la T. S. Eliot that humankind could only bear so much reality. But just occasionally the reality he so ably aired was too much to bear, and could jar. Long before I became his chaplain I had quite a fierce spat with him about some aspect of my parish's policy. 'The role of a diocesan bishop is to save a parish from the good intentions of its vicar,' John concluded, no hint of smile, no whiff of irony. Though it is a fair enough episcopal modus vivendi, at that precise time I found it pretty hard to take. Then, years later, after I had presented him with a copy of my second book, *A Vicar's Diary* (1998), before a meal at our house, he launched into a devastating critique. That critique was undoubtedly accurate, but authors tend to be just a touch vulnerable when their infant novel first hits the shelves. Just occasionally he could say the undoubtedly right thing at the unfortunately wrong time, and I feel this trait has to be reckoned with vis-à-vis his denunciation of the *Crockford* Preface.

But what really needs to be reckoned with is that John, the cool observer of scientific evidence, tirelessly sifting the results before moving to an impeccable conclusion, when it came to guessing the identity of the anonymous author of the infamous Preface, actually got it totally and utterly wrong. From the tone of the Preface, he was almost certain that it was written by Canon Peter Boulton. Canon Boulton, who moved from being Vicar of Worksop to Director of Education for Southwell Diocese in 1987, had been a member of the CAC and the key Synod sub-committees prior to Gareth Bennett taking his place earlier that summer. Boulton was clearly a fierce and splenetic critic of many of the things that John and Runcie stood for, but was a robust person whose track record indicated he could take criticism as well as deal it out. When John released his statement on *Crockford's* publication on 3 December, Boulton was his intended target.

At morning prayers at Bishopthorpe Palace on Tuesday 8 December, Chris Armstrong prayed for the soul of Gareth Bennett, whose body had been discovered the night before. Raymond Parkinson, caretaker at the Palace, recalls the Archbishop's jaw dropping as he heard the news for the first time, and leaving the chapel, his face ashen. In all their years at the Palace, Raymond and Chris had never seen John so shaken.

Why didn't John make his mistake public at the time, rather than waiting 20 years to reveal it to his biographer? Probably because with accusations and counter accusations flying between the press and Bishopthorpe, the heat was so intense that it needed cooling rather than hotting up further by bringing the Preface author-who-never-was into the furnace. John, ever the pragmatist, would realize that revealing who he thought had been the author could hardly reverse Gareth Bennett's death. And it was perhaps not the best time to admit you'd made the wrong call with the decisiveness and judgement of the Church of England's leadership so under the microscope.

A salient question is whether there was anyone advising the intensely self-sufficient John during this unhappy time. The closest thing he had to an adviser was his press officer and lay assistant, Raymond Barker. Raymond's career spanned reading PPE at Magdalen, Oxford, lecturing in the inter-service Russian course for National Service conscripts during the Cold War, being an editor for the BBC World Service and lecturing at Bradford University in comparative government and American politics. John was to comment in his obituary (*Church Times*, 7 January 2005):

> When JF Kennedy was murdered, Raymond was on duty at the World Service and organised their response. All this was valuable preparation for understanding, 20 years later, the complex politics that developed between the Church of England and the Thatcher government.

As if the whole issue of the *Crockford's* Preface wasn't complex enough, there was clearly a political implication. General Synod member and right-wing Tory Peter Bruinvels claimed that the Preface was part of a conspiracy to force Runcie to retire and prevent John succeeding him. Bruinvels, who offered to volunteer as a hangman should the Conservative Government ever reintroduce the death penalty, and whose response to Clare Short's admirable campaign to scrap *The Sun*'s infamous page three was to appear on that page with his favourite 'lovely', may not seem the most reliable of witnesses. But the evidence of someone who became a Church Commissioner and lay canon of Guildford must stand for something. And his triumphant trumpeting of a conspiracy was echoed by Tory Cabinet Minister and Synod member, John Selwyn Gummer. The former cabinet minister and left-wing guru Tony Benn called for the Church of England to immediately disestablish, to free her of such Tory interference and plots.

Raymond Barker was eminently well qualified to steer John through this political morass. Yet he also had some fatal flaws. One, which John mentions in his obituary, was that, surprisingly for a press officer, he could be quite aggressive towards the media. This is an understatement; time and time again I heard Raymond speak to reporters as if he was the cruellest counsel for the prosecution and the reporter was the most heinous criminal in the dock. He could be equally aggressive towards parochial clergy, chiefly for their habit of making uninformed pronouncements that grabbed media attention and hijacked his agenda. I started work at Bishopthorpe in 1991, a former parish priest and budding journalist, so not surprisingly Raymond and I often didn't see eye to eye.

We repeatedly clashed over Raymond's habit to steal into the Archbishop's study whenever he was absent and pore over his private papers. Though I respected the fact that I was a mere Bernard to Raymond's Sir Humphrey, as chaplain I saw myself as the Archbishop's guard dog and was uneasy about what seemed like an act of espionage. The Archbishop's Private Secretary was uneasy about it too, but Raymond would brook no criticism about his action, claiming he needed to know everything, and implying he had the Archbishop's consent anyway. We once called his bluff by planting a spoof letter on the Archbishop's desk, purporting to be from a security firm, and reporting that the first video tapes from the secret surveillance cameras installed in the Archbishop's study, my study and the Palace entrance were now ready for the Archbishop's inspection. When Raymond fell upon this letter, he went into the blue funk of a John le Carré character whose cover had been blown.

Though a sharp critic, who could pounce on a flabby phrase or half-baked idea and suggest a better alternative, Raymond's political machinations, which were used to a world stage in which Kennedys came and went, were perhaps too high octane to fuel a comparatively minor church in a damp and cold island skulking off a land mass in the northern hemisphere. The fluent spontaneity he brought to their lengthy daily meetings might well have dazzled the acutely pensive John. Yet that spontaneity was feigned; behind it lay many hours of reflection, allowing Raymond to weave a web of his own sub-agendas with material to which he should not have had access. This would give his pronouncements a momentum which took John in a direction which his natural cautious wisdom would normally have avoided. And finally Raymond's hatred for the media and for lesser clergy, with an eye for a soundbite, would put him on a collision course with the anonymous author of the over-publicised Preface. 'Full-steam ahead, Archbishop. Let's take the icebergs on!' Left to his own devices, I guess John would have judged the *SS Church of England* as only a coaster, the icebergs mere snowballs.

Who were the icebergs? Who was the *Titanic* back in 1987? Gareth Bennett certainly had the touch of ice about him, but his impressive intellect and historical knowledge could have made him a titan, had disappointment and disillusion not set in. Derek Pattinson, the General Synod's Secretary General, certainly strode around the narrow Church like a titan, and yet there was ice in his commissioning and lack of editing of Bennett's work which could be construed at best as a woeful lack of professionalism, at worst as devilish mischief. Robert Runcie, the chief target of the Preface, had many rights to the accolade titanic. Yet beneath the armour of this former MC-winning tank commander lay an intensely vulnerable soul who was coming under huge pressure from the Thatcherite majority who controlled much of the popular media. That media had recently taken to mocking the eccentricities of Runcie's wife, and John knew only too well how close the insecure Runcie was to utter breaking point, driving him to come to the rescue of his partner in archiepiscopacy. Unlike John, Runcie correctly guessed the Preface author's identity, but would not reveal it.

And what of John? There was undoubtedly ice in his character, but he was titanic in spades. His intellect, his spirituality, his judgement, his knowledge of the Church were all as titanic as his physical stature. Did the whole *Crockford's* Preface episode damage his chances of succeeding Runcie? It hardly facilitated that succession: when the detail of the episode was long forgotten, the abiding memory was that something an archbishop had said had resulted in a clergyman's death.

Did John want Canterbury? Many around him, including Gordon Bates, his suffragan at Whitby, who described him as the best Archbishop of Canterbury we never had, certainly wanted it for him. But John himself remains diffident, wondering whether his self-sufficiency would have remained intact given the plethora of advisors at Lambeth; clearly one Raymond Barker was more than enough for him.

Certainly the whole tragic affair deeply affected John, and brought about a change in course. He resolved to let the beleaguered Anglo-Catholics feel they were being heard. His appointment of George Austin as his archdeacon at York was part of a strategy to bring into his inner circle people who would criticize him, and certainly Austin was no disappointment on that score. Nor was John a disappointment to the Anglo-Catholics. The Act of Synod, of which John was the main architect, gave the Anglo-Catholic integrity a valued place in the Church of

England, causing many Anglo-Catholics to rue the day they had conspired to stop the man who turned out to be their champion acceding to Canterbury.

Gareth Bennett's gripe about Runcie appointing his cronies to high office was off-target, in that Runcie's preference was probably for Oxbridge men. Oxbridge of the mid-1940s to the mid-1960s was a small world, so drawing people from that constituency was bound to attract the charge of cronyism. And Bennett, that most Oxbridge of Oxbridge men, was probably mourning an age that was passing. As John Major and other new men soared through the ranks of government in the latter 1980s, the tide was moving against governance by patricians educated at public school and Oxbridge; Bennett's Preface may have unfortunately accelerated that trend, but certainly didn't create it. On the Saturday of that first week in Advent 1987, as the whole affair raged and accusations and counter accusations flew, as Garry Bennett bought the hosepipe to connect to his car exhaust to bring about his untimely death at his own hand, Robert Runcie took time out from the whole debacle. In Southwark Cathedral he consecrated a little-known theological college principal as Bishop of Bath and Wells. The new bishop's name? George Carey, the priest overwhelmed by one of John's silences prior to his appointment to St Nick's, Durham.

> And as the smart ship grew
> In stature, grace and hue,
> In shadowy silent distance grew the Iceberg too.
> (Thomas Hardy, 'The convergence of the twain')

20

Bishopthorpe John

When Mary Murray became John's PA at Bishopthorpe she inherited several cabinets of files labelled 'Clergy (Deceased) with Permission to Officiate' and a system where she trekked in her wellies to the Dell, the marshlands of the Palace grounds, to light a surreptitious bonfire to burn confidential papers following a Crown Appointments Commission meeting. During the winter, her boss frequently descended unto the flooded basement, rowing to rescue any valuable debris floating on the surface, only to reappear in the office, his suit covered with cobwebs, needing a brisk secretarial dust-down prior to a VIP's visit. A visiting BT engineer puzzled over what an archbishop was: 'Is he some sort of duke?' Mary, her mind still on John's aquatic adventures, thought he said, 'Is he some sort of duck?'

There were so many phone calls complaining about Bishop David Jenkins' latest pronouncements that Mary suggested directing each call to a secretary specializing in (a) resurrection; (b) virgin birth; (c) homosexuality; (d) politics. John laughed and gave her one of his looks, eyebrows raised: 'Maybe we could take advantage of new technology, ask them to press 1, 2, 3 or 4, leave them hanging there for 20 minutes, and then give a quick burst of "You shall go out with joy!" before cutting them off.' The Church Commissioners refused to provide Mary with a replacement office chair, so John, whipping a screwdriver out of his breast pocket, stripped the chair down and repaired it. In so doing he badly stabbed his hand with the screwdriver. 'Oh dear!' he exclaimed, as his blood spurted everywhere. Mary, who could have come up with a stronger exclamation, thought John a saint who wouldn't hesitate to bound out into the grounds in all weathers to rescue threatened wildlife, would humbly use local transport in European cities when the official car failed to turn up at the airport, and would take time out on holidays abroad to buy staff special Christmas presents. He would return from his latest high-powered engagements, no fanfares to greet him, just, 'Mary, a cup of tea would be nice.'

John acknowledged that, too preoccupied with learning the ropes himself, he hadn't delegated sufficient episcopal responsibility to Alec Hamilton in Durham. So in York he allowed his suffragans to run what effectively were three mini-dioceses, using their local expertise to assist his major decisions at monthly staff meetings.

I interviewed Bishops Gordon Bates, Clifford Barker, Humphrey Taylor, James Jones and Glyn Webster, and Archdeacons Leslie Stanbridge, Hugh Buckingham, George Austin and Christopher Hawthorn. All hailed the monthly staff meetings as a master class, bowling John a question, then being patient with the long pause prior to the oracle pronouncing. In Durham, John had an edgy and difficult reputation vis-à-vis meetings, but in Bishopthorpe proved relaxed and happy, as if he had reached his final destination.

John never seemed class conscious, nor condescending, nor hierarchical, nor manipulative, nor with a hidden agenda, but was a confident leader who knew what was the essence, what you could pass by. George Austin reported how he once stood up in General Synod and opposed the stance of his Archbishop. Afterwards, George apologized to John, who assured him that he had nothing to apologize for because he positively welcomed healthy debate in which his views were open to be challenged. Bishop Gordon reflected how,

> prior to his appointment as Archdeacon of York, George had been a severe and very vocal critic of John, waging war on anyone he thought was a dangerous liberal. I believe the appointment was a considerable shock to George himself and caused him to rethink his understanding of John. After appointing him, John must have wondered if he had done the right thing, and there were times when George's involvement in the media caused John much heartache and even, at times, anger. But George became, like the rest of us, deeply grateful to John for his bravery and selflessness. When John was attacked, he did not retaliate, except with kindness and understanding.

Gordon's archdeacon, Chris Hawthorn, shared this view, but also felt that you needed to be very sure of your ground before seeking to argue with John, who nevertheless would listen to you with great care before declaring, 'Your argument is specious!'

The Times' Clifford Longley wrote this (10 November 1983) in his profile on John prior to his enthronement at York:

> The new archbishop has the most logical and sharpest of minds, proved once by means of a first class honours degree at Cambridge and proved again every time he speaks in public. He is a case of 'once a scientist always a scientist' for in matters even of faith or church order Dr Habgood's invariable starting point is factual, and his method to assemble the facts in tidy order. From that his conclusions follow; he is therefore a difficult man to argue with. Other people's looser points can be impatiently swept aside. It was this quality, sometimes mistaken for arrogance, which gave him a reputation for coldness when he first became Bishop of Durham.

Chris recalled how, whenever the senior staff got bogged down in a subject, John would conclude, 'We're making heavy weather of this, let's move on', with the concomitant danger that they papered over the cracks. John's successor, David Hope took a more pragmatic approach: 'Let's get our coats off and sort this out!' A good example of the paralysis that can afflict all ecclesiastical institutions was the Mothers' Welfare Centre in York. Basically it had been founded for a different age, providing care and refuge for single girls who had fallen pregnant and had been kicked out of the parental home. In the 1990s the centre was fully staffed, complete with a matron, excellently equipped, with the Mother's Union and other worthy organizations often arranging services and events to finance the place. The problem was society had moved on in its attitudes to illicit relationships, meaning that no longer did any mothers or babies cross the centre's door. Clearly the centre needed to be closed or its purpose reassigned; after numerous senior staff meetings full of prevarication, John asked his trusty Director of Ministry and Mission, Canon Ron Metcalfe, to visit the place and set its closure in motion. Ron returned, wild-eyed and hair ruffled, looking like a school inspector who had had a harrowing experience inspecting

St Trinians, narrowly escaping with his life and testicles intact. 'You'd have to pay me in gold nuggets ever to visit that place again,' he stammered. John left it at that, and 25 years on, I wouldn't be surprised if the centre was still match-fit should York diocese revert to a 1950s morality.

Notwithstanding his experience at the centre, Ron was a superb fixer, organizing a weekend Lay Assembly of 600 folk in John's first year as Archbishop. He realized that John, and his predecessor Stuart, were not enthusiastic about diocesan campaigns, preferring to leave clergy and parishes to get on with it without bombarding them with archiepiscopal good intentions. Nevertheless, the assembly was a great success, with John circulating around groups over coffee, making them realize that here was an archbishop who listened and responded. The partnership between John and Ron enabled a massive flourishing during John's years in York, lay conferences, preaching courses, management courses, first incumbents' courses, all very fit for purpose and run on a shoestring. The partnership also enabled the appointment of John Young as Diocesan Evangelist, Michael Searle as Director of Training and Simon Stanley as Director of Communications – all of whom proved men for the hour and enabled it to be a truly fantastic hour: 'Bliss was it in that dawn to be alive.'

John insisted that part of every day should be spent doing more or less nothing, dressing down Bishop Roy Williamson for working late into the night. 'Unless you give time to your family, unless you switch off, you're not going to be a good bishop.' Sometimes, however, John's workaholic nature got the better of him. Michael Searle and I devised a contract for curates, working five two-hour sessions a day, only to have John dismiss the proposal with a curt: 'Fourteen hours a day for eating and sleeping seem to me excessive.'

All agreed John allowed everyone to have their say at any meeting (once giving a troubled parish in the South Riding four hours to vent their spleen), but then distilled into a few words what was worthwhile, before moving to a conclusion and commitment to action. All appreciated his tremendous humour, which diffused difficult situations, recalling Boxing Day lunches at Bishopthorpe for clergy spending Christmas alone, with John staging indoor fireworks and having Christmas card competitions, with prizes for the fattest baby, most splendid stagecoach, prettiest Virgin and most appropriate card for Mrs Thatcher.

Pastoral care was patchy. When they stayed the night at Bishopthorpe prior to James Jones's consecration, his little daughter Tabitha had been enchanted with John, following him everywhere, even to the loo! But strangely there was no contact whatsoever following James's wife and daughters' very serious road accident a few days later. Chris Hawthorn, though, received a comforting hand on his shoulder at the end of a meeting, followed by John's handwritten letter after his elderly mother's death. Once when we were confirming in Middlesbrough, I had to prompt a distinctly reluctant John to visit Bishop Gordon, who was recovering from major surgery on his spine, which carried a 50 per cent chance of paralysis. But the visit, though brief since it coincided with glutinous lunch on the ward, went well. Though Bishop Humphrey often asked after John's family, John never asked after his, just once asking him whether he was in pain when he was being treated for a slipped disc, a kindly enquiry that Humphrey suspected was more driven by the physiology than episcopacy.

We were at a service at Leeds Parish Church on the day John's first grandchild was born, and again my suggestion that we detour by Leeds Infirmary to check on mother and baby was met by a look of utter bewilderment. 'What are they naming your grandson?' I asked, when he returned from the briefest of forays into the maternity ward, startled by a swish of purple. 'Elliott,' John replied. 'Oh, after T S?' I asked, priding myself on remembering John's favourite poet's initials in the heat, or rather cool, of the moment. 'I think not,' he pronounced, returning to his usual surly silence. John took a confirmation in my first parish, the date frighteningly coinciding with Rachel's due date for our second child. Fortunately Hannah arrived 20 days early. But when I told John about the near miss in the heavily pregnant pauses in the vestry before the service, he simply said, 'If I had been you, I'd have cancelled me!' Very witty, but no follow-on questions about how the birth had gone, how mother and child were doing, whether he might pop in later in the evening. Hugh Buckingham was in awe when John let slip that sometimes he'd been so busy as a parish priest, he could only manage 30 home visits a week; clearly that thirst for visiting had been eclipsed.

Bishop Clifford considered John to have a penetrating and ordered mind. His advice, though pithily expressed, was always shrewd, challenging and memorable, undergirded by kindness and humour. There was no system of appraisal nor much praise for work well done – 'I work on the basis it's better not to know,' John had replied when Bishop Gordon asked him how he thought he was doing.

> My general reaction is to keep fairly detached. It's important to take neither compliments nor criticisms too seriously because in the end only God knows whether you've done a good job or are likely to do one. To be too worried about the impression you are making is to distance yourself from God and the job.

But everyone thought that if they failed to perform as expected, John would be on to them.

As to what was expected, John didn't give much away when interviewing prospective candidates. 'He didn't tell me how difficult Bishop Donald (known as the Bat out of Hull) was to work with, gave me no personal oversight, so I was on my own,' Hugh Buckingham complained. 'But he would always sort out any muddle. He deserved his nickname "The Saviour", but like all saviours, they end up getting crucified.' Hugh was given short shrift when he asked precisely what an archdeacon did: 'Everyone knows what an archdeacon does, Robin Woods set the precedent.' (Robin Woods had been Archdeacon of Sheffield over a quarter of a century previously). Hugh had enjoyed supper, bed, breakfast and a Eucharist at Bishopthorpe, spending the evening helping care for John's tortoises, having a conducted tour of the palace and listening to John shout at the TV news whenever Mrs Thatcher appeared. 'If you'd like to come, let me know,' were John's final words after the ultimate non-interview. But Hugh realized he had read his papers, been tickled by his book (*How to Be a Christian in Trying Circumstances* (1985)), and simply wanted to check Hugh was the person his record said he was.

Hugh felt that John had a well-deserved reputation for being quite hopeless in private conversation, yet curiously proved quite garrulous in down-at-heel parishes, chatting with parishioners as he never did with him. Bishop Gordon observed the same trait, how John chose the least attractive and deprived parishes for his confirmations, with incumbents, wary of how the visit would go, 'enthusing afterwards how marvellous he had been, talking to all, preaching well, pausing for a photo with each candidate'. Although John offered little feedback or praise, on his retirement he wrote glowingly to all his senior staff, with this letter to Gordon typical:

> You have been a tower of strength through all these years and a wonderful colleague, and I have constantly admired the care you have exercised and the efficiency with which you have organised it. I am sure you could have had a diocese of your own, but selfishly I have been glad you stayed where you are, and this is a view shared by the diocese.

Chris Armstrong, John's domestic chaplain at Bishopthorpe from 1985 until I replaced him in 1991, kept a colourful diary. I conclude this chapter with several extracts from its marvellous blend of the mundane and majestic. Initially depressed by the dowdy chapel, he gets the chauffeur's girlfriend to wash and refresh all the altar linen, prizing some colourful altar frontals from an over-defensive PA, who had presumably secreted them, intending to make curtains for her flat. Chris has run-ins with Rosalie, mostly about keeping his dog (and his children) under control, and consults with Simon Wright, his predecessor, who had been considerably shocked when the Blanch bonhomie was replaced by the Habgood acute shyness. Chris has to mediate with the local junior school, saddened that their access to the grounds was curtailed by the new regime, at the end of his first year arranging a carol concert in the chapel with Rosalie presenting a chocolate bar to each child. The staff Christmas party is fed on royal venison, followed by John showing slides of his foreign travels, which Chris ducks by rushing off to a prior engagement. I wasn't so canny and, along with my infant daughters, over successive Christmases endured gruelling slides of John's visit to Auschwitz (where he dwelt too long on the capacity and purpose of the ovens), as well as a video of John's doctor daughter, Laura, educating Africans about AIDS, complete with Zulu's chanting, 'Say no to sex!' Chris notes that on Christmas Eve, after the office staff had departed, John continued to work, flagging up the holiday by changing his suit for a sports jacket.

Fun moments include a silent ordination retreat turning into an Edwardian House party, as candidates spend the final evening at

Bishopthorpe, entertained by John and Rosalie; a disarmament conference in West Germany, where John joked that they had taken a major role
in draining the EU wine lake; an opening of the first York kite festival
on the Knavesmire, for which Rosalie made John two kites; a millennial
celebration at a church north of Doncaster, where the vicar and the
arrangements proved hopeless, provoking several archiepiscopal raised
eyebrows: 'You'd think after a thousand years they'd have learned something, wouldn't you?!'

John and Rosalie hosted frequent and very happy visits from Michael
Ball, Bishop of Jarrow, who played piano duets with Rosalie and flew kites
with John. Chris felt that Michael's relaxed, easy and humorous air made
John look ten years younger. I too recall Michael staying at Bishopthorpe
Palace whenever General Synod met in York, travelling alongside John in
the car, breaking the silence and ribbing John, making him chuckle as we
drove to the Minster. As you turn through Monk Bar on the approach to
the Minster, you are faced by a massive iconic advert painted on the side
of a house on Lord Mayor's Walk: 'Nightly Bile Beans, keep you healthy,
bright-eyed and slim.' 'Oh John,' Michael piped up, 'I hope you've taken
your Bile Beans to keep you regular. Do you think we should dispense
them nightly to Synod?' There were peals of laughter, especially since you
couldn't think of a bunch of folk who looked less healthy, bright-eyed or
slim. They once returned to Bishopthorpe after a pretty gruelling day of
Synod sessions. 'Now,' Rosalie chirped, 'what have you been talking about
tonight?' The two men looked at each other, brows furrowed, and then
burst into laughter as neither could recall what on earth they had spent
the long day discussing.

Diocesan events included manipulation and deviousness during a visit
to a troubled parish in East Hull, where the churchwarden was convinced
Chris's surname was Newt. Chris bore a passing resemblance to Derek
Nimmo, who played the hapless bishop's chaplain, Newt, in *All Gas and
Gaiters*. Apparently the cruel vicar's wife had dubbed the Archbishop
and his chaplain Nought and Newt, and the churchwarden clearly hadn't
got the joke. In North Hull, John suspended a vicar when a track record
of child abuse came to light, supporting the excellent curate there who
maintained the church's ministry and gave pastoral care to his vicar's
victims, despite being spat at and being verbally abused in the street.

Chris notes that John would clear his diary and see the curate at any time of day, as he would any cleric going through a difficult time. John worked closely with the Humberside police, the vicar was arrested, remanded in Hull jail, where he died of a heart attack before his trial, with John quietly officiating at his funeral at Hull crematorium. Then there was a troubled confirmation west of Hull, where the fiercely protestant PCC had instructed John to wear convocation robes. John refused and wore cope and mitre, preaching that no church could declare UDI, but rather contributed to the wide stream of Christian tradition rather like the small brooks and streams flowing into the nearby Humber.

Personal moments include a return to Durham on St Cuthbert's day, where all and sundry bewail John's leaving them. John preaches about young Adrian's acute loneliness and disorientation on moving to Bishopthorpe, being transformed by making a good friend – as someone who went to seven schools as my father moved from parish to parish, I fully sympathize. John proves surprisingly expansive when driving, talking animatedly about his first curacy, and his wonderful landlady – 'all curates deserve mothering!' On another drive, John jokes as they return from Ripon, inventing examination questions for episcopal candidates: 'What is the relationship between a liturgical smile and an Evangelical smile? Give examples.' John baptizes Chris and Gerry's third child in Bishopthorpe chapel, but then is too busy to attend the christening party. John confirms Francis at Repton School, where Chris overhears the chaplain giving the candidates a terrifying lecture on sin before the service. Elderly Michael and Joan Ramsey are given a final home in a flat at the Palace, with the former archbishop sitting at John's feet, hearing his ordination charge and baffling the ordinands, his eyebrows dancing: 'In my day we sang the Litany in Latin!'

Significant moments include the Easter Vigil in the bowels of dark York Minster, in the crowded crypt, baptizing in the same place where Paulinus had baptized King Edwin and Princess Hild on Easter Eve 627. John had kept an Easter Vigil at Queen's, where a Methodist deaconess had hugged him, crying, 'Thank God for the Church of England!' Given its liberal and ecumenical reputation, Chris was surprised to hear that John often heard confessions at Queen's. Repeatedly, Chris catches his breath, as he realizes, 'John is an instrumental figure at several levels, some too confidential to be committed to paper ... It was definitely John's Synod. Whenever he speaks he commands universal attention.' John had chaired the Women Ordained Abroad debate, about women priested abroad being allowed to minister here. The motion was defeated, the women subdued rather than suicidal or schismatic, with John resolving to assuage their hurt.

On a national level, John launches the Church Urban Fund and preaches movingly at Sheffield Cathedral following the Hillsborough disaster. There were two long hold-ups on the A1, with John ordering Gordon our chauffeur to put his foot down, confident that the South Yorkshire police would be massed in Sheffield and not patrolling the motorways.

The media looms, with John attacked in *The Times* and elsewhere for views ranging from his support for the NUM in continuing to mine major coal reserves to his studied views on embryo research. John's role in the aftermath of the *Crockford's* Preface places them under siege at Bishopthorpe from the *Daily Mail* and he is heavily criticized elsewhere. Chris concludes that John overreacted, soured opinion, resulting in the papers clamouring to block his prospects for Canterbury.

Insightful James Jones observed John's strong suit was delving into the abstract, which rarely communicated well in a media that majored in concrete realities. Chris was impressed by John's performance in 1987 *In Conversation* with Sue MacGregor, where he came across as relaxed, self-contained and someone who thinks, and thinks deeply. When interviewed by Jonathan Dimbleby at the end of 1988 John ominously declared himself 'too old for Canterbury', and on *Any Questions* the following Good Friday (broadcast from Askham Bryan Prison), John's performance was marred by pregnant pauses and defending unpopular causes. His last line, however, stole a show in which Edwina Curry had previously held the stage. Asked how they would eat their Easter eggs, John, mindful of Edwina's gaff over salmonella-infected eggs, quipped, 'I'd curry mine.'

Cardinal Glemp, Archbishop of Warsaw, visited Bishopthorpe, somewhat bewildered to be presented with a leather-bound ASB. He was paving the way for a return visit to Poland in 1992 by John and a joint Anglican/Roman Catholic delegation, which included visits to Krakow and Auschwitz. Archbishops were deemed to be too superior to travel by bus like the rest of the delegation, and were instead transported in chauffeur-driven limos. The aim of the exchange was to explore how, following the democratization of Poland, its persecuted and belittled church could break free and operate in a free society. ASBs notwithstanding, the Cardinal was keen to draw on the Church of England's experience, and move a closed and suspicious Polish church to be more open.

Majestic events in Chris's diary include the opening of General Synod in Westminster Abbey, with the Queen in a bright yellow coat, casting admiring glances at John; Prince Andrew and Sarah Ferguson's royal wedding, with the young Prince William sticking his tongue out as John passed by, and the Moderator of the Church of Scotland looking (and sounding) especially glum; John leading a BCC visit to Russia, which went ahead despite Chernobyl, with John preaching more impromptu sermons than ever before, with KGB minders carefully listening in, curiously describing an angel's statue in Leningrad as life-size – 'How did they know?' quipped John; the Queen opening York Minster's restored South Transept; and John preaching at the five hundred and fiftieth anniversary of Eton, 'If you have been to Eton, the best thing you can do afterwards is accept it, and then forget about it!'

21

Primate John

I've emphasized previously that the same artist, George Bruce, painted Michael Ramsey's and John's portraits for Bishopthorpe, though nearly three decades separated their archiepiscopacy. By deliberately choosing Bruce, I believe John was signalling a strong sense of connection and continuity between him and Ramsey, playing Elisha to his Elijah. Any sense of connection between the cool, calculating, precise scientist and the rambling, at times crazy, mystic may seem surprising. Yet I think Ramsey's strong sense of otherness, which John was first struck by at Madré's way back in his Kensington days, deeply called to him and gave him the nerve to be other too. 'I don't do soundbites, I talk in paragraphs, I don't think I've ever coined an aphorism in my life,' John concluded in an *Observer* interview (11 April 1993). I once commented to John that Ramsey's much-trumpeted *The Gospel and the Catholic Church* struck me as so obvious that I couldn't see what all the fuss was about. John laughed, 'It wasn't so much what he said, but how he said it, so profoundly and authentically, convincing anyone who met him that his God wasn't a might-be but was an is.' Profound and authentic are epithets that apply to John as equally as Ramsey: Bruce gives them different faces, but paints the same soul.

As for the other Primates who crossed John's path, he mainly avoided their wiles rather than follow in their footsteps. He felt Donald Coggan was difficult to get to know, his imagination limited by his conservative Evangelical stable, undoubtedly humble and other-worldly, but not sufficiently decisive. He proffered little advice when John felt he was appointed to Durham too soon, other than that he had a good suffragan. He was a workaholic at Lambeth, insufficiently resourced, seeking to solve every problem by appointing a committee of three wise men, or consulting his chosen five senior bishops to plan strategy.

John found Stuart Blanch to be relaxed and funny, but sensed 'he didn't do an awful lot'. Stuart was fourth choice for York, with Robert Runcie one of those declining because Lindy didn't fancy life by the Ouse.

John respected Robert Runcie for restructuring the staff at Lambeth to free up his main strengths, chiefly his gift for friendship, his consciousness of history and his love of style, especially in speaking. John was critical of Terry Waite's ill-fated Middle Eastern mission, which dominated Lambeth's agenda and staff, when their skills were badly needed to tackle problems nearer home. John felt

Runcie was good at painting the large picture, deflating the pretentious and setting present problems in a historical context. He was dependent on advisors and speech-writers, which he then worked obsessively on to make his own. Chairing meetings clearly bored him; he usually came well advised, although it was not always clear he had read the main documentation, and was apt to state his own conclusions too soon. He summed up well, and our roles, with me having read the papers beforehand, were helpfully complementary. Having wide responsibilities, he used his experience in one field to illuminate issues in another, and at bishops' meetings he would draw on insights from different parts of the world both to entertain us and recall us out of our ecclesiastical ghetto, demonstrating that holiness and humour, breadth and seriousness of purpose belonged together.

The media campaign against him, undoubtedly politically inspired, was a crushing burden, and I know from our frequent telephone conversations, cost him a lot emotionally. This is why I deliberately drew the media away from him over the *Crockford's* affair. The commitment Runcie gave to *Faith in the City* brought out the best in his entrepreneurial skills in getting the process moving, determined that this report was going to result in action. There was nobody with better stature to be Archbishop of Canterbury at the time, a classic Anglican who managed to maintain his balance against all the odds. It was his bad luck that he had to do it during an exceptionally difficult period, undoubtedly damaged by the vicious campaigns against him.

During Runcie's primacy, John served on the planning committee for the 1988 Lambeth Conference and on the steering committee during the conference itself. He was also chair, with Desmond Tutu vice-chair, of one of the four sections of the conference – on Christianity and social order. AIDS loomed large on their agenda, as did the changing nature of marriage, global poverty, peace and human rights. As in 1978, John was the one who burned the midnight oil, drafting the final report.

George Carey, then Bishop of Bath and Wells, felt that Runcie was plainly disenchanted with the House of Bishops, ill at ease with his fellow bishops and unhappy with bureaucracy. In his view John was one of the most capable bishops in the House, more than capable of leading it, doing his best to make the House an efficient tool. He feared that Runcie's ennui and John's business-like approach made proceedings cold and forbidding, freezing out any contributions from new bishops. John Nott, then Bishop of Norwich, felt similarly, that Runcie was like a forbidding headmaster expecting his school to be biddable and obedient. Carey, on the other hand, seemed sufficiently at ease with himself to let John take centre stage, bringing a relaxed, informal air where contributions were welcome.

John's view of Carey was that he had done a superb job at St Nick's in the Marketplace in Durham, and at Trinity College, Bristol, not least in bringing the college back into the Church of England, as well as making striking speeches in Synod as a new bishop, which were measured and conciliatory to other traditions. John realized, in being appointed to Canterbury so soon in his episcopal ministry, Carey had a lot of catching up to do, and deserved nursing. Carey writes:

On being nominated to Canterbury, I stayed overnight with John and Rosalie. If John thought he had been in the running, such a thought was never expressed nor was it shown. Indeed, he was generous to an extreme and gave me very valuable advice, which continued to the end of our time together. I made it my policy that John and I would chair the House of Bishops together. He was always supportive and always generous with his time. John *is* the House of Lords, very much in his element, his ability as a scientist greatly respected. Everything he uttered was carefully measured and expressed lucidly. Yet I found him very difficult to read, always there, ready to support and wise in all his dealings, but giving little of himself away. There were times when I ached to get some appreciation from John, some word of praise, some acknowledgement that things were going well. But this was never his way. I was relaxed about this most of the time, because I too am confident by nature and do not rely on others to affirm me unnecessarily, but it struck me as strange that we were so close as colleagues and so distant as people.

The Archbishop of Canterbury is a favourite target for the media, and there was a flurry of articles in 1993, drawing on unattributed and probably concocted sources, suggesting John, with his personal authority, political experience and intellectual stature, was stealing the headlines and was the de facto head of the Church of England, running it from York. I guess 'Complementary partnership succeeding' doesn't quite steal the headlines in the same way. And there probably was a shift in leadership style in Church and State which made commentators uneasy and yearn, sadly too late, for John's sure touch.

I found George (and Eileen) Carey immensely warm, with a pastoral concern and attention for me and our family outstanding, in stark contrast to John, who often seemed oblivious, preoccupied with matters of state. Watching the two men celebrate at General Synod Eucharists in York Minster was instructive, with Carey relaxed and smiling, often wrong-footed by the Mozart Mass, which a more formal John, steeped in the Classics from infancy, intuitively knew his way around. I recall Carey trying out his good ideas on John, who was impressed by the way Carey handled the Commissioners' £80 million deficit, a headache not of his making. Carey graciously backed down when John was less than enthusiastic. For instance, Carey wanted to give the title 'Spearhead' to the Decade of Evangelism; John feared that such a title, with violent connotations harking back to the Crusades, would send the wrong signals in our multi-faith society. As an alternative, John suggested 'Springboard' (whose only connotations were with *The Magic Roundabout*), with which Carey happily concurred. Carey then proposed making the talented but prickly Michael Green (who had been previously passed over for several bishoprics) the Bishop for Evangelism, with being freed from having an actual see enabling him to be deployed missionally at point of need. John was scathing about bishops who didn't have a diocesan base, arguing that it was a Roman Catholic aberration and distinctly un-Anglican, and again Carey backed off, little realizing that within a year John would be championing such flying bishops.

Speaking of which, Carey was warmly supportive of women's ministry, and highly enthusiastic about women being ordained as priests, to which General Synod under his leadership gave approval by a narrow majority in November 1992. Having labelled opponents as guilty of a very serious heresy, Carey had lost the confidence of the traditional integrity. In the weeks and months following the vote, his understandable euphoria had the downside that he seemed oblivious to the need to retain and give succour to the Church of England's traditionalists. Fortunately a small group chaired by Sir Philip Mawer, then General Secretary to the General Synod, and which included Bishops Alan Chesters and David Hope, Mary Tanner and John, had explored contingencies should the vote go either way, with the widespread expectation it would not be carried.

In the event, the group changed gear exceptionally well, especially as it worked under pressure with the first women's ordinations looming. There was wide consultation, including one where traditionalists packed into the Great Hall at Bishopthorpe in January 1993, a fire blazing in the grate, John alone before them, patiently listening, taking notes and airing possibilities. Realizing traditionalists often ministered in deprived parishes that other priests wouldn't touch with a barge pole, he was keen to deeply affirm them. Another consultation at Kennington Parish Church was similarly constructive.

The deal, which was enshrined in canon law, which in the Established Church has the same force as civil law, was complex. Church Councils would be empowered to vote on three resolutions, whether (a) they did not wish to have a female parish priest, (b) they did not wish a female priest to minister in their parish, or (c) they wished for alternative episcopal oversight by a traditionalist bishop, who would support them liturgically and pastorally. At the same time, measures were passed for priests who in conscience could not continue to serve and therefore needed to seek alternative employment, with generous compensation packages to ease the transition and assist with housing. It is amazing that all this legislation, complete with the consecration of three PEVs (flying bishops) to new suffragan sees, along with housing and support networks, took place in just over 12 months.

Many criticize the Act of Synod as prejudicial against women priests, setting a limit to their ministry, making it subordinate to a PCC vote. They conveniently forget that at the time a hostile Conservative and male-dominated Commons and Lords were highly critical of the Women Priests Ordination Measure, which they undoubtedly would not have passed unless there were concrete assurances that both traditionalists who stayed and traditionalists who left would be respected. The fact that John, whose views were highly respected by Parliament, put his name to the Act of Synod massively reassured them that the Church would be safe in his hands. The highly critical Matthew Parris lauded John as 'the last Anglican theologian I used to make the walk to the Lords' chamber to hear speak'. In a personal letter dated 1 June 2006, the broadcaster and author Jeremy Paxman, scourge of any politicians and public figures with a whiff of hypocrisy or idiocy about them, wrote: 'I am astonished to think that you recall any of my interviews with the Archbishop, but you're right that I found him a clever, kind and very thoughtful man.' That the Act bore John's name also won over a scathing House of Bishops and General Synod, and the ordinations went ahead in March 1994.

David Hope, then Bishop of London, made this comment about the process:

I had already published the London Plan in order to deal with the situation in my then diocese following the ordination of women vote – a diocese greatly divided on the subject. John chaired the small group of which I was a member seeking to work out the terms of the Act of Synod. Although John had voted in favour of the ordination of women he was scrupulously fair (as I anticipated he would be – unlike some bishops!) to ensure a proper hearing and representation of the views of those opposed. I believe it was due to his careful and painstaking efforts that the Act of Synod came to be formulated and passed by the Synod.

Richard Harries, then Bishop of Oxford, had this observation:

In particular I remember the crucial meeting when we agreed to make provision for those opposed to the ordination of women. I think it must have been at the Liverpool Britannia Adelphi – I always thought that the faded glory of this hotel exactly suited us in the Church of England! Many of us were unhappy about the provision for special oversight, but such was the respect in which John was held we agreed to it. I can remember taking him up at one point when he talked about 'alternative episcopal oversight'. I suggested it should rather be 'extended episcopal oversight' – but I don't think I won that one.

In conversation in 2006 John reflected:

The Act of Synod gave the Church of England time to discuss in practice what having ordained women would mean. It was a transitory measure for a five-year period of reception – that's why we appointed PEVs who had no more than five years before their retirement. It enabled a context in which the Church could learn about women priests in practice without dividing itself. The hope and expectation was that those opposed would play their part to discover what it meant, whether women's ministry was blessed and a blessing or not. It very much depended on the bishops creating the right atmosphere, and sadly not a lot of bishops did. David Jenkins was a particular problem, his intolerance incensed traditionalist Catholics. With one exception, I felt I got on with them well, and they trusted me.

Reading those words 13 years on, I sense that John felt the period of reception could go either way. He was an Eton- and King's-educated patrician, and though he had a high view of women, saw their role as complementary to men, a view supported by his grounding in physiology. I believe there was a part of him that felt that after five years the novelty might wear off, women would realize that being a parish priest wasn't all it was cracked up to be, and that they would quietly go away, and the Church could carry on with its main agenda. Of course, the ordination of women wasn't provisional, so you would still have women priests around. But there were other well-intended initiatives which at the time seemed the flavour of the month, but in the course of time disappeared entirely. One example is Ministry in Secular Employment (MSE), which was hailed as a superior sort of priesthood, freed up from all the usual markers (such as liturgy, altars, conventional ministry etc.). Essentially it was priesthood undercover, a sleeper priest functioning below the radar. It died a death, with either all the candidates suffering from burn-out and having to be converted to conventional ministry (because a priest needs the markers), or being so successful at going to ground we lost all contact with them. I'm sure at some stage I will stumble across one, dug into a peat bog on the North York Moors, preaching to the grouse.

I have tried very hard to ponder what John actually said, rather than what I thought he said or what I wanted him to say, even though what I hear goes against my grain. In the event, women's ministry flourished and proved a precious gift on so many levels. In John's view, Forward in Faith, rather than coming to terms with that flourishing, 'had taken their bat and ball home', forcing the Act of Synod to have permanence it was never intended to have. But whatever, John got us through the day and spared us the sort of deadlock that Parliament faced over Brexit in the second half of the 2010s.

The anguish and division faced by the Church over the issue was mirrored in John's marriage, in that Rosalie, who was prone to mistake Bishopthorpe for Barchester, was fiercely against the ordination of women. John adored and deeply respected his wife, and that undoubtedly gave him a heightened sensitivity to, as well as a first-hand experience of, traditionalists. The phrase 'fiercely against' is an understatement. In October 1992, when it looked as if the Synod vote would go against them, we had a meeting of women deacons at Bishopthorpe, to explore how their ministry could be enhanced despite not being priested. After a succession of extremely awkward moments, John piped up, 'David, go and ask Rosalie to prepare tea.' I descended to the kitchens in fear and trepidation, found Rosalie and passed on John's order for fifty cuppas, assisting her, putting cups out on to trays and boiling kettles. 'What's this meeting about?' she breezily asked – clearly John had kept her in the dark.

I explained as gently as I could, but she exploded with rage, 'What, give them tea, I'd rather give them strychnine!' As far as I could make out in such a highly charged kitchen, her fury was fuelled by women clergy causing John a lot of time-consuming trouble, effectively robbing her and the family of his attention. I also detected regret that she had sacrificed her career to enable John, so had no time for those seeking self-promotion and aggrandisement, which she felt was counter-gospel.

York had 39 women ready to be priested. Normally, candidates prior to their ordination spent the final evening dining at Bishopthorpe. But in order to prevent an Edwardian house party turning into Murder on the Ouse Express, we housed the women in a safe house, the diocesan retreat centre nestling in the North York Moors at Wydale, and John drove over to give his customary charge. The women, to say the least, were not pleased at their exile, and the Director of Training running their retreat told me they had deliberately placed two nursing mothers on the front row of the chapel, who in the diarist Francis Kilvert's words, 'displayed their charms liberally', their babies noisily suckling during John's address. John, who had rejoiced to see Rosalie breastfeed their four children, wasn't fazed in the least. Instead he spoke beautifully, for 40 minutes, on how to say and how not to say the dominical words, 'This is my body, this is my blood.'

Chiefly because of his acute domestic situation, John left it to his suffragans to do the ordination, and in fact never ordained a woman as a priest. He left it to me as Director of Ordinands to organize the two historic ordinations in the Minster with 39 women, understandably miffed that their Archbishop wasn't laying his hands on them. I laid hands on them, with a front-page photo in the *Yorkshire Post* – once Rosalie spotted it, she didn't talk to me for a fortnight. I think there is a special place in heaven for John and me, considering we got the Act of Synod and those first ordinations through, with all that going on at home.

As well as a whole load of other stuff. John saw quite a lot of beleaguered PM John Major, of whom he was rather fond, although less so when he heard about his affair with Edwina Currie. Rosalie got on very well with Norma, who in John's words 'seemed bewildered and deserved a bit of mothering'. John told me that Major had talked humbly with him about how he valued the Church, wanted it on his side, wanted people to understand the difficulties of politics, wanted friends who wouldn't rat on him. John, styling himself as a one-nation Tory, corresponded with Major, advocating the changes he enthused about, but advised against rushing things through and not taking people with him. Major thought so highly of John's ecclesiastical and diplomatic skill that he asked him to preach at the National Thanksgiving following the end of the First Gulf War in Glasgow Cathedral, where the congregations included Muslims and Jews as well as Christians, of many different nationalities and walks of life. The iconic phrase that sticks from John's sermon is, 'Who can forget the dying cormorants?' drowned in a sea of oil. It is not so much the words, but the way he said them, with such immense sadness and sorrow, embracing all the pointless loss of war.

In 1995, Graham Usher, now Bishop of Norwich, was a York ordinand training in Cambridge, a senior figure in the Scouting movement. He returned from a humanitarian visit to the Balkans and was so shocked by the violent genocide he encountered first-hand that he wrote to John in great detail, urging him to take action. John immediately arranged an appointment with John Major, taking along with him John Sentamu, then Vicar of Tulse Hill in South London, who had had first-hand experience of another war-torn region in Amin's Uganda. John urged the Prime Minister to deploy British armed forces, assuring him of Church of England support. Major initially thought the Church of England would oppose such armed intervention, so was heartened and indeed given confidence by John's assurance to the contrary. The result was the United Nations Protection Force (UNPROFOR), which had included British troops in a peace-keeping mission since 1992, handed over to NATO's more proactive Implementation Force (IFOR) later in 1995.

On John's retirement, Major wrote: 'I have greatly valued the role you have played in both Church and State. You will go into retirement with the affection and respect of all.'

Once a year the two Archbishops with their wives formed part of the home team, along with the PM and Cabinet, and were invited to Buckingham Palace for a diplomatic reception with ambassadors, their senior staff and families. Later in the evening, the party became more select, just the PM, the Archbishops, the Leader of the House, the Lord Mayor of London and the Queen having a good interchange. At one, John had had a conversation with Margaret Thatcher following a BCC visit to Argentina in the aftermath of the Falklands War, declaring his intention to host a return visit for the Argentinean church, and suggesting that the Government should do a similar thing. Thatcher proceeded to give John a 15-minute lecture on why not. John felt that *Faith in the City* rather soured things for him with Thatcher. As undoubtedly did his scathing article in *The Observer*, following her address to the Church of Scotland Assembly when she dabbled in biblical studies, claiming there was no such thing as society.

There are so many delicious myths around why Thatcher did not prefer omniscient John for Canterbury in 1990, or indeed in 1979, none of which is backed up by any evidence, since the Crown Appointments Commission (CAC) proceedings were confidential. The broadsheets speculated that there was a movement called ABH (Anyone But Habgood) that resisted his appointment to Canterbury, and there certainly was co-ordinated opposition to his appointment as Bishop of London in 1981. John had established a reputation for taking no prisoners – who can forget his 15-page open letter in 1952 condemning the Cambridge Christian Union? He had hardly settled into Auckland Castle before he did a hatchet job on General Synod's Commission on Broadcasting proposals in 1973, followed by his unequivocal championing of the ASB, his bold defence of David Jenkins and his non-interventionist God, and culminating in his staunch defence of Robert Runcie following publication of the 1987 *Crockford's* Preface. So the knives would certainly be out. A very senior priest and academic, for whom I have the highest regard, revealed that in the 1980s he had been invited to join a group called 'The Friends', but left very soon after he discovered it was devoted to preventing John from becoming Archbishop of Canterbury. 'It was a very high-profile group, meeting in London, very hush hush – and posh. Terrible, I don't know why on earth they thought I would agree with them!' Such was the force of the group that even 30 years on, my source wishes to preserve his anonymity.

Whispering campaigns against him notwithstanding, John felt that all those CACs he attended or chaired proceeded with a high degree of integrity, meeting with the Archbishops' Secretary for Appointments beforehand to weed out the non-starters to produce a list of reasonable length for subsequent research and discussion. He stressed that there was never collusion before the meeting between Archbishops, who nevertheless had their preferences, with Runcie being cuttingly dismissive about any non-starters. John felt that Carey didn't have the same deep knowledge that Runcie had of any candidate, which shifted the power base to the Secretaries and the information they chose to disclose. But John found it to be a very prayerful event, spending the first evening reducing the list, then sleeping on it, followed by a dawn Eucharist and further discussions. John took immense care to make sure any diocesan representatives felt involved and satisfied with the final two names. The General Synod representatives brought their own prejudices to the table, but to their credit acquainted themselves with a wide range of candidates to complement the precis the Secretaries gave.

Particular interventions included John and Runcie strongly recommending Bishop Timothy Bavin's translation from Johannesburg to Portsmouth in 1985, to pave the way for Desmund Tutu to be appointed to the former see and take centre stage in leading South Africa out of apartheid. David Jenkins' antics in Durham made the CAC resistant to appointing any more notable theologians, concluding it was highly difficult to combine the role of professor and bishop in these pressured times, with the essential qualification being intelligence rather than scholarship.

Obviously John could not comment on how things played out and whether people acted as honourably as him whenever he was necessarily absent from the CAC as a candidate himself for the post under discussion. Vis-à-vis John not going to Canterbury, one bishop concluded it was simply no longer the shy Etonian patrician's day; Bishop Michael Ball wondered if dear John was loved enough; several describe John as the best Archbishop of Canterbury we never had, Ron Metcalfe as the best Archbishop of Canterbury we should have had. John certainly bore no grudges about the episode, and York lent itself more to John's preferred role of whispering exquisite advice from the wings rather than perpetually being centre stage at Lambeth. By November 1990, Thatcher herself was no longer preferred, and wrote this reply to a kindly letter from John:

Your kind and generous message has given me great strength and encouragement during these difficult days. It was so kind of you to write. I most earnestly hope that the things I have tried to do for Britain will continue. This matters more to me than anything else.

Perhaps John never went to Canterbury because he so obviously would *not* continue the things Thatcher had tried to do for Britain.

22

Just John

The prevailing narrative is that the 1990s senior leadership of the Church was lax in enforcing safeguarding. It appears we were at best naive and easily manipulated, at worst prone to defend our own, wilfully guarding our own dubious reputations as well as the reputation of Mother Church. I fear, however, such a narrative is oblivious to the massive difference in culture between then and now. It was a culture where Jimmy Saville was high priest, a secular saviour urging us to 'Clunk, click every trip', heralding 'the age of the train', assuring us that Jim'll fix our every dream – Archbishop Stuart Blanch had a 'Jim fixed it for me' medallion hanging in his study. Almost weekly, *Top of the Pops* faded out with Saville's arm round a young girl, while Abba trilled 'When I kissed the teacher'. The Church presented a counter view, but was dismissed as being square, uptight, frigid and prudish.

Though John had felt that both the 1973 General Synod Report on the media and the Festival of Light had been too censorious, he embraced a well-thought-through sexual ethic. His line was that when they had sex, a couple were at their most vulnerable and exposed and deserved the legislature afforded by the State and Church to prevent either party being manipulated or abused. He was amazingly devoid of hang-ups, never felt sex was sordid, but rather championed it as sacred. Anything sacred deserves protection from a society all too prone to debase and despoil it, and John believed that marriage, with lifelong vows affirmed by the wider community, was the safest environment for sexual love to flourish. Other environments were obviously possible and indeed could be life-affirming, but did not afford the same level of support or widespread approval.

John's unequivocal ethic drove how we handled the Discipline List, held at Lambeth and Bishopthorpe, detailing sanctions against clergy who had breached the conduct expected of them. When I became chaplain in 1991, I expected the discipline system to reflect the more re-laxed attitudes emerging in other professions, where people were allowed to have a private life and make foolish mistakes without it impacting on their career. I couldn't have been more wrong. John's take was that it was the greatest privilege to be a priest, giving access to people at the most vulnerable times in their lives; any priest who abused that trust deserved the severest penalty, quickly and openly administered, so that the public could continue to have confidence in the Church's ministry. Most of the cases we dealt with were marital irregularity, in the vicar-runs-off-with-organist genre. The bishop whose northern diocese the vicar served in would give a detailed report to John, who would then dismiss the vicar and require him and his family to vacate their vicarage with immediate effect. While the Church had limited access to counselling and financial support for the spouse the vicar had betrayed, John made it very clear that the prime responsibility for maintenance of his estranged spouse and family rested firmly with the vicar.

I operated the system in the Northern Province under John's explicit instruction, although it did strike me as very harsh. Normally any adul-terous cleric was out of stipendiary ministry for five years, and only if he proved contrite was then gradually reintroduced. I recall one cleric under discipline desperately seeking permission to baptize his grandchild, who had miraculously survived a difficult birth. John refused, point-blank, on the grounds that any practice of priesthood, even contained within the family, could be taken as turning a blind eye to behaviour that demand-ed prohibition. We had another case where an ordinand ran off with a curate, and both were prohibited, with John's classic comment, 'What bi-zarre concept of Christianity do such people hold?'

Other cases on the Discipline List were more complex, with some errant clerics almost acting out a death wish. One vicar had put an advert in his local newsagents for a mistress, and surprisingly had several applicants. Any cases involving child abuse led to Deposition (nullifying) of Orders. I only recall two live cases involving child abuse in my time, Jan Knoss in Hull and Trevor Ward in Middlesbrough; both cases immediately were re-ferred to the police to deal with as soon as the abuse came to light.

I read and memorized all the files, chiefly so I could know my foes. Many of the clerics, having made a big lie their reality, were manipulative and strangers to the truth, and were capable of applying for jobs in other dioceses while they were still prohibited from ministry. Twenty-five years on, I am still wary of applicants who explain a gap in employment as 'Taking time out to find myself/reassess my faith/rediscover my vocation'. I am mindful of the story of the young monk who told the Abbot of Ampleforth that he felt life had wider horizons for him than that of a monastery. 'Really, what's her name?' the canny Abbot replied.

In 1994 we received an edict from Lambeth that all the files of deceased clergy, including discipline files, should be destroyed, in accordance with the latest Data Protection Guidelines. The edict required the person in charge of the files to sign an undertaking that it had been and would be enforced. At the time, it struck me as totally crazy, not least because the cleric in the discipline files might have died, but any victims might still be alive, with the discipline file the only objective record we had of such cases. In the end, the Archbishop's PA signed the edict while I, who was employed by no one but the Archbishop and certainly under no obligation to Lambeth, retained the files under lock and key in my office.

I was always very grateful that John supported me as his Director of Ordinands whenever I had misgivings about a candidate. Initially I was the new kid on the block, with the process of formation and selection a steep learning curve for me. Even so, I felt very strongly that once you ordained someone, the eternal destiny of thousands of vulnerable souls was in their hands, so you needed to be as sure as you could be that that ordinand was not intent on mischief. Often it was just a hunch, a CV that was too squeaky clean, or a person's body language didn't quite ring true, or they were too complimentary or flattering, to the point of sycophancy. My line was 'if in doubt, out', and John backed me, despite the barrage of protests from the candidate and their vociferous supporters. I even received two death threats from such candidates, which I guess proved my point. One candidate I wrote to the Advisory Board of Ministry (ABM) about, since I suspected he would emerge in another diocese. ABM, though very scathing about my lack of evidence, did note my concerns and in time he did emerge elsewhere and attend a conference. He was not recommended, chiefly because the selectors trusted John's endorsement of my reservations. Years later, the candidate received a long custodial sentence for historic child abuse that had been committed within another profession prior to his appearing on my screen.

Under current guidelines I would refer such a matter to the Diocesan safeguarding team, who would involve the statutory authorities. Back then, we had no safeguarding team, and the police, themselves coming up to speed with successive Data Protection Acts, refused to run any checks for us. Nor would the Department of Education allow us access to their List 99 of banned teachers. We paid for a DHSS check on current clergy and ordinands, but the check seemed perfunctory, with the standard response 'Nothing contrary held', coming back about folk whom I held substantial adverse details on. In the BBC series *Life on Mars*, Manchester Police Officer Sam Tyler flips back from 2006 to 1973 to a very different world with very different policing. I empathize with him, in that the Church is judged for not flipping forward from 1993 to 2019 and operating the safeguarding policy in force a quarter of a century later. We could only live in 1993, where we were actually ahead of the game.

As for protecting the reputation of the Church, it would be a poor archbishop who didn't include that as his role, in balance with other concerns. In the second book of Samuel my namesake David, the shepherd boy, used his staff to take out lions and bears who threatened the flock, a crucial role for any shepherd. In a keynote address for the Decade of Evangelism in 1994, John, as well as sneering at *Guardian* readers in the superior manner that only an Old Etonian could carry off, quoted Professor David Martin, who described churches 'as the only institutions that deal in tears and concern themselves with the breaking points of human existence'. Such institutions deserve defending, especially when those who inflict the tears and break humans hardly desire the Church's flourishing. I recall attending a stormy meeting in Thirsk, where I was under repeated criticism for not promoting the cause of candidates 'who had a right to be ordained'. A wonderful curate came to my rescue. 'What about the Church's rights? She's an organism, she's the Body of Christ, surely she has rights too?'

Did John turn a blind eye when senior clergy misbehaved? On the contrary, he threw the book at them. One archdeacon, who chaired the Church's watchdog on IT and the emerging internet, was found to have compromising material on his own PC, and was immediately dismissed.

Another archdeacon was also dismissed when his girlfriend complained that he was having an affair with another woman; the details were kept out of the media, not to protect the Church's reputation but rather to protect the reputation of the ethnic minority to which he belonged.

And what of Bishop Peter Ball, twin brother of Michael, John's former suffragan in Durham? With the appointment of Basil Hume, Abbot of Ampleforth, to be Cardinal Archbishop of Westminster in 1976, suddenly monasticism was cool, with monastic bishops and their gnomic brand of spirituality quite the fashion. A monk-bishop, who gathered around him a community of vibrant young men, more than dazzled a church establishment depressed by declining attendance and decreasing impact among the young. Hardly an edition of the *Church Times* went by that didn't include some vignette eulogizing the twin monk-bishops.

But there is no excuse whatsoever, in any age, when clerics exploit their position and abuse those under their authority or care, with our Lord himself setting the bar: 'Whoever causes one of these little ones who believe in me to stumble, it would be better for them that a large millstone were tied around their neck and they were thrown into the sea' (Mark 9.42). And a faith whose focus is the ultimate victim on the cross should be acutely sensitive to, rather than oblivious of, any victims.

I have checked with Mary Murray, John's PA, and we have no recollection whatsoever that once Peter Ball was under investigation by the police that John intervened to plead his cause. Even though John advised George Carey during his early years at Lambeth, George does not recall John contacting him or giving him a steer about Peter Ball's case, and hadn't even realized that John and Michael Ball were such good friends. John's track record with any cleric under investigation by the police was to maintain a necessary independence and impartiality and let the law take its course, and then take things from there. Besides, John did not know Peter as well as he did Michael, and certainly had no knowledge of what has emerged since, for which he would have had a zero tolerance.

Former Archbishop of Canterbury, Rowan Williams, sees John as:

representing at its best a sort of mandarin culture which justified an element of leaving it to the Chaps-who-know, incarnating the best and most intellectually vigorous version of Coleridge's ideal of the Church as the critical friend to the Establishment. The problem is that when this becomes unaccountable, when there is real risk of ignorance and/or manipulation, it doesn't make for a healthy political culture. Mandarinism is just about defensible if you have a cast-iron system for guaranteeing the intelligence and independence of the mandarinate. We don't any longer.

Any mandarinate should be, like Caesar's wife, above suspicion, an aspiration shattered by Bishop Peter Ball's catalogue of abuse. Any cast-iron system for guaranteeing that mandarinate should really have included rigorous accountability for religious houses, greater scrutiny and appraisal of candidates for high office (using my 'if in doubt, out' criterion), and giving voiceless victims a voice. Though approaching the mandarinate from different directions – Carey respected it, John was part of it – I fear there was a certain naivety in both men in accepting it at face value, as if it were as honourable as themselves. Not the most grievous of faults, but sadly one with the most grievous consequences.

23

Retiring John

John was planning to retire in the summer of 1994, but postponed it for a year in order to steer the Church through unchartered waters following the 1992 General Synod vote in favour of women priests. He and Rosalie explored various places to live on retirement – Rosalie hoped to continue teaching at the Minster School and, with orchestral commitments in York, living a shortish distance from York was a necessity. They eventually plumped for Malton, east of York, with a regular rail service to the city. John saw retiring within the diocese as a welcome excuse for setting his face against doing anything further in the diocese, in order to give his successor the necessary space. Other than helping out at Malton Parish Church (where he hid behind a pillar when he was not leading worship), John declined any official engagements whatsoever in the diocese, and resolutely refrained from passing comment on the state of the Church of England both locally and nationally.

Following his retirement, he was made a Life Peer and sat on the cross-benches. In the House of Lords he had always been active in debates on ethical and scientific issues, playing a decisive and much-criticized part on the Committee of Inquiry into Human Fertilisation and Embryology 1982–84, culminating in the so-called Warnock Report. This led up to the Human Fertilisation and Embryology Act 1990, followed by the setting up of the Human Fertilisation and Embryology Authority a year later. Thousands of couples in Britain, desperate to have children, have benefited from John's steady hand steering this legislation.

He was also a member of the Select Committee on Medical Ethics, which published a highly regarded report on euthanasia in 1994. As patron of National Family Mediation he was much involved in all stages of the Family Law Bill, making radical changes to divorce procedures, which, though passed, did not come into effect until the advent of New Labour. Along with Mary Warnock, John was a member of the Archbishop of Canterbury's Medical Ethics Advisory Group, which met quarterly at Lambeth from 1993 to 2006, chaired by Professor Robin Gill. Gill observed:

> Warnock and Habgood spoke in very similar ways, offering staccato, highly logical, and always compassionate opinions on a variety of issues in medical ethics – genetics, health rationing, persistent vegetative states, stem-cell research, assisted dying, pre-implantation genetic diagnosis, and many other topical issues. They did not always reach the same conclusion and, even when they did, they typically reached it by a different but ingenious route. They manifestly respected each other deeply. I found it a joy to hear them contribute, knowing that any bishops present would deepen their knowledge of the ethical issue at stake before a debate in, say, the House of Lords, fully aware of the informed eloquence of these two formidable members of the House. Warnock and Habgood were also quite alike in their lack of religious dogmatism, with an early commitment to careful, empirical science making him cautious of religious dogmatism – in a House of Lords debate on legalising euthanasia Habgood famously proclaimed (unlike other bishops who spoke) that he would make no reference to God. For Warnock and Habgood, public ethics was not to be confused with preaching to the faithful.

In his retirement, John prioritized time 'to capitalize on my experience by writing and catching up on the things I didn't know and ought to know'. As Archbishop, John had published two books of occasional writings, lectures and sermons, *Confessions of a Conservative Liberal* (1988) and *Making Sense* (1993). He also delivered Sheffield University's Stephenson Lectures and Exeter University's Prideaux Lectures, as well as numerous individual lectures, ranging from the Conservative Philosophy Group to the Royal College of Physicians. Following his retirement, he published *Faith and Uncertainty* (1997), a collection of occasional addresses in-cluding the Idreos Lectures on Science and Religion, delivered in 1994 at Manchester College, Oxford. He delivered Newcastle University's Riddell

Lectures on Science and Religion, expanding them into *Being a Person: Where Faith and Science Meet* (1998). His Oxford University Bampton Lectures were published as *Varieties of Unbelief* (2000), and his Aberdeen University's Gifford Lectures were published in *The Concept of Nature* (2002), including chapters on environmental issues, genetic manipulation and the concept of a natural moral law especially in its application to sexuality, declaring his deep sympathy for same-sex marriage. From 1997 he served as the churches' representative on a government think-tank, advising all branches of the government on environmental matters. From 1997, he also chaired the Department of Health UK Xenotransplantation Interim Regulatory Authority (UXIRA), advising Health Ministers on all matters concerning transplantation of animal tissues and organs into humans. So much for a quiet retirement!

In that retirement John spent more time on hobbies such as carpentry and art, the latter developing the high promise in drawing and sketching he had shown at prep school. When he was painting John's portrait at Bishopthorpe, George Bruce inspired him to explore painting in oils, with John watching and learning. Bruce generously gave John an easel, paints and brushes as a surprise birthday present. Thereafter John eagerly set up his easel at sundry vantage points, oblivious of his effect on passers-by, including the top floor of York's M & S (for his Minster-scape) and a lay-by on the A64 to catch the Yorkshire Wolds at their best. John enjoyed regularly sketching on family holidays, as his father had done.

Finally, John saw retirement as time to invest in the family, an opportunity to recover lost time and a chance to get to know his own children better. There were regular visits to Laura, Francis and Adrian, well within reach in the UK, and to Ruth, further afield in South Africa. Worshipping in Capetown Cathedral, John coincided with a visit by a distinctly miffed Tony Blair, upstaged by John getting a far warmer greeting than him from Archbishop Desmond Tutu. Tutu and John were old friends who had taken successive Lambeth Conferences by the scruff of the neck. And Tutu remained deeply grateful to John, whose fast footwork in the UK enabled him to become Bishop of Johannesburg and take the world by storm.

John's former vicar at Malton, Canon Bob Rogers, preached at John's funeral and caught his retirement years marvellously:

It was at Malton that Jacqui and I came to know them. It was a happy home. They were so content there: apart from visits to Ruth in South Africa, and what turned out to be a final holiday in Northumberland with Francis and Nicolette, they rarely left it for any length of time, enjoying short trips in their beloved campervan (restored by John), and picnics on the moors or at Castle Howard; never happier than when members of the family joined them. Though I have to say that there were occasions when Rosalie was not pleased with John: for when the kettle or hairdryer broke he would repair it, when all she longed for was to buy a new one: his workshop was an important part of his life and meticulously ordered – like his library! On one occasion when we were invited with family members, for a meal in their home, peals of laughter were heard coming from the direction of the kitchen where John and Rosalie happened to be preparing the meal. In summer days they would spend much time out on the patio enjoying a leisurely lunch. John enjoyed painting, usually on Saturday mornings framed in his study window. Rosalie once bought some cushion covers with biblical quotes and challenged John to name chapter and verse – she was never able to catch him out!

To me he was a delight: so kind and supportive, and worshipped in his parish church each week, except when delivering a prestigious sermon somewhere or other in the country, or supporting Rosalie who was involved in the orchestra which accompanied Minster services at the major festivals. He would preach from time to time and took the Parish Communion when we were on holiday, and on our return, awaiting us would be a delicious meal prepared by Rosalie, and an offer to preach on the Sunday morning from John, which he announced to the congregation as a 'benefit sermon for the Vicar, who would otherwise have had to spend the final part of this holiday preparing one'. Returning home, we would find he had placed lights on timers throughout the house – part of his quiet caring for us.

We always looked forward to receiving his Christmas card, taken from a painting done during the year. He wrote a Christmas letter, and in the year when Rosalie was taken ill it read, 'You may recognize our card from a previous year. The only painting John has been able to do this year is rather too bleak for what should be a joyful occasion.' Rosalie's illness hit him hard. He visited her each day spending several hours with her, usually walking the two miles there and the same distance back. Then came the time when John needed care and he joined Rosalie in the residential home, facing her increasing frailty and her death; whilst he himself was moving away from our shared reality into one we couldn't enter. John is now safe with our Lord in heaven, having entered that inheritance which nothing can destroy or spoil or wither; re-united with Rosalie led out of darkness by the One who endured the deep darkness of the cross.

John's successor and his archbishop for the first decade of his retirement was David Hope, who wrote very movingly following John's death:

Being a very new bishop and having come straight to Wakefield from being a parish priest and never having encountered very much of the synodical system either at diocesan or national level I was obviously on a very steep learning curve. It was always reassuring though to know that John was there at York and readily available for advice. I recall having turned to him on one or two occasions for his reflections on particular situations in the diocese and always feeling that I had received a well-considered response.

I recall too at one of the ecumenical Scargill meetings having been asked by John to give a paper on the Uniqueness of Christ, which I found a bit forbidding but afterwards he came up and thanked and congratulated me on it.

One very special occasion was when we celebrated the Centenary of the Diocese in 1988. We cancelled all the morning services in the Diocese in favour of every parish coming to Huddersfield Football Ground. John came and preached a memorable sermon. He also came to Ravensthorpe which even in those days had a large Muslim population – he came with me and one or two others to the local mosque for prayers (sitting on the floor of the mosque) and then together with the Muslim leaders moved across the road to the parish church and had a time of prayer there also.

Although appearing to be somewhat forbidding and with little small talk, nevertheless I found that people soon warmed to him and held him in considerable respect and esteem. On my appointment to London, he wrote a hugely encouraging letter in his own hand, with thanks for what I had done in Wakefield and expressing his sadness on losing me to the other Province.

So far as the General Synod was concerned, my impression is that he was always perceived to be a reassuring presence and whenever he spoke he was listened to with great care. He was a good foil to George Carey. If ever the Synod got into a muddle or there were complex matters to deal with, it would be to John that the Synod would turn for advice and comment – though they would not necessarily follow his wisdom, such is the perversity of Synods!

On my appointment to York again he wrote a personal letter of welcome – he said being Archbishop of York was one of the best appointments in the C of E. I had the impression that in fact he was quite glad not to have gone to Canterbury but rather remain at York. Two bits of advice in particular I remember: 'Learn to be a lazy archbishop and remember you are doing a long-distance race and not a hundred-yard sprint!'

During his retirement, he never ever intruded in any way. For me, it was actually immensely reassuring to have him in the Diocese, and I turned to him for advice on a number of occasions, not least when having to deal with more complex applications from those who had been divorced and remarried seeking a formal Faculty to allow them to proceed to ordination training, and also on other disciplinary matters.

I have the highest regard for John. His was a reassuring presence, often seeming somewhat distant and lacking in small talk – I suspect quite a shy person, until you got to know him and he you. I felt there was a hugely caring pastoral heart, a deeply spiritual and prayerful person as evidenced in the quiet and reflective way he conducted worship not least his celebration of the Eucharist – and in marked contrast to the mateyness and noisiness of some! Of his intellectual capacity there was no rival on the bench of bishops. Although often labelled as a 'liberal' my own view is much more nuanced than that – I believe he respected 'tradition' and the 'traditional' much more than he was ever given credit for. Overall a person of great integrity, someone to be trusted absolutely, always available for others, a great encourager, a good and attentive listener and with apparent boundless patience.

Retired John was also more relaxed, complimentary and expansive with former colleagues: in my four years working as his chaplain, there was actually very little personal exchange, barely sentences, but in his retirement I spent days talking with him. In sharp contrast to when John was in archiepiscopal harness and we travelled around 20,000 miles each year, with silence in the car an absolute rule. It made for 400 hours, 40 working days if you work 10 hours a day, a Lent every year. Forty days of silent fast, since we never ate in the car. I once came armed with a pack of bacon sandwiches and offered one to the Boss. 'No thank you,' he replied, giving me the withering look Saul must have given to David when he'd asked for his daughter's hand. 'I've put tomato ketchup in them,' I reassured him. 'That makes me even more determined to resist.' We broke our fast only once, on a tortuous 12-hour journey to Oswestry, at a Little Chef outside Wrexham. It was Sunday lunchtime, the place was packed, but within one minute of me and John striding in in his gorgeous purple cassock – Rosalie's phrase – the cafe emptied. I guess the punters feared it was a Fresh Expression and John had a tambourine hidden in his cassock's ample folds, little knowing that John wasn't a tambourine sort of guy.

I used to sit in the front and watch him in the rear-view mirror. We were jumpy about being ambushed – the IRA were active at that time – so I had to keep an eye out for what was hurtling towards us. Gordon, an ex-sergeant major on the look-out for a skirmish, even used to poke a stick under the car with a mirror on the end checking for bombs. Never mind the IRA, John had said some cutting things about Evangelicals and you do not want to mess with those guys.

Whatever, I watched him for four silent Lents. Often he was pouring over the Bible thinking of something arresting, which would refresh the Gospel and refresh his audience: 'Tell the truth, but tell it slant . . .' On the way home he pored over the *New Scientist*, hallowing it like Scripture.

Always he'd be either thinking or praying. When he was fashioning the Act of Synod, his eyes darted around, his eyebrows danced, a veritable Einstein figuring out his theory of relativity. When he returned home to Rosalie from Wydale Hall after giving his charge to York's first 39 women priests, he had that look of an errant husband concocting an excuse to pull the wool over his wife's eyes: 'This had better be good.'

Whenever we neared home, our journey almost complete, John looked like a boy, anticipating Christmas Day's dawn. All archbishops eventually have to return to base. Late December 1953, Archbishop Cyril Garbett, looking piqued, anticipating a ship's biscuit with his acerbic sister, the chaplain shivering, thinking, 'Oh God, we've still got to say Evensong.' Garbett piping up, 'Thank God, we've still got to say Evensong!' Archbishop Donald Coggan once lectured clergy: 'When I return to a chilly Bishopthorpe, there's nothing I like better than rushing upstairs with Jean, stripping off our outer garments and having a stiff and vigorous game of table tennis. That soon warms me up.' How we laughed! How Donald sadly didn't.

John looked like Odysseus sighing with relief, his long epic journey over, yearning for Rosalie, Laura, Francis, Ruth, Adrian, hoping his lovely family would remember him. The Border Terriers, probably mere pups when he had left, yapping down the corridors at his return. Such long absences.

To the Bishop: Are you going out *again* tonight?
Can Laura and I watch Top of the Pops, *please*?
I hope you are well! See you soon!
All best wishes, Francis

He'd briefly greet the family, and then straight up to the office to answer mail and write the latest talk. 'Oh, a cup of tea would be nice, Mary.'

He always had that same look, as when he celebrated communion or confirmed a child. A happy-in-his-skin look, a look of wonder. I once spotted him over our garden wall, looking at his pet tortoise. For 15 minutes, just wondering at it.

We so need bishops to be silent like John, silent like Mark's women at the tomb rendered mute by the sheer stupendousness of the Easter God.

Silent like Christ on trial: for Rowan Williams, Christ's silence is eloquent because otherwise

> What is *said* will take on the colour of the world's insanity. It will be another bid for the world's power, another identification with the unaccountable tyrannies that decide how things shall be. Jesus described in the ways of this world would be a competitor for a space in it, part of its untruth.

On his sixty-fifth birthday we were both travelling by train to London and I tried to get him a place in the driver's cab. British Rail declined. I guess they didn't think the driver could bear John's silence all the way down the East Coast. Instead they treated us to a First Class breakfast complete with a loquacious hostess called Karen, whom we'd picked up outside W H Smith's kiosk. Karen encouraged John to dunk his eggs as we sped through Doncaster. 'What's that you're reading, Luv,' she chirped. 'Hansard,' came the ice-cold reply. 'Not very chatty, your Boss, is he?' she said when John had gone to the loo at Grantham. He always went to the loo at Grantham. I guess it was his way of paying the place back for spawning Margaret Thatcher.

It was a fearful and terrible thing to fall into the hands of one of John's silences. All sorts of reactions: you felt judged, you felt an idiot, you filled the silence with babble. But also you felt affirmed, tremendously affirmed with a love beyond words. The word became flesh and was stunned into silence.

In this biography and in *Archbishop's Diary* (1995) and in my *Church Times* Diaries from 1996 to 2008, I have painted many pictures of John. If I had to sum him up, it would be a picture of a visit to Whitehaven in 1994. A Sri Lankan priest there had had major brain surgery, and hadn't got long. He was mute, in a wheelchair, with his dear wife tending him, looking so very sad. John commissioned him for a ministry of prayer, and then knelt down before him almost in homage, held his hands in his and looked into his eyes, saying nothing. The silent before the silenced, now both basking in the eternal silence, to which John's marvellous and immense life beckons us all.

Bibliography

Books

Religion and Science (London: Mills and Boon, 1964; London: Hodder & Stoughton, 1972).

Truths in Tension (New York: Holt, Rinehart & Winston, 1964).

A Working Faith (London: DLT, 1980).

Church and Nation in a Secular Age (London: DLT, 1983).

Confessions of a Conservative Liberal (London: SPCK, 1988).

Making Sense (London: SPCK, 1993).

Faith and Uncertainty (London: DLT, 1997).

Being a Person: Where faith and science meet (Riddell Lectures) (London: Hodder & Stoughton, 1998).

Varieties of Unbelief (Bampton Lectures) (London: DLT, 2000).

The Concept of Nature (Gifford Lectures) (London: DLT, 2002).

Changing Britain: Social diversity and moral unity (Board for Social Responsibility, 1987).

Contributed chapters

Vidler, A. R. (ed.), 'The uneasy truce between science and theology', *Soundings* (Cambridge: CUP, 1962).

Loukes, H. (ed.), 'A scientist looks at authority', *The Bible Tells Me So* (London: SPCK, 1967).

Rowe, T. (ed.), 'What is preaching?', *Queen's Sermons* (London: Epworth Press, 1973).

Catterall, R. D. and Nichol, C. S. (eds), 'Society's responses', *Sexually Transmitted Diseases* (New York: Academic Press, 1976).

Duncan, A. S. (ed.), 'Christianity', *Dictionary of Medical Ethics* (London: DLT, 1977, 1981).

Morley, D. (ed.), *The Sensitive Scientist* (London: SCM Press, 1978).

Turner, J. M. (ed.), 'Can science survive?', *Queen's Essays* (Queen's College Birmingham, 1980).

Sims, N. (ed.), 'Theological reflections of compromise', *Explorations in Ethics and International Relations* (London: Croom Helm, 1981).

'Before it's too late', *The Challenge of Nuclear Disarmament* (WCC, 1981).

Richardson, A. and Bowden, J. (eds), 'Creation'; 'Evolution'; 'God of the gaps'; 'Model'; 'Paradigm'; 'Science and religion', *A New Dictionary of Christian Theology* (London: SCM Press, 1983).

McQuarrie, J. and Childress, J. F. (eds), 'Science and ethics'; 'Brainwashing'; 'Indoctrination', *A New Dictionary of Christian Ethics* (London: SCM Press, 1986).

Moss, T. (ed.), 'Discovering God in action', *In Search of Christianity* (London: Firethorn Press, 1986).

Cosstick, V. (ed.), 'Facing moral dilemma', *AIDS – Meeting the Community Challenge* (Homebush, Kenya: St Paul Publications, 1987).

Bailey, S. (ed.), several chapters, *Human Rights and Responsibilities in Britain and Ireland* (London: Macmillan, 1988).

Brown, S. (ed.), 'Peace and justice', *My World* (Abingdon: BRF, 1989).

Cohn-Sherbook, D. (ed.), 'Our inheritance', *Breadth and Sanity Sermons from All Saints Margaret Street, 1989*, reprinted in *Tradition and Unity: Sermons published in honour of Robert Runcie* (New York: Bellow, 1991).

Birch, C. (ed.), 'A sacramental approach to environmental issues', *Liberating Life: Contemporary approaches to ecological theology* (New York: Orbis, 1990).

Edwards, D. (ed.), 'Canterbury and York', *Robert Runcie: A Portrait by his friends* (London: HarperCollins, 1990).

Holloway, R. (ed.), 'Church and risk', *The Divine Risk* (London: DLT, 1990).

Hardy, D. W. and Sedgewick, P. H. (eds), 'Reflections on the liberal position', *The Weight of Glory: Essays for Peter Baelz* (Edinburgh: T & T Clark, 1991).

Mott, Sir N. (ed.), 'The scientist as priest', *Can Scientists Believe?* (Abingdon: Routledge, 1991).

'Nature', *Dictionary of the Ecumenical Movement* (WCC, 1991).

Grubb, A. (ed.), 'Legislative criteria: The human fertilisation and embryology bill', *Challenges in Medical Care* (Chichester: John Wiley & Sons, 1992).

John, J. (ed.), 'Catholicism and the living Christ', *Living Tradition: Affirming Catholicism in the Anglican Church* (London: DLT, 1992).

Brodie, D. and McConnell, R. (eds), 'Invention of the method of invention', *Selected Sermons for Christian Students on Campus* (Lampeter: Mellen Press, 1993).

Brown, S. (ed.), 'Meditations', *Lent for Busy People* (Abingdon: BRF, 1993).

Davie, G. et al. (eds), 'The role of the churches in promoting human rights in the development of the new Europe', *Christian Values in Europe* (Cambridge: Westcott House, 1993).

Gillett, D. and Scott-Joynt, M. (eds), 'In season and out of season', *Treasure in the Field* (London: HarperCollins, 1993).

'Learning to like each other', *Explorations in Science and Theology* (London: Royal Society of Arts, 1993).

Spurway, N. (ed.), 'Is there reliable knowledge about God?' (Gifford Lecture), *Humanity, Environment and God* (Oxford: Blackwell, 1993).

Whitbourn, J. (ed.), 'A prayer for today', *A Prayer in the Life* (London: SPCK, 1993).

'Democracy: A Christian perspective', *World Faiths Encounter* (World Congress of Faiths, 1994).

Gillon, G. (ed.), 'An Anglican view of the four principles', *Principles of Health Care Ethics* (Chichester: John Wiley & Sons, 1994).

McGregor, G. (ed), 'Religious education: The way ahead', *Towards True Education* (College of Ripon and York St John, 1994).

Nelson, J. R. (ed.), 'A danger of knowing too much?', *On the New Frontiers of Genetics and Religion* (Grand Rapids: Eerdmans, 1994).

Yeats, C. (ed.), 'Foreword', *Veritas Splendor – A Response* (Canterbury: Canterbury Press, 1994).

Brown, D. (ed.), 'The sacramentality of the natural world', *The Sense of the Sacramental* (London: SPCK, 1995).

Bunting, I. (ed.), 'Church and society', *Celebrating the Anglican Way* (London: Hodder & Stoughton, 1996).

Pyper, H. (ed.), 'The family in the new social order', *The Christian Family: A Concept in Crisis* (Canterbury: Canterbury Press, 1996).

Platten, S. (ed.), 'A mirror of eternity', *Seeing Ourselves* (Canterbury: Canterbury Press, 1998).

Hastings, A. et al. (ed.), 'Euthanasia'; 'Medical ethics'; 'Suicide', *The Oxford Companion to Christian Thought* (Oxford: OUP, 2000).

'Ago ut Intelligam', *Reflections on Ministry: Essays in honour of William Strawson* (Durham: Church in the Market Place Publications, 2004).

Lorimer, D. (ed.), 'Science and human responsibility', *Science, Consciousness and Ultimate Reality* (Exeter: Imprint Academic, 2004).

Dales, D. (ed.), 'Michael Ramsey – man of God', *Glory Descending* (Canterbury: Canterbury Press, 2005).

Published lectures, essays and so on

'The electrical activity of the brain', *Science and Religion*, Autumn 1949.

'Aunt Sally', *The Pilgrim News Letter*, 33.4.50.

'Brains', *The Pilgrim News Letter*, 28.3.50.

'The scientific attitude', *The Pilgrim News Letter*, 31.3.50.

'Sensitization of sensory receptors in the frog's skin', *Journal of Physiology*, Vol 111, 1950.

'Static or dynamic', *The Pilgrim News Letter*, 36.4.50.

'On the virtuous life', *The Pilgrim News Letter*, 42.4.51.

'Personality', *The Pilgrim News Letter*, 46.5.51.

'Antidromic impulses in the dorsal roots', *Journal of Physiology*, Vol. 121, 1953.

'The attractions of science', *Theology*, December 1958.

'Leisure' (Cambridge University Sermon), *The Cambridge Review*, 1960.

'Slow fuse?', *Crucible*, September 1965.

'Moral discovery', *Theology*, June 1966.

'Censorship', *Theology*, November 1966.

'Guilt and forgiveness', *Theology*, Sept 1968.

'Euthanasia: A Christian view', *Royal Society of Health Journal*, June 1974.

'Does God throw dice?', *Frontier*, Autumn 1975.

'Directions for the Church of England', *Theology*, May 1976.

'Experimentation on human beings', *The Franciscan*, Jan. 1977.

'Some thoughts on unemployment', *C of E Men's Magazine*, Winter 1977.

'Psychology and the nature of life', *The Christian Parapsychologist*, March 1978.

'Technology and politics: Ethical reflections on the arms race', *Crucible*, Jan. 1978.

'On being a liturgical reviser', *Theology*, March 1979.

'A Christian approach to justice', *Ampleforth Journal*, 1984.

'Search for our moral roots', *British Medical Journal*, 1986.

'Establishment', *The House Magazine*, July 1988.

'Mediation on creation', *One World*, WCC, June 1988.

'What is authority for?', *Christian*, May 1988.

'An old friend', *Browning Society Notes*, 1990.

'Are moral values enough?', *British Journal of Education Studies*, 1990.

'God and evolution', Keene Lectures, Chelmsford Cathedral, 1990.

'Can science survive without religion?', *Royal Society of Arts Journal*, 1991.

'The end of life in medical practice', *Journal of the Royal College of Physicians*, February 1993.

'The moral baseline', *The Tablet*, Easter 1993.

'On being a primate', Cambridge, Winter 1994.

'What does it mean to love God?', *Home and Family*, December 1994.

'The cause of truth', *Third Way*, September 1995.

'On war', *Theology*, July 1996.

'The moral haze', *Parliamentary Review*, Autumn 1996.

'Do too many rights make a wrong?', *Crucible*, October 1998.

'Ethical issues in genetic engineering', *Proceedings of the Diagnostic Club*, 2000.

'Theology and the sciences' (1st Athenaeum Lecture), *Interdisciplinary Science Reviews*, Spring 2000.

'Peter Baelz: An obituary', *Crucible*, July 2000.

'Science, consciousness and ultimate reality', *The Christian Parapsychologist*, 2002.

'A Christian approach to bioethics', *Human Fertility*, 2003.

'The memory of God', York Minster Lecture, 2003.

'Fundamentalism', *Gay and Lesbian Christians*, Spring 2004.

Plus numerous reviews in *Prism, Frontier, The Expository Times, Crucible, Theology, Church Times, The Tablet, TLS*.

WE HAVE A VISION OF A WORLD IN WHICH EVERYONE IS TRANSFORMED BY CHRISTIAN KNOWLEDGE

As well as being an award-winning publisher, SPCK is the oldest Anglican mission agency in the world.

Our mission is to lead the way in creating books and resources that help everyone to make sense of faith.

Will you partner with us to put good books into the hands of prisoners, great assemblies in front of schoolchildren and reach out to people who have not yet been transformed by the Christian faith?

To donate, please visit www.spckpublishing.co.uk/donate or call our friendly fundraising team on 020 7592 3900.